THE CHRYSOSTOM BIBLE
A Commentary Series for Preaching and Teaching
Romans: A Commentary

THE CHRYSOSTOM BIBLE

A Commentary Series for Preaching and Teaching

Romans: A Commentary

Paul Nadim Tarazi

OCABS PRESS
ST PAUL, MINNESOTA 55112
2010

THE CHRYSOSTOM BIBLE
ROMANS: A COMMENTARY

Copyright © 2010 by
Paul Nadim Tarazi

ISBN 1-60191-011-8

PRINTED IN THE UNITED STATES OF AMERICA

For Archbishop Philip Saliba
pastor, preacher, teacher

Other Books by the Author

I Thessalonians: A Commentary

Galatians: A Commentary

The Old Testament: An Introduction

Volume 1: Historical Traditions, revised edition

Volume 2: Prophetic Traditions

Volume 3: Psalms and Wisdom

The New Testament: An Introduction

Volume 1: Paul and Mark

Volume 2: Luke and Acts

Volume 3: Johannine Writings

Volume 4: Matthew and the Canon

The Chrysostom Bible

Genesis: A Commentary

Philippians: A Commentary

Land and Covenant

The Chrysostom Bible
Romans: A Commentary

ISBN 1-60191-011-8

Published by OCABS Press, St. Paul, Minnesota.
Printed in the United States of America.

Books are available through OCABS Press at special discounts
for bulk purchases in the United States by academic institutions,
churches, and other organizations. For more information please
email OCABS Press at press@ocabs.org.

Abbreviations

Books by the Author

1 Thess   *1 Thessalonians: A Commentary,* Crestwood, NY: St. Vladimir's Seminary Press, 1982

Gal   *Galatians: A Commentary,* Crestwood, NY: St. Vladimir's Seminary Press, 1994

OTI₁   *The Old Testament: An Introduction, Volume 1: Historical Traditions,* revised edition, Crestwood, NY: St. Vladimir's Seminary Press, 2003

OTI₂   *The Old Testament: An Introduction, Volume 2: Prophetic Traditions,* Crestwood, NY: St. Vladimir's Seminary Press, 1994

OTI₃   *The Old Testament: An Introduction, Volume 3: Psalms and Wisdom,* Crestwood, NY: St. Vladimir's Seminary Press, 1996

NTI₁   *The New Testament: An Introduction, Volume 1: Paul and Mark,* Crestwood, NY: St. Vladimir's Seminary Press, 1999

NTI₂   *The New Testament: An Introduction, Volume 2: Luke and Acts,* Crestwood, NY: St. Vladimir's Seminary Press, 2001

NTI₃   *The New Testament: An Introduction, Volume 3: Johannine Writings,* Crestwood, NY: St. Vladimir's Seminary Press, 2004

NTI₄   *The New Testament: An Introduction, Volume 4: Matthew and the Canon,* St. Paul, MN: OCABS Press, 2009

C-Gen   *The Chrysostom Bible - Genesis: A Commentary,* St. Paul, MN: OCABS Press, 2009

C-Phil   *The Chrysostom Bible - Philippians: A Commentary,* St. Paul, MN: OCABS Press, 2009

LAC   *Land and Covenant,* St. Paul, MN: OCABS Press, 2009

Abbreviations

Books of the Old Testament*

Gen	Genesis	Job	Job	Hab	Habakkuk
Ex	Exodus	Ps	Psalms	Zeph	Zephaniah
Lev	Leviticus	Prov	Proverbs	Hag	Haggai
Num	Numbers	Eccl	Ecclesiastes	Zech	Zechariah
Deut	Deuteronomy	Song	Song of Solomon	Mal	Malachi
Josh	Joshua	Is	Isaiah	Tob	Tobit
Judg	Judges	Jer	Jeremiah	Jdt	Judith
Ruth	Ruth	Lam	Lamentations	Wis	Wisdom
1 Sam	1 Samuel	Ezek	Ezekiel	Sir	Sirach (Ecclesiasticus)
2 Sam	2 Samuel	Dan	Daniel	Bar	Baruch
1 Kg	1 Kings	Hos	Hosea	1 Esd	1 Esdras
2 Kg	2 Kings	Joel	Joel	2 Esd	2 Esdras
1 Chr	1 Chronicles	Am	Amos	1 Macc	1 Maccabees
2 Chr	2 Chronicles	Ob	Obadiah	2 Macc	2 Maccabees
Ezra	Ezra	Jon	Jonah	3 Macc	3 Maccabees
Neh	Nehemiah	Mic	Micah	4 Macc	4 Maccabees
Esth	Esther	Nah	Nahum		

Books of the New Testament

Mt	Matthew	Eph	Ephesians	Heb	Hebrews
Mk	Mark	Phil	Philippians	Jas	James
Lk	Luke	Col	Colossians	1 Pet	1 Peter
Jn	John	1 Thess	1 Thessalonians	2 Pet	2 Peter
Acts	Acts	2 Thess	2 Thessalonians	1 Jn	1 John
Rom	Romans	1 Tim	1 Timothy	2 Jn	2 John
1 Cor	1 Corinthians	2 Tim	2 Timothy	3 Jn	3 John
2 Cor	2 Corinthians	Titus	Titus	Jude	Jude
Gal	Galatians	Philem	Philemon	Rev	Revelation

Following the larger canon known as the Septuagint.

Contents

Preface

The present Bible Commentary Series is not so much in honor of John Chrysostom as it is to continue and promote his legacy as an interpreter of the biblical texts for preaching and teaching God's congregation, in order to prod its members to proceed on the way they started when they accepted God's calling. Chrysostom's virtual uniqueness is that he did not subscribe to any hermeneutic or methodology, since this would amount to introducing an extra-textual authority over the biblical texts. For him, scripture is its own interpreter. Listening to the texts time and again allowed him to realize that "call" and "read (aloud)" are not interconnected realities; rather, they are one reality since they both are renditions of the same Hebrew verb *qara'*. Given that words read aloud are words of instruction for one "to do them," the only valid reaction would be to hear, listen, obey, and abide by these words. All these connotations are subsumed in the same Hebrew verb *šama'*. On the other hand, these scriptural "words of life" are presented as readily understandable utterances of a father to his children (Isaiah 1:2-3). The recipients are never asked to engage in an intellectual debate with their divine instructor, or even among themselves, to fathom what he is saying. The Apostle to the Gentiles followed in the footsteps of the Prophets to Israel by handing down to them the Gospel, that is, the Law of God's Spirit through his Christ (Romans 8:2; Galatians 6:2) as fatherly instruction (1 Corinthians 4:15). He in turn wrote readily understandable letters to be read aloud. It is in these same footsteps that Chrysostom followed, having learned from both the Prophets and Paul that the same "words of life" carry also the sentence of death at the hand of the scriptural God, Judge of all

(Deuteronomy 28; Joshua 8:32-35; Psalm 82; Matthew 3:4-12; Romans 2:12-16; 1 Corinthians 10:1-11; Revelation 20:11-15).

While theological debates and hermeneutical theories come and go after having fed their proponents and their fans with passing human glory, the Golden Mouth's expository homilies, through the centuries, fed and still feed myriads of believers in so many traditions and countries. Virtually banned from dogmatic treatises, he survives in the hearts of "those who have ears to hear." His success is due to his commitment to exegesis rather than to futile hermeneutics. The latter behaves as someone who dictates on a living organism what it is supposed to be, whereas exegesis submits to that organism and endeavors to decipher it through trial and error. There is as much a far cry between the text and the theories about it as there is between a living organism and the theories about it. The biblical texts are the reality of God imparted through their being read aloud in the midst of the congregation, disregarding the value of the sermon that follows. The sermon, much less a theological treatise, is at best an invitation to hear and obey the text. Assessing the shape of an invitation card has no value whatsoever when it comes to the dinner itself; the guests are fed by the dinner, not by the invitation or its phrasing (Luke 14:16-24; Matthew 22:1-14).

This commentary series does not intend to promote Chrysostom's ideas as a public relation manager would do, but rather to follow in the footsteps of his approach as true children and heirs are expected to do. He used all the contemporary tools at his disposal to communicate God's written instruction to his hearers, as a doctor would with his patients, without spending unnecessary energy on peripheral debates requiring the use of professional jargon incomprehensible to the commoner. The writers of this series will try to do the same: muster to the best of their ability all necessary contemporary knowledge to communicate to the general readers the biblical message without burdening them with data unnecessary for that purpose. Whenever it will be deemed necessary or even helpful to do so, and in order to curtail burdensome and lengthy technical asides within the commentaries, specialized monographs related either to specific topics or to the scriptural background—literary, socio-political, or archeological—will be issued as companions to the series.

Paul Nadim Tarazi
Editor

Introduction

Paul's letter to the Romans, the longest of the Pauline correspondence, is placed in the Canon at the beginning of that corpus. The reason is evident. It is addressed to citizens of Rome, assumedly patricians in their majority. The bulk of Paul's correspondence is addressed to the capitals (Thessalonica, Corinth, Ephesus) and two cities (Philippi and Colossae) of the most important eastern Roman provinces covering the originally Hellenic areas of Macedonia, Achaia, and Ionia. After having covered the regions that lie in the easternmost part of the empire in Asia, Paul is about to embark on his journey westward all the way to Spain, thus passing through Rome (Rom 15:18-24).

In writing his letters to the churches of the East, Paul tried to steer them away from his opponents' teaching and keep them faithful to the true gospel he was preaching. In so doing he was scripturalizing his teaching (Gal 1:6-9; 5:2; 6:11) so that the future as well as the contemporary generations of all churches, and not only the expressed addressees (Col 4:16),[1] would hear it time and again until the Lord returns: "My little children, with whom I am again in travail until Christ be formed among you!" (Gal 4:19). The reason behind Paul's decision to write was to have his epistles read together with the Old Testament scripture at church gatherings. In this manner, after his death, his followers would be protected from his opponents' pressures. As 2 Peter clearly states, Paul's epistles are put on the same level as the Old Testament books: "So also our beloved brother Paul wrote to you according to the wisdom given him, speaking of this as he does in all his letters. There are some things in them hard to understand, which the ignorant and unstable twist to their own

---

[1] See also Rev 1:4, 11; 2:7, 11, 17, 23, 29; 3:6, 13, 22; 22:16.

destruction, *as they do the other scriptures.*" (3:15-16) The
corollary to this policy is the irrelevance of the perennial
question, "How could Paul write to churches he did not found,
such as those in Colossae and Rome?"

    After having been let down in Antioch by his colleagues, Peter
and Barnabas, and by the Jerusalemite leaders around James (Gal
2:11-14), Paul establishes his headquarters in Ephesus, the
capital of the Roman province Asia, according to the witness of
both Acts and Revelation. In Acts, Paul bids his last farewell to
the elders of the church of Ephesus (20:17-38) telling them how
he toiled for the gospel in Asia and addresses them as the
"overseers ... of the church of God which he obtained with the
blood of his own Son" (v.28), that is to say, as though they were
the leaders of the church universal. The Book of Revelation
witnesses to the fact that the earliest Roman persecution against
the Christian faithful and their leaders took place in that same
province (Rev 1-3). It is to seven churches of that province,
beginning with Ephesus (1:11; 2:1-7), that the "bound" John in
Patmos writes, as a potential testament, his seven letters just as
the "soon-to-be-bound" Paul (Acts 20:22) delivers his testament
to the elders of the same capital city. In order for Paul to impress
upon the Asian churches, his churches in a special way, that the
message he brought them is the one gospel meant for the all the
nations living in the Roman empire East and West, he wrote a
letter to the capital of the empire intending that it be read in all
the churches. This policy he set forth in Colossians 4:16.[2] The
letter being addressed to Rome and thus to the entire empire,
according to the Roman tradition of the senatorial or imperial

---

[2] Actually, in *NTI₄*, I defended the thesis that, except for the letter to the Galatians, all
his other letters Paul (or his followers, in his name) wrote to the capitals of Roman
provinces with the intention that they be read in his Asian churches.

urbi et orbi (to the city [of Rome] and to the entire orb), explains why it incorporates most of the points he had made in his other letters addressed to the capitals of provinces, why it sounds as a magisterial treatise addressed to "all the nations among whom are the citizens of Rome" (Rom 1:5-6), and why it was put in the place of honor at the head of Pauline corpus.

In this commentary series, I have included both Greek and English texts for each verse. The English is the RSV translation, which I have been using in my writings. In my comments, however, I often defer to the Greek with my own translation in order to render the meaning as close as possible to the original text.

Chapter 1

Vv. 1-7 ¹ Παῦλος δοῦλος Χριστοῦ Ἰησοῦ, κλητὸς ἀπόστολος ἀφωρισμένος εἰς εὐαγγέλιον θεοῦ,Παῦλος δοῦλος Χριστοῦ Ἰησοῦ, κλητὸς ἀπόστολος ἀφωρισμένος εἰς εὐαγγέλιον θεοῦ, ² ὃ προεπηγγείλατο διὰ τῶν προφητῶν αὐτοῦ ἐν γραφαῖς ἁγίαις ³ περὶ τοῦ υἱοῦ αὐτοῦ τοῦ γενομένου ἐκ σπέρματος Δαυὶδ κατὰ σάρκα, ⁴ τοῦ ὁρισθέντος υἱοῦ θεοῦ ἐν δυνάμει κατὰ πνεῦμα ἁγιωσύνης ἐξ ἀναστάσεως νεκρῶν, Ἰησοῦ Χριστοῦ τοῦ κυρίου ἡμῶν, ⁵ δι' οὗ ἐλάβομεν χάριν καὶ ἀποστολὴν εἰς ὑπακοὴν πίστεως ἐν πᾶσιν τοῖς ἔθνεσιν ὑπὲρ τοῦ ὀνόματος αὐτοῦ, ⁶ ἐν οἷς ἐστε καὶ ὑμεῖς κλητοὶ Ἰησοῦ Χριστοῦ, ⁷ πᾶσιν τοῖς οὖσιν ἐν Ῥώμῃ ἀγαπητοῖς θεοῦ, κλητοῖς ἁγίοις, χάρις ὑμῖν καὶ εἰρήνη ἀπὸ θεοῦ πατρὸς ἡμῶν καὶ κυρίου Ἰησοῦ Χριστοῦ.

¹Paul, a servant of Jesus Christ, called to be an apostle, set apart for the gospel of God ²which he promised beforehand through his prophets in the holy scriptures, ³the gospel concerning his Son, who was descended from David according to the flesh ⁴and designated Son of God in power according to the Spirit of holiness by his resurrection from the dead, Jesus Christ our Lord, ⁵through whom we have received grace and apostleship to bring about the obedience of faith for the sake of his name among all the nations, ⁶including yourselves who are called to belong to Jesus Christ; ⁷To all God's beloved in Rome, who are called to be saints: Grace to you and peace from God our Father and the Lord Jesus Christ.

As he does only in Philippians, Paul introduces himself as merely "a servant [slave] of Christ Jesus." In Philippians he wanted to drive home this message to his hearers; assumedly most of them were Roman soldiers.[1] Here, the addressees are

---

[1] See my comments in *C-Phil* 134, 182.

citizens of the city of Rome itself, assumedly mostly Roman patricians. For Paul to introduce himself as a slave and then speak with authority is unwarranted boldness. But, to present himself as the slave of someone believed to be a Jewish messiah whom the Romans put to the most abject and shameful death of crucifixion and still speak with authority is committing outright *lèse majesté* impertinence. Paul should be ashamed to do this, and yet, to the contrary, a few verses later he asserts that he is "not ashamed" at all (Rom 1:16). Consequently, his authority comes from another source, higher than Rome itself and its emperor.

The same Paul, the little one,[2] in spite of being a slave, is "called" into a higher position of being an emissary.[3] As he explicates in 1 Corinthians 9, Paul views his being an apostle equivalent to that of *oikonomos* (chief steward of the house) in a Roman household.[4] As the Greek title *oikonomos* entails, he is the one who puts, or at least enforces, the rules of the house that maintain the good order in daily life.[5] The office to which he is commissioned by his master would be the *oikonomia* (the economics; the house ruling), as Paul refers to his apostolate:

> For if I preach the gospel, that gives me no ground for boasting. For necessity is laid upon me. Woe to me if I do not preach the gospel! For if I do this of my own will, I have a reward; but if not of my own will, I am entrusted with a commission (*oikonomian*). (1 Cor 9:16-17)

---

[2] Which is the meaning of the Latin *paulus*.
[3] Which is the meaning of the Greek *apostolos*.
[4] A position similar to that of butler in an aristocratic house or a majordomo (senior of the house) in an Italian or Spanish rich household.
[5] The patrician, in comparison, would be the *oikodespotēs* (master or owner of the house)

As we learned from the Lukan parable, the chief steward was granted full authority over his peers. However, together with full authority, came full accountability:

> Who then is the faithful and wise steward (*oikonomos*), whom his master will set over his household, to give them their portion of food at the proper time? Blessed is that slave (*doulos*) whom his lord (*kyrios*) when he comes will find so doing. Truly, I say to you, he will set him over all his possessions. But if that slave says to himself, "My lord is delayed in coming," and begins to beat the menservants and the maidservants, and to eat and drink and get drunk, the master of that slave will come on a day when he does not expect him and at an hour he does not know, and will punish him, and put him with the unfaithful. And that slave who knew his lord's will, but did not make ready or act according to his will, shall receive a severe beating. But he who did not know, and did what deserved a beating, shall receive a light beating. Every one to whom much is given, of him will much be required; and of him to whom men commit much they will demand the more. (Lk 12:42-48)

Full accountability is evident in that, should the lord's will not be carried out, the steward will receive a beating, whether he was aware of that will or not. The reason is that, in his position, he is supposed to have been aware of it.[6]

The absolute authority of the apostle lies in that he is commissioned by God himself, who is the God not only of the Jews, but also of the Gentiles (Rom 3:29), among whom are included the citizens of Rome (1:5-6). The gospel with which Paul is entrusted (1 Cor 9:16-17) is God's (the gospel of God;

---

[6] A similar teaching is found in the Matthean parable of the judgment of all nations (Mt 25:31-46) where both the righteous (vv.37-39) and the cursed (v.44) are presented as not having been aware of their judge's will.

Rom 1:1), with God's presence already being felt by the use of the adjective "called" (*klētos*), since God is the "caller" (the one who calls; *kalōn, kalountos*) according to Paul (Rom 4:7; 9:12; Gal 5:8; 1 Thess 2:12; 5:24).[7] Usually Paul speaks of being "entrusted" with the gospel (1 Cor 9:17; Gal 2:7; 1 Tim 1:11; 2 Tim 1:12; Tit 1:3). Here, uniquely, he uses the term *aphōrismenos* (set apart, assigned, designated; Rom 1:1). This is done in view of his mission, which is related to the fact that his "lord" (1:1, 4) through whom he became an apostle (v.5) was himself *horisthentos* (designated, assigned, set apart; v.4).[8] I will discuss the meaning of Paul's being set apart when I deal with Christ's resurrection in v.4.

The Greek verb *evangelizō* (Rev 10:14) and more commonly *evangelizomai* means bring good news worthy of the sacrifice of thanksgiving to the deities (*evangelion*); by extension, the term *evangelion* (gospel) came to refer to the good news itself. The news that Paul was commissioned with is usually mistaken, in theological circles, for something "new" as though he was spreading a novelty. If that were the case, then Paul would have been an innovator, and thus a heretic. And this is precisely what he has been accused of all along by his opponents. The misunderstanding of *evangelion* in classical theology was forced upon Romans by making it expressive of an insurmountable tension between "law" and "gospel" or "grace." However, for Paul, "the law is holy, and the commandment is holy and just and good" (Rom 7:12) to the extent that "in Christ Jesus" we are

---

[7] See also the instances of the aorist *kalesas, kalesantos* (the one who has called) in Gal 1:6, 15; 2 Tit 1:9. See also 1 Peter (1:15; 2:9; 5:10) and 2 Peter (1:3), which are the products of the Pauline school as is argued for by many scholars. See my *NTI₄* 25-106.

[8] Both verbs *aphorizō* and *horizō* are from the same root, the first having the added preposition *apo*. Our English noun "horizon" is from the same root which connotes "putting a limit, border around" and thus "separating from something else."

under "the *law* of the Spirit of life" (8:2). Consequently, the novelty of the news is not to be understood as a new "teaching," but rather is to be viewed as new from the perspective of its hearers: the *evangelion* is news for its recipients who are hearing it for the first time, not for its source (God) or its promoter (the apostle). This technicality is prominent in Acts where Luke uses the verb *evangelizomai* to speak of the first encounter between the apostle and his hearers (13:32; 14:7, 15, 21; 16:10), whereas he uses the verbs *(epi)stērizō* (14:22; 15:32, 41; 18:23) or *stereō* (16:5), whose meaning is "strengthen, confirm" to refer to the subsequent apostolic visits.[9]

For God and for Paul the "good news" was not—actually could not have been—news, since God had already spoken it, and it was inscribed in scripture which Paul had heard and read. Indeed, the *evangelion* was "promised beforehand by God in the holy scriptures" (Rom 1:2). What is striking is the addition "through his prophets." It is not, however, totally unexpected when one remembers that Romans is an expansion of the gospel laid down in writing once and for all (Gal 6:11-16) in Galatians. In that epistle Paul presented the gospel of God as being his promise inscribed in scripture (3:1-4:28), and at the end of his argumentation, just before his concluding remark where we hear the last mention of the term "promise" (4:28), he quotes from Isaiah: "Rejoice, O barren one who does not bear; break forth and shout, you who are not in travail; for the children of the desolate one are many more than the children of her that is married." (54:1)   The reason is that the verb *evangelizomai* (Hebrew *biśśer*) occurs, in the prophetic scrolls, only in Isaiah in conjunction with the divine good news encompassing Gentiles as well as Israel through the preaching of God's "law" to both (40:9

---

[9] See the detailed discussion in *Gal* 1-2.

[twice]; 52:7 [twice]; 60:6; 61:1).[10] In Romans, due to the generalization inherent to "holy scriptures," Paul uses the generic "prophets" to refer to the prophetic literature. This, in turn, will allow him in Romans 9-11 to appeal to the other prophetic books, in addition to his frequent quotations from Isaiah, as we shall see.[11]

The content of Romans 1:3-4 is at the same time scriptural and anti-imperial. Though the priority is to scripture, it is through and through anti-kingly, and Paul's specific terminology brings out the anti-imperial edge. The reason for this is that the epistle is primarily addressed to patricians of Rome. Besides *evangelion*, which rings a bell reminiscent of the first emperor Caesar Augustus,[12] Paul will use, in conjunction with it, the nouns *dynamis* and *sōtērian* (v.16) that are also imperial as well as divine terminology. So, immediately counteracting any possible reference to the Roman emperor as being the "divine son," Paul speaks of the scriptural God's son as being a descendant of the seed of David, the scriptural king of Judah and Israel. In so

---

[10] In Jer 20:15 the reference is to bad news. In Nah 2:1 the good news is addressed to Judah and against the Assyrians. In Joel 2:32 the original of the LXX *evangelizomenoi* is the Hebrew *śeridim* meaning "fleers, survivors."

[11] Actually, he will quote part of Joel 2:32 between two Isaianic quotations, which confirm the LXX understanding that the "survivors" are considered as the recipients of the good news of salvation that comes from God, on the condition that they put their trust in him.

[12] His birth was hailed as *evangelion* (good news) in an inscription, from ca. 9 B.C., found at Priene in Turkey: "Since Providence, which has ordered all things and is deeply interested in our life, has set in most perfect order by giving us Augustus, whom she filled with virtue that he might benefit humankind, sending him as a savior, both for us and for our descendants, that he might end war and arrange all things, and since he, Caesar, by his appearance excelled even our anticipations, surpassing all previous benefactors, and not even leaving to posterity any hope of surpassing what he has done, and since the birthday of the god Augustus was the beginning of the good tidings (gospel) for the world that came by reason of him."

doing, he is immediately compelling his addressees to hear what scripture, through the prophets, is saying "concerning" (*peri*) that son. Now, in scripture, there are two Davids. The first one is the father of the kingly dynasty that ended in disaster. When that David was a simple shepherd and the least among his brothers (1 Sam 16:11), he was granted an impossible feat: to overcome Goliath and save his people with a shepherd's sling (17:1-54). The moment he became a king and took too seriously his being a "proprietor," which is the meaning of the Hebrew *melek* (king), and started behaving as though he owned his subjects, he and his dynasty were doomed: God alone is the *melek* of his and all peoples. Out of the ashes and dry bones brought about by David's behavior, God will bring about his new people who will be led by a new David, the shepherd after the heart of the sole shepherd, God himself (Ezek 37). It is under the aegis of this new David that all nations will join God's fold:

> Incline your ear, and come to me; hear, that your soul may live; and I will make with you an everlasting covenant, my steadfast, sure love for David. Behold, I made him a witness to the peoples, a leader and commander for the peoples. Behold, you shall call nations that you know not, and nations that knew you not shall run to you, because of the Lord your God, and of the Holy One of Israel, for he has glorified you. (Is 55:3-5)

This scriptural text clearly emulates the *pax Romana* promoted by Rome and its emperors.

God's real son is from David's seed, to be sure, yet is only so through what was left of that seed: the dry bones in the valley. That is why God's intervention was implemented through his spirit (Rom 1:4) which was the same agent through which he "raised the dead bones" (Ezek 37:1-14). Still, the terminology used to qualify God's raising Jesus from the dead is intentionally

Roman. Just as a Roman general is "hailed" by his troops into the office of emperor, so is Jesus "designated" (*horisthentos*) as son of God, the Christ and the Lord of all. The intention is clearly to pin the lordship of Jesus against that of the Roman emperor. Nevertheless, unlike both the first David and the Roman emperor who both need a dynasty to perpetrate their rule, Jesus Christ will remain the Lord forever without need of a dynasty to ensure the perpetuity of his realm; he has no need of a "seed."[13] And just as a shepherd precedes the flock in the sense that without him there is no flock, merely sheep scattered unto oblivion and death, so also Jesus Christ, the shepherd forever, was raised as "first fruits," leading the way for his sheep to join him (1 Cor 15:20-28). This reading is confirmed in the passage that forms an *inclusio* with Romans 1:1-7. At the end of the argumentation that culminates in the last verses of Romans 8, we hear of God being the judge and Christ being our defense attorney, in these terms:

> What then shall we say to this? If God is for us, who is against us? He who did not spare his own Son but gave him up for us all, will he not also give us all things with him? Who shall bring any charge against God's elect? It is God who justifies; who is to condemn? Is it Christ Jesus, who died, yes, *who was raised from the dead*, who is at the right hand of God, who indeed intercedes for us? Who shall separate us from the love of Christ? (vv.31-35)

Then, immediately, Paul adduces a scriptural quotation where we are spoken of as sheep: "As it is written, 'For thy sake we are being killed all the day long; we are regarded as sheep to be slaughtered.'" (v.37) Yet, due to "the love of God in *Christ Jesus*

---

[13] Later Paul writes: "For we know that Christ being raised from the dead *will never die again*; death no longer has dominion over him." (Rom 6:9)

our Lord[14] (v.39) through which "he loved us" (v.37) "we are more than conquerors" (v.37). Conquest, another classical Roman imperial terminology, is also found thrice at the end of 1 Corinthians 15 (vv.54-57).[15]

What is telling, however, is that the metaphor used by Paul in Romans 8:31-35, in conjunction with God's raising of Jesus Christ from the dead, is a legal one (justifies; condemn; intercedes). Nonetheless, that should not be strange to someone versed in scripture. Indeed, the background of all scriptural stories and statements is the court of law where God is seated as judge and where we all appear "before" him to be condemned or acquitted. Actually, the entire letter to the Romans is imbued, as no other letter is, with terminology related to the Greek root *dik*—[16] whose essential connotation is "legal justice," "court of law justice." So, just as Paul used household (slave; lord) and imperial (gospel; power; salvation) terminology to intertwine Roman culture with scriptural background, he does the same in his use of the legal setting, which is scriptural and at the same time fits perfectly in the Roman worldview.

So what is the meaning and function of Christ's being raised from the dead *beforehand* and, thus, *now* for us? Before answering this question one is to dispel a common misunderstanding, namely, that "rose" (*anestē*) and "was raised" (*ēgerthē*) are equivalent, if not synonymous. The first is from the intransitive (stative) verb *anistēmi* describing the state of standing up, whereas the second is the passive of the transitive verb *egeirō*

---

[14] Which is found verbatim in Rom 1:4.

[15] *Hypernikōmen* of Rom 8:37 and *nikos* (translated "victory") in 1 Cor 15:54-57 are from the same root in Greek.

[16] Theodicy is the transliteration of the Greek *theodikē* meaning "God's justice, divine justice."

describing the action of raising someone or something, and thus *making* someone or something stand. The outcome is the same but the agent of the action is not: one *raises* (makes stand) someone else who, in turn, *stands* due to his being raised. In order to fully grasp the correlation, one is to revert to the original Hebrew whence the scriptural Greek is translated. The intransitive *anistēmi* is the Hebrew first (*qal*) verbal form *qam* whereas the transitive *egeirō* is the Hebrew fifth (*hiphil*) verbal form *heqim*, both from the same root *qum*. Actually the Hebrew background is reflected in the use of *anistēmi* in the transitive form, whose meaning is "stand" in the sense of "make stand,"[17] to speak of God's raising Christ (Acts 2:24, 32; 3:26; 13:33, 34; 17:31) and thus corresponds to *egeirō* (raise). The two instances of *anistēmi* in Acts 13:33 and 34 are actually sandwiched in the same context between two occurrences of *egeirō*, one in v. 30 and the other in v.37

Consequently, when one takes seriously the legal tone of the scriptural stories and statements, the issue of Christ's death is not a matter of whether God's Christ can or cannot die. Rather, the issue is the death of the "righteous" who is condemned to death unjustly (Mt 27:4, 19; Lk 23:47; Acts 3:14; 7:52; 22:14; 1 Pet 3:18; 1 Jn 2:1). Jesus, God's Christ, was condemned to death, and thus "struck down," by a verdict of "guilty" (unrighteous) issued by the leaders of both Israel and the nations.[18] However, that verdict was "ungodly" in the sense that God was not consulted. The reason for this was that Jesus was accused of presenting himself as God's emissary. Consulting with God would have been risky: Jesus may have been proven right and

---

[17] My English speaking readers are familiar with the similar case of the verb "stand," which is usually used as intransitive, but obtains also in the transitive form.
[18] See e.g. Acts 4:27

Chapter 1

37

thus righteous. This understanding is reflected in the stories of Jesus' trial in the New Testament: it takes place "at night" and "hurriedly." However, although according to scripture God may be "absent," thus giving the impression that he does not see or hear,[19] ultimately he judges not only the earthly authorities, but the "divine" as well:

> A Psalm of Asaph. God has taken his place in the divine council; in the midst of the gods he holds judgment: "How long will you judge unjustly and show partiality to the wicked? Selah *Give justice to the weak and the fatherless; maintain the right of the afflicted and the destitute. Rescue the weak and the needy; deliver them from the hand of the wicked.*" They have neither knowledge nor understanding, they walk about in darkness; all the foundations of the earth are shaken. I say, "You are gods, sons of the Most High, all of you; nevertheless, you shall die like men, and fall like any prince." Arise, O God, judge the earth; for to thee belong all the nations! (Ps 82:1-8)

And this is what he scripturally did in the case of his chosen one who "was despised and rejected by men" (Is 53:3).[20] God intervened as the supreme court of appeal and reversed the verdict by "raising up" the one whom the court of Israel and the nations unjustly "struck down." In other words, God made Jesus "stand" in a way that would make it impossible for any court to render a verdict of condemnation to death. Later in the letter Paul will write: "Christ was raised (*ēgerthē*) from the dead by the glory of the Father ... For we know that Christ being raised (*egertheis*) from the dead will never die again; death no longer has dominion over him." (Rom 6:4, 9) In turn, this irrevocable intervention *now* on God's part gives us a conditional hope that,

---

[19] See e.g. Ps 22:1-2.
[20] See earlier my comments on Rom 1:2 concerning the importance of Isaiah.

in the future, the same will be done for us: "For *if* we have been united with him in a death like his, we shall certainly be united with him in a resurrection like his ... But *if* we have died with Christ we believe that we shall also live with him." (vv.5, 8)

This understanding of the text fits perfectly with the meaning and function of *horisthentos* (designated, assigned, ordained, showed openly, declared officially; 1:3) in conjunction with the raising of Jesus Christ: the raising is an action by God through which he "showed" and "declared officially" Jesus as his "Son," that is, his messiah. Put otherwise, through his raising of Jesus, God is "anointing" him before all as his plenipotentiary messiah, as is expressed in Psalm 2. This is precisely what one finds in Acts in the passages that use a terminology parallel to that found in Romans 1:1-4. In two of the references from Acts cited earlier where the raising of Jesus is mentioned, it is done in conjunction with the verb *horizō* (appoint, designate, ordain), which is found in Romans 1:4:

> ... this Jesus, delivered up according to the definite (ordained) plan (*hōrismenē boulē*) and foreknowledge of God, you crucified and killed by the hands of lawless men. But God raised him up, having loosed the pangs of death, because it was not possible for him to be held by it. (Acts 2:23-24)

> The times of ignorance God overlooked, but now he commands all men everywhere to repent, because he has fixed a day on which he will judge the world in righteousness by a man whom he has appointed (*hōrisen*), and of this he has given assurance to all men by raising him from the dead. (Acts 17:30-31)[21]

---

[21] See also the parallel text, "And he commanded us to preach to the people, and to testify that he is the one ordained (*hōrismenos*) by God to be judge of the living and the dead" (Acts 10:42).

What is telling, however, is that in a parallel passage speaking about God's intervention on behalf of Jesus, we find not only the verb *horizō* coupled with the verb *khriō* (anoint), but also in conjunction with a reference to Psalm 2:

> And when they heard it, they lifted their voices together to God and said, "Sovereign Lord, who didst make the heaven and the earth and the sea and everything in them, who by the mouth of our father David, thy servant, didst say by the Holy Spirit, 'Why did the Gentiles rage, and the peoples imagine vain things? The kings of the earth set themselves in array, and the rulers were gathered together, against the Lord and against his Anointed (*Khristou*)'[22]—for truly in this city there were gathered together against thy holy servant Jesus, whom thou didst anoint (*ekhrisas*),[23] both Herod and Pontius Pilate, with the Gentiles and the peoples of Israel, to do whatever thy hand and thy plan (*boulē*) had predestined (*proōrisen*)[24] to take place." (Acts 4:24-28)

Moreover, as indicated earlier, God's intervention was against the verdict emitted by "Herod and Pontius Pilate," the representatives of "the Gentiles and the peoples of Israel."

The news had to be brought to both Jews and Gentiles that they issued an unrighteous verdict against God's chosen one. At the same time, included in this news would be an invitation for them to confess their misdeed and put their trust in the corrective verdict of God whose "kindness is meant to lead to repentance" (Rom 3:4). And in order to implement the spreading of this message of forgiveness, God empowered two emissaries: Peter for the diaspora Jews and Paul for the Gentiles

---

[22] Ps 2:1-2.

[23] In Greek "anoint" and "Christ" are from the same root; thus, Christ means "anointed."

[24] A combination of the verb *horizō* and the preposition *pro* (before), which we shall encounter later in Rom 8:29.

(Gal 2:7-8). That is precisely what Paul is saying to his
addressees and, by the same token, justifying his writing to them
without having known them: "[Jesus Christ our Lord] through
whom we have received grace and apostleship[25] to bring about
the obedience (submission) of trust[26] for the sake of his name
among all the nations, among whom are also yourselves who are
called to belong to Jesus Christ." (Rom 1:5-6) Since Paul is the
apostle to the Gentiles, then the Romans are part of his turf. And
in order to underscore the fact that there is only *one* way for the
Gentiles to receive the "truth of the gospel" (Gal 1:5, 14), i.e.,
through Paul himself, he introduces his calling with a verb
similar to the one he uses to speak of how Christ became the
subject content of that gospel: *aphorizomai* (set apart; Rom 1:1),
corresponding to *horizomai* (v.4). Put otherwise, for a Gentile,
God communicates what he did through his messiah via Paul's
lips (Gal 4:19-20), just as God communicated his will to Judah
through Isaiah's lips (Is 6:5-8). The one gospel, the one Christ,
and the one spirit of holiness (Rom 1:1-4) originate with Paul
and no one else (2 Cor 11:2-4). The one God and the one Christ
proclaimed in the one gospel are inseparable from the *one*
apostle.[27] Actually, God's having designated Paul as apostle is the
guarantee that the same God has designated Jesus as his messiah
and son. From the perspective of the Gentile hearers, if Paul is
not their *one* apostle, then God has not shown Jesus to be also
their Lord, and the corollary would be that Jesus *is actually not*

---

[25] This is a Semitism meaning "the grace of apostleship."

[26] This is also a Semitism meaning "trusting obedience" or, even better, "trusting
submission." I am opting for translating *pistis* as "trust" rather than "faith" because the
latter has unfortunately become synonymous with a "credal formula" that is to be
endorsed mentally.

[27] See my article "Paul, the One Apostle of the One Gospel." *The Journal of the
Orthodox Center for the Advancement of Biblical Studies* (*JOCABS*) 2 (2009) 3, 10.

their Lord whom they have to obey and submit to, the way slaves in the Roman Empire submit to the emperor.[28]

Paul was called to be God's apostle (Rom 1:1) by sheer grace. For him, part of acknowledging that grace was to share it by informing the Roman Gentiles that they also are "called," since the God of *all* is essentially the caller and thus *all*, including the apostle, are ultimately invited into God's kingdom through his call. And the calling to *all* who are in Rome is issued because they are God's "beloved" in spite of their enmity with God (Rom 5:10), just as Paul was called when he was still persecuting God's church (Gal 1:13; Phil 3:6). Furthermore, the call is for all to become God's "holy ones" in order for them to be part of the retinue of the one who alone is holy, God himself: "For God has not called us for uncleanness, but unto holiness." (1 Thess 4:7) It is by abiding in this holiness (Rom 6), which is expressed in following the dictates of the law of the spirit of life (8:2), that anyone who will have trusted in the gospel will attain the peace of God's kingdom that is yet to come (5:1-5).[29]

Vv. 8-15 [8] Πρῶτον μὲν εὐχαριστῶ τῷ θεῷ μου διὰ Ἰησοῦ Χριστοῦ περὶ πάντων ὑμῶν ὅτι ἡ πίστις ὑμῶν καταγγέλλεται ἐν ὅλῳ τῷ κόσμῳ. [9] μάρτυς γάρ μού ἐστιν ὁ θεός, ᾧ λατρεύω ἐν τῷ πνεύματί μου ἐν τῷ εὐαγγελίῳ τοῦ υἱοῦ αὐτοῦ, ὡς ἀδιαλείπτως μνείαν ὑμῶν ποιοῦμαι [10] πάντοτε ἐπὶ τῶν προσευχῶν μου δεόμενος εἴ πως ἤδη ποτὲ εὐοδωθήσομαι ἐν τῷ θελήματι τοῦ θεοῦ ἐλθεῖν πρὸς ὑμᾶς. [11] ἐπιποθῶ γὰρ ἰδεῖν ὑμᾶς, ἵνα τι μεταδῶ χάρισμα ὑμῖν πνευματικὸν εἰς τὸ στηριχθῆναι ὑμᾶς, [12] τοῦτο δέ ἐστιν συμπαρακληθῆναι ἐν ὑμῖν διὰ τῆς ἐν ἀλλήλοις πίστεως ὑμῶν

---

[28] This will be detailed in Rom 6.

[29] As for the grace and the peace Paul wishes on his addressees, and how the eschatological peace functions together with the original grace, see my detailed comments in *C-Phil* 68-71.

τε καὶ ἐμοῦ. ¹³ οὐ θέλω δὲ ὑμᾶς ἀγνοεῖν, ἀδελφοί, ὅτι
πολλάκις προεθέμην ἐλθεῖν πρὸς ὑμᾶς, καὶ ἐκωλύθην ἄχρι
τοῦ δεῦρο, ἵνα τινὰ καρπὸν σχῶ καὶ ἐν ὑμῖν καθὼς καὶ ἐν
τοῖς λοιποῖς ἔθνεσιν. ¹⁴ Ἕλλησίν τε καὶ βαρβάροις, σοφοῖς
τε καὶ ἀνοήτοις ὀφειλέτης εἰμί, ¹⁵ οὕτως τὸ κατ' ἐμὲ
πρόθυμον καὶ ὑμῖν τοῖς ἐν Ῥώμῃ εὐαγγελίσασθαι.

*⁸First, I thank my God through Jesus Christ for all of you,
because your faith is proclaimed in all the world. ⁹For God is my
witness, whom I serve with my spirit in the gospel of his Son,
that without ceasing I mention you always in my prayers,
¹⁰asking that somehow by God's will I may now at last succeed
in coming to you. ¹¹For I long to see you, that I may impart to
you some spiritual gift to strengthen you, ¹²that is, that we may
be mutually encouraged by each other's faith, both yours and
mine. ¹³I want you to know, brethren, that I have often
intended to come to you (but thus far have been prevented), in
order that I may reap some harvest among you as well as among
the rest of the Gentiles. ¹⁴I am under obligation both to Greeks
and to barbarians, both to the wise and to the foolish: ¹⁵so I am
eager to preach the gospel to you also who are in Rome.*

The Greco-Roman epistolary protocol required that a letter start
with thanksgiving to the gods for their gift of health or fortune
or victory or the like. Being an apostle Paul thanks *his* God for
the trust his addressees have put in the message of the gospel.
And since whatever happens in Rome has a value *urbi et orbi* (for
the city [of Rome] and the entire Roman orb), he tells them that
the reason behind his thanksgiving is that this trust of theirs "is
proclaimed (*katangelletai*) in all the world." The use of a verb
that is from the same root as *evangelizomai* (evangelize) and
evangelion (gospel) makes his compliment to the Romans all the
more impressive: their positive response to the gospel has become

a gospel.[30] This is understandable given that the events of the capital city are usually spread throughout the province. By the same token, he is putting pressure on his addressees to continue on the path they already started; any change in their resolve and behavior may affect the province or, in the case of the citizens of Rome, the entire empire and, consequently, may jeopardize the gospel.

What is more important, however, is that Paul is raising a prayer of thanksgiving to God in the Romans' name as well as for their sake. In so doing, he considers himself, as will be made clear in Romans 15:16, as the high priest of the heavenly city that defines the citizenship of the believers.[31] This is confirmed in that he refers to his apostolic activity as an act of "worship" (*latrevō*; 1:9), which is nothing other than the "worship connected to the (apostolic) word" (*logikēn latreian*) he will mention later (12:2). Since he has not yet reached Rome and is only hoping to get there (15:23-24), his prayer concerning the Romans is "that somehow by God's will I may now at last be granted the way of coming to you" (1:10). And as their apostle, his interest in not in their health or fortune, but in the gospel he is bound to share with them. So, if he "longs to see" them, it is solely with the intention to "impart to you some spiritual gift (*kharisma*) to strengthen you" (v.11). The Greek *kharisma* being the product of the *kharis* (grace, gift), it ensues that Paul was intending to come to Rome, if not to preach the gospel—since the assumption is that the recipients are already believers—, then definitely to strengthen them in its teaching, as is clear from

---

[30] See especially 1 Thess 3:6: "But now that Timothy has come to us from you, and has brought us the good news (*evangelisamenou*) of your faith and love…"

[31] More on this matter in my discussion of Rom 12:2 and 15:16. Furthermore, see my discussion in *C-Phil* 137-9 in conjunction with Phil 2:17 where Paul uses cultic terminology.

v.13. In other words, he is intending to make sure that what they received is indeed "the truth of the gospel," the gospel's truthful teaching. He has the authority to do so since he is the apostle to *all* Gentiles, as he established a few verses earlier. In order not to offend them, he explicates "that we may be mutually comforted (*symparaklēthēnai*) in each other's faith, both yours and mine" (v.11). This is not to be understood as though Paul was expecting to learn something from the Romans in matter of the gospel teaching. Rather, should Paul find the Romans on the true path, he would be comforted that the gospel seed has brought about fruit as it did among the other Gentiles to whom Paul preached (v.13), which would be tantamount to Paul's sharing in the joy that the gospel brings. Elsewhere, he outright says:

> For this reason, when I could bear it no longer, I sent that I might know your faith, for fear that somehow the tempter had tempted you and that our labor would be in vain. But now that Timothy has come to us from you, and has evangelized (*evangelisamenou*) us (with the news of) your faith and love and reported that you always remember us kindly and long to see us, as we long to see you—for this reason, brethren, in all our distress and affliction we have been comforted (*paraklēthēmen*) about you through your faith; for now we live, if you stand fast in the Lord. For what thanksgiving can we render to God for you, for all the joy which we feel for your sake before our God, praying earnestly night and day that we may see you face to face and supply what is lacking in your faith? (1 Thess 3:5-10)

In Romans 1:14-15, Paul explains the reason behind his eagerness to travel to Rome: as apostle to all the Gentiles, not only does he have the authority, but as *oikonomos* he is "under obligation" (*opheiletēs*), to do so. At this point, he says openly that he is coming also to "evangelize" them (v.15), and not only that he and they may be mutually comforted. And to make sure that they not misunderstand his intention, he indicates that his coming to Rome is an honor for the citizens of that city, not for him. From the perspective of scripture, the Greco-Roman differentiation between Greeks and barbarians, the first being wise and the latter foolish (*anoētois*), does not hold: both parties are equally Gentiles "separated from Christ, alienated from the commonwealth of Israel, and strangers to the covenants of promise, having no hope and without God in the world" (Eph 2:12). As Gentiles, they do not have the true wisdom that is embedded "in the holy scriptures" which the apostle has been set apart to bring to them (Rom 1:2).[32] Moreover, just as in the case of Galatians, it is the letter itself, officially addressed to all the Romans *urbi et orbi*,[33] that is "the gospel of God."

Vv. 16-17 [16] Οὐ γὰρ ἐπαισχύνομαι τὸ εὐαγγέλιον, δύναμις γὰρ θεοῦ ἐστιν εἰς σωτηρίαν παντὶ τῷ πιστεύοντι, Ἰουδαίῳ τε πρῶτον καὶ Ἕλληνι. [17] δικαιοσύνη γὰρ θεοῦ ἐν αὐτῷ ἀποκαλύπτεται ἐκ πίστεως εἰς πίστιν, καθὼς γέγραπται· ὁ δὲ δίκαιος ἐκ πίστεως ζήσεται.

> [16]*For I am not ashamed of the gospel: it is the power of God for salvation to every one who has faith, to the Jew first and also to the Greek.* [17]*For in it the righteousness of God is revealed through faith for faith; as it is written, "He who through faith is righteous shall live."*

Paul starts his exposition of the gospel with a compendium saying, in a nutshell, that the gospel of God is addressed to all, to the Jew first, but also to the Gentile. Just as Roman imperial edicts apply to all those who live within the boundaries of the empire, so also the gospel applies to all. Again, using imperial

---

[32] This theme is developed in 1 Cor 1-3.
[33] See the Introduction for details.

terminology, Paul asserts that the gospel is the "power" (*dynamis*) of God unto the securing safety from all harm (*sōtērian*; salvation) to everyone that puts his trust in the message of that gospel. This message applies first to the *trusting* Jews because they "were *entrusted* with the oracles (words, speeches) of God" (3:2) and consequently with the gospel contained in them (1:1-2).[34] But, according to Isaiah and the other prophets, the same message of salvation is addressed also to the Gentiles, to whom Paul was sent with the mission to deliver that message to them.

But why does Paul stress the fact that he is not "ashamed" to bring that gospel to the Roman patricians? The reason is that the apostolic "word" of preaching is closely linked to the cross: "For Christ did not send me to baptize but to preach the gospel, and not with eloquent wisdom, lest the cross of Christ be emptied of its power. For the word, namely (the word) of the cross, is folly to those who are perishing, but to us who are being saved it is the power of God." (1 Cor 1:17-18) For Paul, the cross is a reason for boasting: "But far be it from me to glory except in the cross of our Lord Jesus Christ, by which the world has been crucified to me, and I to the world." (Gal 6:14) The clue to making sense out of this factual equation between "gospel" and "cross" lies in the aspect of shameful death linked to the cross in the Roman empire. Crucifixion was intended for public humiliation and was the punishment administered to slaves,

---

[34] In Greek both the noun *pistis* (trust, faith) as well as the verb *pistevō* (put one's trust; have faith in) are from the same root as the verb *epistevthēsan* (were entrusted). The latter is, furthermore, the same verb Paul uses to speak of his having been entrusted with the apostolic mission (1 Cor 9:17; Gal 2:7; 1 Thess 2:4) just as Peter was (Gal 2:7). Both Peter and Paul were "Jews by birth and not Gentile sinners" (Gal 2:15). It stands to reason that they would not have been entrusted with the mission of spreading the gospel that is embedded in scripture (Rom 1:1-2) had they not been entrusted first with that scripture. Hence Paul's repeated stress on this matter (Rom 11:1; 2 Cor 11:22; Gal 1:13-14; Phil 3:5).

foreigners, and those involved in a revolt against the legal authority. It was the opposite of the soldier's glorious death for the sake of a noble cause: martyrdom for one's own country or nation or empire. Crucifixion was a death unto total oblivion of someone whose life was unworthy of remembrance: an unworthy end of an unworthy life, shame ending in shame. So Paul here is making sure that his Roman patrician hearers not be mistaken that, should they fully endorse his preaching, they will be considered as having committed the sin of *lèse majesté* against the emperor and might end up in the arena of the Coliseum.

The gospel is God's (Rom 1:1). If any deity's, and for that matter any king's (Ps 72), basic function is to judge and dispense justice, it is more so for the scriptural God (Ps 82). This is precisely what Paul will categorically remind us of: "But if our wickedness serves to show the righteousness (*dikaiosynēn*) of God, what shall we say? That God is unrighteous (*adikos*) to inflict wrath on us? I speak in a human way. By no means! For then how could God judge the world?" (Rom 3:5-6) That is why, here in Romans 1:16, Paul says that what is revealed in the gospel is God's righteousness (*dikaiosynē*), showing indeed that he is God and has all the right to send forth his message throughout the whole world, let alone the Roman empire. However, since he is no idol, God can only be heard, not seen. Furthermore, his message sounds "unacceptable" (Ezek 3:4-7), and only those who trust it will receive the life that it promises. It is a message *ek pisteōs* (out of [originating in] the trust the messenger [apostle] has put in it) *eis pistin* (unto [calling for] a similar trust on the part of the recipient).

At this point one can see another reason why Paul added "through his prophets" before "in the holy scriptures" at the beginning of the letter (Rom 1:2). The first scriptural reference is

taken from the prophetic Book of Habakkuk: "The righteous out
of trust (*ek pisteōs*) shall live." (2:4). It clearly indicates the origin
of the phrase *ek pisteōs* Paul just used and which is going to
control the entire argumentation. However, there is more to this
than meets the eye. The sequence of "righteous(ness)," "trust,"
and "life" is actually the blueprint of the argumentation in
Romans 1-8. A look at a biblical concordance will readily show
that these chapters are built in the following manner: a high
incidence of words from the root *dikaio*— (right[eous]) is
followed by a high incidence of words from the root *pist*—
(trust, faith), which in turn is followed by a high incidence of
words referring to the noun *zōē* (life) and the verb *zō* (live). It is
the message of God's righteousness, which requires trust on our
part. In turn, this trust, if sustained through full submission to
the law of God's spirit, will lead us into life eternal. The fact that
this same quotation from Habakkuk was already the basis of the
argument of Galatians (3:11) is a clear indication that Romans
was conceived as a magisterial extended *apologia* for Galatians.

The first and foremost "righteous one," as we shall see, is Jesus
Christ himself, who put all his trust in God's command without
opening his mouth (Is 53:7). But the example of Christ is not
communicated to us except through the medium of the apostle:
"Be imitators of me, as I am of Christ." (1 Cor 11:1) So in
practice, from the perspective of the letter's hearers, the
"righteous one" *par excellence* is Paul himself. It is only then that
the hearers are required to trust in the message propounded to
them by the apostle. Still, in Galatians, the blueprint for
Romans, our father and thus prime example in the matter of
trust in God's message is Abraham:

Thus Abraham "believed God, and it was reckoned to him as
righteousness." So you see that it is men of faith (*ek pisteōs*) who

are the sons of Abraham. And the scripture, foreseeing that God
would justify the Gentiles by faith, preached the gospel
beforehand to Abraham, saying, "In you shall all the nations be
blessed." So then, those who are men of faith (*ek pisteōs*) are
blessed with Abraham who had faith. (Gal 3:6-9)

This explains why, in the part where *pistis* has the lion's share, an
entire chapter will be dedicated to Abraham, the father of both
Gentiles and Jews (Rom 4).

Vv. 18-32 ¹⁸ Ἀποκαλύπτεται γὰρ ὀργὴ θεοῦ ἀπ᾽ οὐρανοῦ ἐπὶ
πᾶσαν ἀσέβειαν καὶ ἀδικίαν ἀνθρώπων τῶν τὴν ἀλήθειαν ἐν
ἀδικίᾳ κατεχόντων, ¹⁹ διότι τὸ γνωστὸν τοῦ θεοῦ φανερόν
ἐστιν ἐν αὐτοῖς· ὁ θεὸς γὰρ αὐτοῖς ἐφανέρωσεν. ²⁰ τὰ γὰρ
ἀόρατα αὐτοῦ ἀπὸ κτίσεως κόσμου τοῖς ποιήμασιν νοούμενα
καθορᾶται, ἥ τε ἀΐδιος αὐτοῦ δύναμις καὶ θειότης, εἰς τὸ
εἶναι αὐτοὺς ἀναπολογήτους, ²¹ διότι γνόντες τὸν θεὸν οὐχ
ὡς θεὸν ἐδόξασαν ἢ ηὐχαρίστησαν, ἀλλ᾽ ἐματαιώθησαν ἐν
τοῖς διαλογισμοῖς αὐτῶν καὶ ἐσκοτίσθη ἡ ἀσύνετος αὐτῶν
καρδία. ²² φάσκοντες εἶναι σοφοὶ ἐμωράνθησαν ²³ καὶ
ἤλλαξαν τὴν δόξαν τοῦ ἀφθάρτου θεοῦ ἐν ὁμοιώματι εἰκόνος
φθαρτοῦ ἀνθρώπου καὶ πετεινῶν καὶ τετραπόδων καὶ
ἑρπετῶν. ²⁴ Διὸ παρέδωκεν αὐτοὺς ὁ θεὸς ἐν ταῖς ἐπιθυμίαις
τῶν καρδιῶν αὐτῶν εἰς ἀκαθαρσίαν τοῦ ἀτιμάζεσθαι τὰ
σώματα αὐτῶν ἐν αὐτοῖς· ²⁵ οἵτινες μετήλλαξαν τὴν ἀλήθειαν
τοῦ θεοῦ ἐν τῷ ψεύδει καὶ ἐσεβάσθησαν καὶ ἐλάτρευσαν τῇ
κτίσει παρὰ τὸν κτίσαντα, ὅς ἐστιν εὐλογητὸς εἰς τοὺς
αἰῶνας, ἀμήν. ²⁶ Διὰ τοῦτο παρέδωκεν αὐτοὺς ὁ θεὸς εἰς
πάθη ἀτιμίας, αἵ τε γὰρ θήλειαι αὐτῶν μετήλλαξαν τὴν
φυσικὴν χρῆσιν εἰς τὴν παρὰ φύσιν, ²⁷ ὁμοίως τε καὶ οἱ
ἄρσενες ἀφέντες τὴν φυσικὴν χρῆσιν τῆς θηλείας
ἐξεκαύθησαν ἐν τῇ ὀρέξει αὐτῶν εἰς ἀλλήλους, ἄρσενες ἐν
ἄρσεσιν τὴν ἀσχημοσύνην κατεργαζόμενοι καὶ τὴν
ἀντιμισθίαν ἣν ἔδει τῆς πλάνης αὐτῶν ἐν ἑαυτοῖς
ἀπολαμβάνοντες. ²⁸ Καὶ καθὼς οὐκ ἐδοκίμασαν τὸν θεὸν
ἔχειν ἐν ἐπιγνώσει, παρέδωκεν αὐτοὺς ὁ θεὸς εἰς ἀδόκιμον
νοῦν, ποιεῖν τὰ μὴ καθήκοντα, ²⁹ πεπληρωμένους πάσῃ ἀδικίᾳ
πονηρίᾳ πλεονεξίᾳ κακίᾳ, μεστοὺς φθόνου φόνου ἔριδος

δόλου κακοηθείας, ψιθυριστάς   ³⁰ καταλάλους θεοστυγεῖς
ὑβριστὰς ὑπερηφάνους ἀλαζόνας, ἐφευρετὰς κακῶν, γονεῦσιν
ἀπειθεῖς, ³¹ ἀσυνέτους ἀσυνθέτους ἀστόργους ἀνελεήμονας· ³²
οἵτινες τὸ δικαίωμα τοῦ θεοῦ ἐπιγνόντες ὅτι οἱ τὰ τοιαῦτα
πράσσοντες ἄξιοι θανάτου εἰσίν, οὐ μόνον αὐτὰ ποιοῦσιν
ἀλλὰ καὶ συνευδοκοῦσιν τοῖς πράσσουσιν.

¹⁸ For the wrath of God is revealed from heaven against all
ungodliness and wickedness of men who by their wickedness
suppress the truth. ¹⁹For what can be known about God is plain
to them, because God has shown it to them. ²⁰Ever since the
creation of the world his invisible nature, namely, his eternal
power and deity, has been clearly perceived in the things that
have been made. So they are without excuse; ²¹for although they
knew God they did not honor him as God or give thanks to him,
but they became futile in their thinking and their senseless
minds were darkened. ²²Claiming to be wise, they became fools,
²³and exchanged the glory of the immortal God for images
resembling mortal man or birds or animals or reptiles.
²⁴Therefore God gave them up in the lusts of their hearts to
impurity, to the dishonoring of their bodies among themselves,
²⁵because they exchanged the truth about God for a lie and
worshiped and served the creature rather than the Creator, who
is blessed for ever! Amen. ²⁶For this reason God gave them up to
dishonorable passions. Their women exchanged natural relations
for unnatural, ²⁷and the men likewise gave up natural relations
with women and were consumed with passion for one another,
men committing shameless acts with men and receiving in their
own persons the due penalty for their error. ²⁸And since they did
not see fit to acknowledge God, God gave them up to a base
mind and to improper conduct. ²⁹They were filled with all
manner of wickedness, evil, covetousness, malice. Full of envy,
murder, strife, deceit, malignity, they are gossips, ³⁰slanderers,
haters of God, insolent, haughty, boastful, inventors of evil,

disobedient to parents, [31]foolish, faithless, heartless, ruthless. [32]Though they know God's decree that those who do such things deserve to die, they not only do them but approve those who practice them.

What is astonishing for a 21st century reader is that Paul explains[35] God's saving justice unto life on the basis of God's wrath unto destruction:

> For in it the righteousness of God is revealed through faith for faith; as it is written, "The righteous one through faith shall live." *For* the wrath of God is revealed from heaven against all ungodliness and wickedness of men who by their wickedness suppress the truth. (Rom 1:17-18)

However, such comes as a surprise only to someone who is not privy to the scriptural story. As I explain in detail elsewhere,[36] human stories start at point A and end with point Z: human kingdoms and empires begin as small entities,[37] rise to their apex and then fall into oblivion. The scriptural story, on the other hand, starts with the destruction of God's city for its sins (Ezek 16 and 23) and ends with the promise of its eventual pardon unto a new life (Is 1). Consequently, Romans 1:17 concerning God's righteousness introduces not just v.18, but the entire passage 1:18-2:16, where both Gentiles and Jews are presented as liable to God's condemning justice that punishes them for their infractions of God's will expressed in his law. When one follows the overarching biblical story, one cannot escape the fact that before the introduction of scriptural Judaism through circumcision in Genesis 17, the hearers are overwhelmed with

---

[35] Notice the explicative *gar* (for, since, because) at the beginning of v.18.

[36] *C-Phil* 47-9.

[37] E.g. the beginnings of the later great Rome were so negligible: the twin brothers Romulus and Remus are sustained by a she-wolf.

the report of a series of divine punishments over the human beings in general, who function scripturally as "uncircumcised" Gentiles: against Adam, representative of the entire humanity (Gen 3); against his descendants in Noah's times (Gen 6-8); against Babel, the center of human arrogance (Gen 10); against Egypt (Gen 12); and finally against a coalition of the Mesopotamian kingdoms (Gen 14). After the institution of circumcision, we have the beginning of the scriptural saga that revolves around Jacob (Israel) and his progeny. This saga follows the blueprint of Ezekiel 16, the *mašal* (parable; exemplar story) around which was woven the scriptural story of three sisters: Samaria, Jerusalem, and Sodom.[38] It starts with the punishment of Sodom (Gen 19), followed by that of Samaria (2 Kg 17), and culminating in the demise of Jerusalem (2 Kg 25).

Romans 1:18 zeroes in on the "ungodliness and wickedness of *the human beings (anthrōpōn)*", thus recapitulating the first chapters of Genesis. The terminology is based on the prophetic precedent, where the Gentiles are dubbed as being basically polytheistic, which is a flagrant infringement of the strict scriptural monotheism. However, in preparation for Romans 2, where he is going to include the Jews in the de facto infringement of God's will in spite of their knowledge thereof, Paul dubs the sin of men not only as "ungodliness" (*asebeian*) but also as "wickedness" (*adikia*; unlawfulness) (1:18); *asebeia* (Latin *impietas*) is a classic term in Greco-Roman society, whose positive counterpart is *evsebeia* (Latin *pietas*). Being "pious" means to have reverence toward the gods, the dead, and the elders. Thus, *evsebeia* amounts to the respect due to those in a higher position compared to us; *asebeia* is the lack of such reverence. It was assumed that one was "blessed" so long as one

---

[38] See *OTI₁* 22-25.

was "pious," which explains why this title was linked with the rulers. The gods would keep a ruler so long as he showed "piety." The generalization of this sin to "all men" is corroborated in that the first "word" or "commandment" in the Decalogue pertaining to our relation to other human being is: "Honor your father and your mother, *that your days may be long* in the land which the Lord your God gives you" (Ex 20:12); "Honor your father and your mother, as the Lord your God commanded you; *that your days may be prolonged, and that it may go well with you,* in the land which the Lord your God gives you." (Deut 5:16) By the same token, when viewed scripturally, the *asebeia* becomes also *adikia* (unlawfulness; unrighteousness; wickedness), thus applying in a specific way to the Jew.[39] That is why, in preparation for Romans 2, where Paul discusses the *adikia* of the Jew, and in Romans 3, where he concludes that "all, both Jews and Greeks, are under the power of sin," *asebeia* is totally discarded in favor of *adikia*. Actually, already at the end of Romans 1:18 men are presented as "suppressing the truth by their wickedness (*en adikia*)."

Unfortunately in many instances, Platonic Greek philosophy and terminology have become the lens through which scripture is read. Consequently, Romans 1:19-23 have been subjected to a philosophical reading and have been made to sound as though these verses are a philosophico-theological treatise concerning "godhead" or the "divinity" of God. However, all scripture is intended to invite, if not persuade, the hearers not to "fathom God in his eternal mystery," but simply to do his will. The "truth" for Paul is always the "truth of the gospel" (Gal 2:5, 14) which is to be "obeyed" (5:7). And this truth lies in the teachings

---

[39] Scripturally, the wicked is an insider who knows the rule, yet decides to behave as an outsider that is ignorant of the rule.

of "the prophets in the holy scriptures" (Rom 1:2). Consequently, Romans 1:18-32, which is introduced with "as it is written" in v.17, is to be heard as a reminder of how those scriptures perceive the ungodliness and wickedness of men.

In both the Law and the Prophets the oneness of the universal God is a given. Polytheism is introduced later only as something to be discarded. In the Law (Pentateuch) the first time we hear of gods is in the story of Rachel's stealing her paternal house gods (Gen 31:19-35). A few chapters later we hear the following:

> God said to Jacob, "Arise, go up to Bethel, and dwell there; and make there an altar to the God who appeared to you when you fled from your brother Esau." So Jacob said to his household and to all who were with him, "Put away the foreign gods that are among you, and purify yourselves, and change your garments; then let us arise and go up to Bethel, that I may make there an altar to the God who answered me in the day of my distress and has been with me wherever I have gone." So they gave to Jacob all the foreign gods that they had, and the rings that were in their ears; and Jacob hid them under the oak which was near Shechem. (Gen 35:1-4)

The same scenario is repeated in the prior Prophets (Joshua through 2 Kings). It is after the tribes are settled in Canaan that we hear of the foreign gods only in preparation for the request to discard them (Josh 23:6, 15-16; 24:14-23). However, if monotheism is the rule in scripture, it does not ensue that it is self-evident. It is rather a scriptural premise that is introduced as a challenging novelty, as is clear from the following: "Thus says the Lord, the God of Israel, '*Your fathers* lived of old beyond the Euphrates, Terah, the father of Abraham and of Nahor; and they *served other gods*.'" (Josh 24:2) Indeed, the rule is that the nations each have their god: "When the Most High gave to the nations their inheritance, when he separated the sons of men, he fixed the bounds of the peoples according to the number of the sons of God. For the Lord's portion is his people, Jacob his allotted heritage." (Deut 32:8-9) Consequently, the monotheism of scriptural Israel is imposed upon it:

> I am the Lord your God, who brought you out of the land of Egypt, out of the house of bondage. *You shall have no other gods before me.* You shall not make for yourself a graven image, or any likeness of anything that is in heaven above, or that is in the earth beneath, or that is in the water under the earth; *you shall not bow down to them or serve them*; for I the Lord your God am a jealous God, visiting the iniquity of the fathers upon the children to the third and the fourth generation of those who hate me, but showing steadfast love to thousands of those who love me and keep my commandments. (Ex 20:2-6; Deut 5:6-10)

The "unseen" God of Genesis 1-11 is, scripturally speaking, none other than the God who said to Israel:

> Therefore take good heed to yourselves. Since you saw no form on the day that the Lord spoke to you at Horeb out of the midst of the fire, beware lest you act corruptly by making a graven image for yourselves, in the form of any figure, the likeness of male or female, the likeness of any beast that is on the earth, the likeness of any winged bird that flies in the air, the likeness of anything that creeps on the ground, the likeness of any fish that is in the water under the earth. (Deut 4:15-18)

Still, this God, though "un-iconic," is, by definition, the maker of everything, since creativity is the attribute of any god. Notice how the power of this unseen God to make everything is mentioned in parallel with his divineness (*theiotēs*; quality of

being divine) (Rom 1:20).[40] Put otherwise, being the sole God
does not make the scriptural God less of a god and thus in need
to prove himself. This is corroborated in v.21 where we are told
that men, including Israel, did not treat God *as (a) God* (*hōs
theon*) by glorifying him. And then there is the addition "and
thank him," which does not make sense except against the
scriptural background whereby God makes himself the God of
men, Israel as well as Adam, by granting them the "gift" of
knowledge of his will through a command; it is only by their
obedience to that "law" that life will be vouchsafed in Canaan or
in the garden, respectively.[41] Later, Paul will explain that the Law
is actually the icon of the "unseen" scriptural God (2:17-23).
What went wrong is that men, including Israel, "became futile in
their mental debates (*dialogismois*)," and in so doing "their
foolish mind was darkened" (v.21). Considering that in scripture
kardia (heart) is actually the translation of the Hebrew *leb* (core,
center), the organ with which one thinks and takes decisions,
then these two phrases are actually the two sides of the same
coin. Men decided to cogitate without reference to God's
command. Instead of following the wisdom of God's law[42] they
went after their own thoughts and "claiming to be wise, they
(actually) ended up as fools" (v.22).[43]

This reading of Romans 1:18-23 against the background of the
scriptural story line, rather than in terms of a series of

---

[40] It is important to note that the Greek used here is *theiotēs* and not *theotēs*. While the
latter connotes "(the) divine being," the former refers rather to "being godly" and thus
"acting divinely."

[41] My reading will be corroborated in how, later in Rom 5, Adam will be introduced in
conjunction with the discussion of the Mosaic law.

[42] See *OTI₃* 107-128.

[43] As I indicated earlier, the same theme is found in 1 Cor 1-3.

philosophic-theological statements,[44] is corroborated in v.24, which introduces the way God implements his punishment: let men proceed on the path they have chosen and suffer the consequences or, as Paul puts it, "For this reason God gave them up (*paredōken*) in the desires (*epithymias*) of their hearts unto uncleanness (*akatharsian*), to the dishonoring (*atimazesthai*) of their bodies among themselves." First, it is clear that it is the same heart which is the culprit here as it was in v.21. Secondly, the heart's desires are linked in Galatians 5:16-17 to the flesh, which is tantamount to the human will that works against God's will.[45] Thirdly, the resulting "uncleanness" is the opposite of the holiness to which the believers are called (1 Thess 4:7). The same thought is repeated almost verbatim in Romans 1:26 with "passions" (*pathē*) instead of "desires": "For this reason God gave them up to passions of dishonor (*atimias*)." The closeness is actually tighter than meets the eye when one considers that, in the passage in Galatians referred to earlier, "passions" and "desires" are used as having parallel meanings: "And those who belong to Christ Jesus have crucified the flesh with its passions (*pathēmasin*)[46] and desires (*epithymiais*)." (5:24) Thus God's punishment in scripture, especially in the Prophets, sounds thus: "You want it your way and not mine, then have it your way and you shall bear the consequences." The most classical instance is found in 1 Samuel 8:

> Then all the elders of Israel gathered together and came to Samuel at Ramah, and said to him, "Behold, you are old and your sons do

---

[44] Which ironically corresponds to what went wrong according to vv.21-22: human dialogical thought took precedence over God's authoritative command.

[45] The Hebrew *basar* refers to the meat of earthly mammals including humans and, consequently, to the realm of creatures as is clear from the statement "The Egyptians are men, and not God; and their horses are flesh, and not spirit" (Is 31:3).

[46] From the same root as *pathē*.

not walk in your ways; now appoint for us a king to govern us like
all the nations." But the thing displeased Samuel when they said,
"Give us a king to govern us." And Samuel prayed to the Lord.
And the Lord said to Samuel, "Hearken to the voice of the people
in all that they say to you; for they have not rejected you, but they
have rejected me from being king over them. According to all the
deeds which they have done to me, from the day I brought them
up out of Egypt even to this day, forsaking me and serving other
gods, so they are also doing to you. Now then, hearken to their
voice; only, you shall solemnly warn them, and show them the
ways of the king who shall reign over them." So Samuel told all
the words of the Lord to the people who were asking a king from
him. He said, "These will be the ways of the king who will reign
over you ... And in that day you will cry out because of your king,
whom you have chosen for yourselves; but the Lord will not
answer you in that day." But the people refused to listen to the
voice of Samuel; and they said, "No! but we will have a king over
us, that we also may be like all the nations, and that our king may
govern us and go out before us and fight our battles." And when
Samuel had heard all the words of the people, he repeated them in
the ears of the Lord. And the Lord said to Samuel, "Hearken to
their voice, and make them a king." (vv.4-11, 19-22)

In opting for their ways, men were ironically committing the sin
of *asebeia* while they were practicing their own *evsebeia* toward
the idols: "they exchanged the truth of[47] God for a lie and
honored piously (*esebasthēsan*)[48] and worshiped the creature
rather than the Creator, who is blessed for ever! Amen." (Rom
2:25) Their apparent *evsebeia* was simply a "lie" and thus
factually *asebeia*.

---

[47] Notice RSV has "about" instead of "of," thus making of "the truth of God" a matter
of philosophical theology rather than the dictates of the gospel for men to abide by.
[48] The verb *sebazomai* is from the same root as *evsebeia* (and *asebiea*) and means "to
worship piously."

Paul's intention is to steer the "wise" Roman patricians (Rom 1:14) away from the cogitative wisdom of the dialogical discourse (*dialogismois*; v.21) to doing God's will expressed in his *torah*. This becomes clear the third time he uses the phrase "God gave them up": "And since they did not consider it proper (*edokimasan*) to acquire the right knowledge of God, God gave them up to an inconsiderate (*adokimon*) mind in order to do (*poiein*) the improper things." (v.28). This statement makes sense only to the one who is familiar with scripture, where the right knowledge of God is equivalent to the knowledge of his *torah*. Since the *torah* is a set of commandments to be followed, then the true knowledge of God is expressed in doing his will. In the list of wrongdoings of vv.29-30, it is wickedness (*adikia*; unrighteousness) that is the first and summing up element; all others wrongdoings are expressions of it.[49] This is corroborated in that the perpetrators of such wrongdoings are acting against God's *dikaiōma* (righteous decree; v.32). Even worse: "although they are fully aware of that decree namely, that those who practice such wrongdoings are liable of death, not only do they do them, but also approve of those who practice them." (v.32) Thus, toward the end of his indictment against all men Paul squarely brings to the fore the two verbs "do" (*poiein*) and "practice" (*prassein*), which will take center stage when he will begin in Romans 2 his indictment of the Jews who know God's law yet do not do or practice its requirements.

---

[49] Regarding the first item of a series being the controlling one, see my comments in *Gal* 293-301 on *porneia* (fornication; harlotry; Gal 5:19) and *agapē* (love; Gal 5:22).

Chapter 2

Vv. 1-16 ¹ Διὸ ἀναπολόγητος εἶ, ὦ ἄνθρωπε πᾶς ὁ κρίνων· ἐν ᾧ γὰρ κρίνεις τὸν ἕτερον, σεαυτὸν κατακρίνεις, τὰ γὰρ αὐτὰ πράσσεις ὁ κρίνων. ² οἴδαμεν δὲ ὅτι τὸ κρίμα τοῦ θεοῦ ἐστιν κατὰ ἀλήθειαν ἐπὶ τοὺς τὰ τοιαῦτα πράσσοντας. ³ λογίζῃ δὲ τοῦτο, ὦ ἄνθρωπε ὁ κρίνων τοὺς τὰ τοιαῦτα πράσσοντας καὶ ποιῶν αὐτά, ὅτι σὺ ἐκφεύξῃ τὸ κρίμα τοῦ θεοῦ; ⁴ ἢ τοῦ πλούτου τῆς χρηστότητος αὐτοῦ καὶ τῆς ἀνοχῆς καὶ τῆς μακροθυμίας καταφρονεῖς, ἀγνοῶν ὅτι τὸ χρηστὸν τοῦ θεοῦ εἰς μετάνοιάν σε ἄγει; ⁵ κατὰ δὲ τὴν σκληρότητά σου καὶ ἀμετανόητον καρδίαν θησαυρίζεις σεαυτῷ ὀργὴν ἐν ἡμέρᾳ ὀργῆς καὶ ἀποκαλύψεως δικαιοκρισίας τοῦ θεοῦ ⁶ ὃς ἀποδώσει ἑκάστῳ κατὰ τὰ ἔργα αὐτοῦ· ⁷ τοῖς μὲν καθ᾽ ὑπομονὴν ἔργου ἀγαθοῦ δόξαν καὶ τιμὴν καὶ ἀφθαρσίαν ζητοῦσιν ζωὴν αἰώνιον, ⁸ τοῖς δὲ ἐξ ἐριθείας καὶ ἀπειθοῦσι τῇ ἀληθείᾳ πειθομένοις δὲ τῇ ἀδικίᾳ ὀργὴ καὶ θυμός. ⁹ θλῖψις καὶ στενοχωρία ἐπὶ πᾶσαν ψυχὴν ἀνθρώπου τοῦ κατεργαζομένου τὸ κακόν, Ἰουδαίου τε πρῶτον καὶ Ἕλληνος· ¹⁰ δόξα δὲ καὶ τιμὴ καὶ εἰρήνη παντὶ τῷ ἐργαζομένῳ τὸ ἀγαθόν, Ἰουδαίῳ τε πρῶτον καὶ Ἕλληνι· ¹¹ οὐ γάρ ἐστιν προσωπολημψία παρὰ τῷ θεῷ. ¹² Ὅσοι γὰρ ἀνόμως ἥμαρτον, ἀνόμως καὶ ἀπολοῦνται, καὶ ὅσοι ἐν νόμῳ ἥμαρτον, διὰ νόμου κριθήσονται· ¹³ γὰρ οἱ ἀκροαταὶ νόμου δίκαιοι παρὰ [τῷ] θεῷ, ἀλλ᾽ οἱ ποιηταὶ νόμου δικαιωθήσονται. ¹⁴ ὅταν γὰρ ἔθνη τὰ μὴ νόμον ἔχοντα φύσει τὰ τοῦ νόμου ποιῶσιν, οὗτοι νόμον μὴ ἔχοντες ἑαυτοῖς εἰσιν νόμος· ¹⁵ οἵτινες ἐνδείκνυνται τὸ ἔργον τοῦ νόμου γραπτὸν ἐν ταῖς καρδίαις αὐτῶν, συμμαρτυρούσης αὐτῶν τῆς συνειδήσεως καὶ μεταξὺ ἀλλήλων τῶν λογισμῶν κατηγορούντων ἢ καὶ ἀπολογουμένων, ¹⁶ ἐν ἡμέρᾳ ὅτε κρίνει ὁ θεὸς τὰ κρυπτὰ τῶν ἀνθρώπων κατὰ τὸ εὐαγγέλιόν μου διὰ Χριστοῦ Ἰησοῦ.

¹Therefore you have no excuse, O man, whoever you are, when you judge another; for in passing judgment upon him you condemn yourself, because you, the judge, are doing the very same things. ²We know that the judgment of God rightly falls upon those who do such things. ³Do you suppose, O man, that when you judge those who do such things and yet do them yourself, you will escape the judgment of God? ⁴Or do you presume upon the riches of his kindness and forbearance and patience? Do you not know that God's kindness is meant to lead you to repentance? ⁵But by your hard and impenitent heart you are storing up wrath for yourself on the day of wrath when God's righteous judgment will be revealed. ⁶For he will render to every man according to his works: ⁷to those who by doing patiently (the) good work seek for glory and honor and immortality, he will give eternal life; ⁸but for those who are factious and do not obey the truth, but obey wickedness, there will be wrath and fury. ⁹There will be tribulation and distress for every human being who does evil, the Jew first and also the Greek, ¹⁰but glory and honor and peace for every one who does good, the Jew first and also the Greek. ¹¹For God shows no partiality. ¹²All who have sinned without the law will also perish without the law, and all who have sinned under the law will be judged by the law. ¹³For it is not the hearers of the law who are righteous before God, but the doers of the law who will be justified. ¹⁴When Gentiles who have not the law do by nature what the law requires, they are a law to themselves, even though they do not have the law. ¹⁵They show that what the law requires is written on their hearts, while their conscience also bears witness and their conflicting thoughts accuse or perhaps excuse them ¹⁶on that day when, according to my gospel, God judges the secrets of men by Christ Jesus.

Paul explains that the Jew, who knows God's will expressed in the Law, is prone to be judgmental. However, God alone is the judge, before whom the Jew is as "without excuse" (*anapologētos*; Rom 2:1) as the Gentiles (1:20). The reason is obvious: divine judgment is not based on one's knowledge of the Law, but on one's practice thereof:

> Therefore you have no excuse, O man, whoever you are, when you judge another; for in passing judgment upon him you condemn yourself, because you, the judge, are practicing the very same things. We know that the judgment of God rightly falls upon those who practice such things. Do you suppose, O man, that when you judge those who practice such things and yet do them yourself, you will escape the judgment of God? (2:1-3)

Still, this is not a general philosophical statement. Rather, it is a "reading" of scripture itself, as will be made amply clear in 3:10-18. And scripture functions as a double jeopardy against the Jew. Not only has the Law been given to him (3:2), but he learned from scripture itself that he was granted time and again the possibility to repent of his wrongdoings, through "God's kindness and forbearance and patience" (2:4). However, time and again the Jew contravened God's law and, in so doing, he was "storing up wrath for [him]self on the day of wrath when God's righteous judgment will be revealed" (v.5). And God will judge, rendering to each according to one's deeds (v.6).

The terminology Paul uses to describe positive and negative behaviors is very interesting in that it paves the way for his detailed argument in Romans 5-6. The mention of patience at the outset and in conjunction with good work reminds the hearers that the path toward "glory and honor and incorruptibility" is a long one and does not end until God renders his verdict "on that day when God judges the secrets of men" (2:16). Nothing is settled until that day, as Paul underscores in 1 Corinthians 4:1-5. It is only then, and not before then, that "life eternal" is granted. The use of the singular "good work" (Rom 2:7) is telling: it is neither a once for all deed,

nor a quota of deeds, rather it is the *same work* that has to be
patiently *sustained* until the end.

What this sustained good work is all about can be gathered
from the terminology used to speak of its opposite: "but for
those who are factious and do not obey (*apeithousi*; put their
trust in) the truth, while obeying (*peithomenois*; being convinced
by) wickedness, there will be wrath and fury." (v.8) The use of
the verb *peithō* (trust) in the Pauline epistles corresponds
functionally to the verb *pistevō* (believe, put one's trust in). Its
translation as "obey" in RSV is functionally correct since the
truth (of the gospel) is a behavioral teaching rather than a mental
or philosophical proposal. This is confirmed in that the opposite
of truth is wickedness (*adikia*), which is an attitude expressed in
actions condemnable by justice (*dikē*). A further corroboration is
found in the phrase "those who are factious" (*tois ex eritheias*)
that is found elsewhere only in Philippians where it is used in
conjunction with preaching the gospel:

> Some indeed preach (*kēryssousin*) Christ from envy and rivalry, but
> others from good will. The latter do it out of love, knowing that I
> am put here for the defense of the *gospel; the former* proclaim
> (*katangellousin*) Christ *out of partisanship* (*hoi ex eritheias*), not
> sincerely but thinking to afflict me in my imprisonment. (Phil
> 1:15-17)

As for the rule regarding the good and the evil work, it applies to
both Jew and Gentile since God shows no partiality. Still, as Paul
underscored earlier (Rom 1:16), the Jew is first in line, either to
damnation or to the peace of the Kingdom, because he is fully
aware of what is required, given that he is "entrusted with the
oracles (*logia*; speeches, words) of God" (3:2).

Then Paul concludes by saying that if God is impartial, it is because,[1] whether one is aware of God's law or not, God will judge *according to that Law* (2:12-16). Just as 1:18-32, this passage is to be understood scripturally, not philosophically or ethically. The meaning of 2:12 is crucial to the entire argumentation. It is more often than not translated in a manner similar to that found in RSV: "All who have sinned without the law (*anomōs*) will also perish without the law (*anomōs*), and all who have sinned within (the domain of) the law (*en nomō*) will be judged through the law (*dia nomou*)." First and foremost, the parallel between Gentile and Jew is established by the same "have sinned" (*hēmarton*), meaning that in both cases there is sin, that is, contravention of God's will. Consequently, whereas those who are within the domain of the Law will be "judged" by that Law, those who have sinned, albeit without the Law, will nevertheless perish (by condemnation) (*apolountai*). Later, Paul will repeat the same argument: "through one man sin came into the world and death through sin … all men sinned (*hēmarton*) *for* until the law sin was in the world … death [as a consequence of sin] reigned from Adam to Moses, even over those whose sins were not like the transgression of Adam." (5:12-14) As I indicated in my discussion of 1:18-32, when men misbehaved before the Law they were punished. In the case of Adam, which sets the tone for the following stories, sin was actually a contravention of an express commandment. That is why 5:14 refers to Adam's sin as a "transgression" (*parabaseōs*), which is a legal term. The conclusion is evident: in scripture, the ultimate reference for the "good" and "evil" is the Law.[2] And since the Law is a set of commandments rather than informational

---

[1] Notice the *gar* (for, because, since) opening 2:12.

[2] See my *C-Gen* where I show that all the sins of Jacob as well as those before him up until Adam are cast as transgressions of Mosaic commandments.

statements, "it is not the hearers of the law who are righteous
before God, but the doers of the law who will be declared
righteous" (2:13). And even the Gentiles are bound by this
reality since, although they "have not a law," nevertheless they
are righteous only insofar as they "*do the matters (prescriptions) of
the law*" (v.14). This is corroborated in the following v.15 where
reference is made to "the work (deed) of the law" (*to ergon tou
nomou*).[3] At this point, Paul uses the terminology of the
Jeremianic "new covenant" where the Law is written on the
hearts (Jer 31:33). So, by doing God's will inscribed in the Law
without being privy to that Law, the Gentiles would be behaving
like someone who is under the aegis of the new covenant:
without being "taught by others" (Jer 31:34) they follow the
dictates of their own conscience and accept its verdict whenever
it accuses or excuses them (Rom 2:15).

All this stands to "scriptural" reason since on his day God will
judge "the hidden matters (secrets; *ta krypta*) of men" (2:16) in
order to bring them to light and reveal them: "Therefore do not
pronounce judgment before the time, before the Lord comes,
who will bring to light *the things now hidden* (*ta krypta*) in
darkness and will reveal the purposes *of the heart*. Then every
man will receive his commendation from God." (1 Cor 4:5) But
this judgment will be done *according to Paul's gospel* with the
Christ preached therein functioning as the muster (*dia Iēsou
Khristou*) (Rom 2:16). This phraseology recalls the terminology
of 1:1-4 and there Paul's gospel is nothing else than what was
taught "through his prophets in the holy scriptures" and was
preserved in the *torah* which, according to Isaiah, was slated to

---

[3] In both these instances we have the double definite article: *the* (matters) of *the* Law"
and "*the* work of *the* Law." In the remainder of the passage *nomos* is without the
definite article.

be carried out to the ends of the earth.[4] However, the question remains, "Why should Paul be preaching to the Gentiles something that seems ultimately to be gathered from the dictates of the human conscience?" Put otherwise, "What is the need for the gospel if it does not offer anything special or, at least, more?" And ultimately, "Shouldn't we be left to behave after our conscience?" These questions if conceived ethically, or philosophically, or anthropologically, or the like, are irrelevant from the perspective of scripture. Scripture can answer only from its own perspective. In other words, unless a question is within the purview of scripture, scripture cannot answer it. So the only valid question to scripture cannot but be, "What is scripture saying?"

The scriptural premise is that "man" (Adam) was given a commandment to abide by in order to secure a peaceful life for himself in the garden he was assigned to live in together with all that lived there—the fauna and flora. Adam faltered and then tried to "excuse" himself. His son Cain did the same; he killed his own brother and then tried to "excuse" himself (Gen 4:9). This produced a genealogy that culminated with Lamech who "excused" his propensity to massive killing (vv.23-24). Man's conscience was not functioning properly: it "excused" and never "accused." The result was that humankind virtually "perished" (Gen 6-8). So God decided to proceed on a path that culminated with the "gift" of the Law with its express commandments in order to secure that man, or at least Israel, would not rely on his own "excusing" conscience, but would follow the Law's instructions unto life rather than unto death. However, the "children of Israel" did not heed the Law and ended up exiled from Canaan, just as Adam was exiled from the garden, and

---

[4] See my comments above on Rom 1:1-4.

Cain was doomed to roam as a wanderer. To get out of that impasse, God devised a new plan: the *same* Law would be written this time indelibly on men's hearts (Jer 31:31-34), with the Isaianic proviso that it would be shared with the nations. And this is precisely what Paul's mission was all about. The Gentiles *could* have lived righteously without the Law (*anomōs*), even the new one, but scripture has shown that "men" never succeeded in such an endeavor. Paul was commissioned to "secure" their salvation, just as Peter was commissioned to secure that of the circumcised (Gal 2:7-8), "on that day when, according to my gospel, God judges the secrets of men by Christ Jesus" (Rom 2:16).

Vv. 17-29 *¹⁷Εἰ δὲ σὺ Ἰουδαῖος ἐπονομάζῃ καὶ ἐπαναπαύῃ νόμῳ καὶ καυχᾶσαι ἐν θεῷ ¹⁸ καὶ γινώσκεις τὸ θέλημα καὶ δοκιμάζεις τὰ διαφέροντα κατηχούμενος ἐκ τοῦ νόμου, ¹⁹ πέποιθάς τε σεαυτὸν ὁδηγὸν εἶναι τυφλῶν, φῶς τῶν ἐν σκότει, ²⁰ παιδευτὴν ἀφρόνων, διδάσκαλον νηπίων, ἔχοντα τὴν μόρφωσιν τῆς γνώσεως καὶ τῆς ἀληθείας ἐν τῷ νόμῳ· ²¹ ὁ οὖν διδάσκων ἕτερον σεαυτὸν οὐ διδάσκεις; ὁ κηρύσσων μὴ κλέπτειν κλέπτεις; ²² ὁ λέγων μὴ μοιχεύειν μοιχεύεις; ὁ βδελυσσόμενος τὰ εἴδωλα ἱεροσυλεῖς; ²³ ὃς ἐν νόμῳ καυχᾶσαι, διὰ τῆς παραβάσεως τοῦ νόμου τὸν θεὸν ἀτιμάζεις· ²⁴ τὸ γὰρ ὄνομα τοῦ θεοῦ δι᾽ ὑμᾶς βλασφημεῖται ἐν τοῖς ἔθνεσιν, καθὼς γέγραπται. ²⁵ Περιτομὴ μὲν γὰρ ὠφελεῖ ἐὰν νόμον πράσσῃς· ἐὰν δὲ παραβάτης νόμου ᾖς, ἡ περιτομή σου ἀκροβυστία γέγονεν. ²⁶ ἐὰν οὖν ἡ ἀκροβυστία τὰ δικαιώματα τοῦ νόμου φυλάσσῃ, οὐχ ἡ ἀκροβυστία αὐτοῦ εἰς περιτομὴν λογισθήσεται; ²⁷ καὶ κρινεῖ ἡ ἐκ φύσεως ἀκροβυστία τὸν νόμον τελοῦσα σὲ τὸν διὰ γράμματος καὶ περιτομῆς παραβάτην νόμου. ²⁸ οὐ γὰρ ὁ ἐν τῷ φανερῷ Ἰουδαῖός ἐστιν οὐδὲ ἡ ἐν τῷ φανερῷ ἐν σαρκὶ περιτομή, ²⁹ ἀλλ᾽ ὁ ἐν τῷ κρυπτῷ Ἰουδαῖος, καὶ περιτομὴ καρδίας ἐν πνεύματι οὐ γράμματι, οὗ ὁ ἔπαινος οὐκ ἐξ ἀνθρώπων ἀλλ᾽ ἐκ τοῦ θεοῦ.*

¹⁷But if you call yourself a Jew and rely upon the law and boast of your relation to God ¹⁸and know his will and approve what is excellent, because you are instructed in the law, ¹⁹and if you are sure that you are a guide to the blind, a light to those who are in darkness, ²⁰a corrector of the foolish, a teacher of children, having in the law the embodiment of knowledge and truth— ²¹you then who teach others, will you not teach yourself? While you preach against stealing, do you steal? ²²You who say that one must not commit adultery, do you commit adultery? You who abhor idols, do you rob temples? ²³You who boast in the law, do you dishonor God by breaking the law? ²⁴For, as it is written, "The name of God is blasphemed among the Gentiles because of you." ²⁵Circumcision indeed is of value if you obey the law; but if you break the law, your circumcision becomes uncircumcision. ²⁶So, if a man who is uncircumcised keeps the precepts of the law, will not his uncircumcision be regarded as circumcision? ²⁷Then those who are physically uncircumcised but keep the law will condemn you who have the written code and circumcision but break the law. ²⁸For he is not a real Jew who is one outwardly, nor is true circumcision something external and physical. ²⁹He is a Jew who is one inwardly, and real circumcision is a matter of the heart, spiritual and not literal. His praise is not from men but from God.

Having established that the Gentiles are bound by the law of the new covenant written on their hearts, Paul elaborates how the same applies to the Jews, thus sealing the oneness of the gospel he untiringly fought for since the Jerusalem summit (Gal 2:1-10). In preparation for his conclusion concerning the true Jew who is not so just in appearance (Rom 2:28-29), Paul begins with the Jew in name only. This Jew's boast over the Gentile revolves not so much around God, but rather around the Law which is mentioned no less than ten times in eleven verses (17-

27).[5] The reason is evident: since God is non-iconic in scripture, his "shape" or "appearance" is the Scroll of the Law. Indeed the Law is the "embodiment" (*morphōsin*; shaping, forming) of the knowledge and the truth pertaining to the scriptural God. Since knowledge of the Lord and that of his *torah* are equivalent in scripture, and the truth is embedded in that same *torah* preached as his gospel to the nations, then God's *morphē* (shape; form; reflection) lies in the words of the *torah*. This is corroborated in the full equivalence between the two in the phrases "you boast in God" (*kavkhasai en theō*; v.17) and "you boast in the law" (*en nomō kavkhasai*; v.23).[6]

The Jew does not need to delve into his own conscience to test (*dokimazeis*) matters to figure out the better ones (*diapheronta*) in order to do them. He already knows God's will since he is instructed out of (the contents of) the Law (*ek tou nomou*; v.18), and he can impart this knowledge to others (vv.19-20a) precisely because he has the Law (v.20b). Still, he does not abide by the Law's instructions (vv.21-22), thus committing transgressions against it (v.23). Consequently, he ends up by boasting in the Law and God, flashing his own superiority over the Gentiles, yet, at the same time, dishonoring that same God (v.23) in the eyes

---

[5] God is referred to only twice (vv.17 and 23) outside his mention in the scriptural quotation in v.24.

[6] Another example of how translations distort the original is evident in how RSV renders Rom 2:17 and 20. Both verses use the same phrasing in Greek. However, in the first case, RSV has "boast of your relation to God" and, in the second, it reads "boast in the law." By adding the unwarranted "your relation to" in v.17, RSV "personalized" God, while viewing the Law as an impersonal set of rules, thus blurring an essential scriptural datum of the full equivalence between the scriptural God and the Law, and between that God and his will. By personalizing God and impersonalizing the Law, the RSV translation reflects a theological bias that prepares the way for discarding the Law or, at least, for considering it as secondary, if not unnecessary. This is a stand which Paul would never concede to. For Paul, disobeying God's will expressed in his commandments is tantamount to dishonoring him (v.24)!

of those same Gentiles (v.24)! By expressly quoting scripture here, Paul is appealing to God himself in order to preempt any accusation to the effect that he is giving his own personal opinion.

Then Paul moves to tackle the matter of circumcision, which is the tangible expression of being a Jew and was a reason for boasting (Phil 3:19). And since circumcision is Abrahamic, he introduces the terminology he will be using in Romans 4 dedicated to Abraham (Rom 2:25-26): circumcision, uncircumcision, and especially the verb *logizomai* (account). Already in the case of Abraham, the point was established that, unless one abides by God's will, circumcision is of no avail:

> Now there was a famine in the land, besides the former famine that was in the days of Abraham. And Isaac went to Gerar, to Abimelech king of the Philistines. And the Lord appeared to him, and said, "Do not go down to Egypt; dwell in the land of which I shall tell you. Sojourn in this land, and I will be with you, and will bless you; for to you and to your descendants I will give all these lands, and I will fulfil the oath which I swore to Abraham your father. I will multiply your descendants as the stars of heaven, and will give to your descendants all these lands; and by your descendants all the nations of the earth shall bless themselves: *because[7] Abraham obeyed my voice and kept my charge (what is to be kept), my commandments, my statutes, and my laws.*" So Isaac dwelt in Gerar. (Gen 26:1-6)

If obedience applies to Abraham, it is the more so binding on every Jew. Otherwise, the circumcised is as good as an uncircumcised (Rom 2:25) as Jeremiah, the prophet of the new covenant, taught:

---

[7] The original *'eqeb 'ašer* is forceful; it means "the preceding being the consequence of that…"

Behold, the days are coming, says the Lord, when I will punish all those who are circumcised but yet uncircumcised—Egypt, Judah, Edom, the sons of Ammon, Moab, and all who dwell in the desert that cut the corners of their hair; for all these nations are uncircumcised, and all the house of Israel is uncircumcised in heart. (Jer 9:25-26)

And conversely, as he already wrote earlier (Rom 2:14), Paul surmises that if the uncircumcised "keeps the (lawful) precepts (*dikaiōmata*) of the Law" and thus "fulfills the Law" (v.27), then his uncircumcision "will be accounted (*logisthēsetai*)[8] as circumcision" (v.26), and he will even function as a muster for God in his case against the Jew who "transgresses the Law" and thus will prove at judgment to be simply a Jew "through the letter (of the Law) and circumcision," that is to say, someone who is outwardly circumcised, but not "in heart," that is, someone who can outwardly recite the Law, but does not practice it. Indeed, he will merely appear to be Jew to the outside world (v.28). God, who "judges 'the hidden matters (secrets)' (*ta krypta*) of men" (v.16), will be able to point out the Jew who is so "inwardly" (*en tō kryptō*; in the secret, v.29), as opposed to the Jew who is so "outwardly" (*en tō phanerō*, v.28). For true circumcision cannot be outwardly given; it is "in the heart," which is at the center of the human thought, will, and resolve.

Paul explicates the circumcision in heart as being "in the spirit, not in the letter" (v.29). In order to understand what he means one is to appeal to Ezekiel who mentions both spirit and heart in conjunction with the new covenant:

---

[8] Notice the future tense, which is a reference to God's judgment on his day (v.16; 1 Cor 4:1-5). This means that true circumcision is to be expressed through a sustained obedience to God's will until judgment day, as I indicated in my comments on Rom 2:7-11.

And I will give them one heart, and put a new spirit within them;
I will take the stony heart out of their flesh and give them a heart
of flesh, that they may walk in my statutes and keep my
ordinances and obey them; and they shall be my people, and I will
be their God. (11:19-20; see also 36:26-27)

Therefore I will judge you, O house of Israel, every one according
to his ways, says the Lord God. Repent and turn from all your
transgressions, lest iniquity be your ruin. Cast away from you all
the transgressions which you have committed against me, and get
yourselves a new heart and a new spirit! Why will you die, O
house of Israel? For I have no pleasure in the death of any one,
says the Lord God; so turn, and live. (18:30-32)

These texts make it clear that it is God's spirit that ensures that
his will be inscribed on hearts (of flesh) and not on (hearts of)
stone. This rejoins Jeremiah's statement regarding the new
covenant:

Behold, the days are coming, says the Lord, when I will make a
new covenant with the house of Israel and the house of Judah, not
like the covenant which I made with their fathers when I took
them by the hand to bring them out of the land of Egypt, my
covenant which they broke, though I was their husband, says the
Lord. But this is the covenant which I will make with the house of
Israel after those days, says the Lord: I will put my law within
them, and I will write it upon their hearts; and I will be their God,
and they shall be my people. (31:31-33)

The reason behind the insufficiency of the heart is that the
human heart can make "unwise" decisions (Rom 1:21) and even
be unrepentant (2:15) when summoned to do so (Ezek 18:30-
32). It is solely God's spirit that is granted after the punishment
for wrongdoing (Ezek 37:1-15) which will ensure that the heart
not only remember the letter of the Law, but also remember to

keep it as Deuteronomy insistently requires. That is why Paul will refer to the Law that saves from condemnation as "the law of the spirit of life" (Rom 8:2). It is abiding by this law that will ultimately ensure commendation from God (2:29b) on judgment day (1 Cor 4:5).

Chapter 3

Vv. 1-8 ¹ Τί οὖν τὸ περισσὸν τοῦ Ἰουδαίου ἢ τίς ἡ ὠφέλεια τῆς περιτομῆς; ² πολὺ κατὰ πάντα τρόπον. πρῶτον μὲν [γὰρ] ὅτι ἐπιστεύθησαν τὰ λόγια τοῦ θεοῦ. ³ τί γάρ; εἰ ἠπίστησάν τινες, μὴ ἡ ἀπιστία αὐτῶν τὴν πίστιν τοῦ θεοῦ καταργήσει; ⁴ μὴ γένοιτο· γινέσθω δὲ ὁ θεὸς ἀληθής, πᾶς δὲ ἄνθρωπος ψεύστης, καθὼς γέγραπται· ὅπως ἂν δικαιωθῇς ἐν τοῖς λόγοις σου καὶ νικήσεις ἐν τῷ κρίνεσθαί σε. ⁵ εἰ δὲ ἡ ἀδικία ἡμῶν θεοῦ δικαιοσύνην συνίστησιν, τί ἐροῦμεν; μὴ ἄδικος ὁ θεὸς ὁ ἐπιφέρων τὴν ὀργήν; κατὰ ἄνθρωπον λέγω. ⁶ μὴ γένοιτο· ἐπεὶ πῶς κρινεῖ ὁ θεὸς τὸν κόσμον; ⁷ εἰ δὲ ἡ ἀλήθεια τοῦ θεοῦ ἐν τῷ ἐμῷ ψεύσματι ἐπερίσσευσεν εἰς τὴν δόξαν αὐτοῦ, τί ἔτι κἀγὼ ὡς ἁμαρτωλὸς κρίνομαι; ⁸ καὶ μὴ καθὼς βλασφημούμεθα καὶ καθὼς φασίν τινες ἡμᾶς λέγειν ὅτι ποιήσωμεν τὰ κακά, ἵνα ἔλθῃ τὰ ἀγαθά; ὧν τὸ κρίμα ἔνδικόν ἐστιν.

¹*Then what advantage has the Jew? Or what is the value of circumcision? ²Much in every way. To begin with, the Jews are entrusted with the oracles of God. ³What if some were unfaithful? Does their faithlessness nullify the faithfulness of God? ⁴By no means! Let God be true though every man be false, as it is written, "That thou mayest be justified in thy words, and prevail when thou art judged." ⁵But if our wickedness serves to show the justice of God, what shall we say? That God is unjust to inflict wrath on us? (I speak in a human way.) ⁶By no means! For then how could God judge the world? ⁷But if through my falsehood God's truthfulness abounds to his glory, why am I still being condemned as a sinner? ⁸And why not do evil that good may come? —as some people slanderously charge us with saying. Their condemnation is just.*

Earlier Paul said that "circumcision is of value if you obey the law" (Rom 2:25). So the second part of his question in 3:1

75

regarding the value of circumcision has already been answered. The main issue is the first part of the question "What is the advantage (*to perisson*) of the Jew (over the Gentile)?" or more precisely, "What does the Jew have more (over the Gentile)?" That is why, although Paul begins by saying "Much in every way" followed by "to begin with," he actually adduces only one element, "the oracles (*logia*; words, statements, speeches) of God" with which the Jews were entrusted specifically. It is actually from those scriptures that the "Israelites" are informed of "the sonship, the glory, the covenants, the giving of the law, the worship, and the promises to the patriarchs, and even of the Christ" (9:4-5). But, and more importantly, they are informed that God is the *judge* and he "*judges* the secrets of men through this Christ" (2:16). The main point of Paul's question in 3:1 is to introduce God's righteous judgment. This is confirmed in that the rest of the chapter revolves around the root *dik*— whose basic connotation is justice or righteousness, which is the crimson thread that runs through the Law. This, in turn, explains why Paul added the question regarding the value of circumcision after the one concerning the Jew. By definition the Jew is one who is circumcised, and consequently any question about the Jew entails a question about circumcision. Conversely, as circumcised, the Jew is bound by obedience to the Law (2:25) which is found precisely in "the oracles of God." Besides *dik*—, the other root that is overwhelmingly used in Romans 3 is *pist*— (trust) which is precisely the second element of the scriptural quotation in 2:17: "The righteous one through trust (faith) will live."

Although the Jews were entrusted with the oracles of God, they proved in their actions not to abide by them and thus to be untrustworthy. However, this unfaithfulness does not annul God's faithfulness to his word of teaching, a topic which will be revisited in Romans 11. Man's wickedness is just an *opportunity* for God to *show forth* his justice and is not to be equated with God's *needing* that opportunity to *prove* that he is just. His just wrath is a function of his justice, as was shown in Romans 2. If God were unfaithful to his word that he would implement his justice according to our actions, then his word of judgment would be false! Such thought is plainly oxymoronic since God is by definition the (just) judge.[1] Were it not so, then he will not be able to judge righteously the world as he does in Psalm 82. But if God is shown in all his glory whenever he judges the world and thus asserts himself as the God of all and everything, and since being sinful allows him this opportunity, why should sinfulness be condemnable (Rom 3:7)? This seems to be the argument of Paul's opponents who accuse him as de facto saying, "Let us do evil that good may come." Paul retorts that such accusation is false, and its promoters are justly liable to divine condemnation.

This sudden aside against the opponents, a unique instance in this epistle, is reminiscent of Galatians:

> We ourselves, who are Jews by birth and not *Gentile sinners*, yet who know that a man is not justified by works of the law but through faith in Jesus Christ, even we have believed in Christ Jesus, in order to be justified by faith in Christ, and not by works of the law, because by works of the law shall no one be justified (*ex ergōn nomou ou dikaiōthēsetai pasa sarx*). But if, in our endeavor to be justified in Christ, *we ourselves were found to be sinners*, is Christ then a servant (*doulos*) of sin? By no means! (2:15-17)

The fact that Galatians is in the background is corroborated in that the following passage (Rom 3:9-20) ends with the same

---

[1] See earlier my discussion of Romans 1:18-2:16.

scriptural quotation "by works of the law shall no flesh (human being) be justified" (*ex ergōn nomou ou dikaiōthēsetai pasa sarx*; Ps 143:2) found in Galatians 2:16. Consequently, in Romans 3:7-8, Paul is defending himself against the accusation of making God condone sin if the Jew is put on an equal footing with the Gentile "sinner." But it is clear that this is not what Paul is saying. Rather, Paul contends, it is scripture that evidences that both Jew and Gentile *did* sin. Already he made this point in Galatians when he wrote: "But the scripture consigned *all* (*ta panta*) *under sin* (*hypo hamartian*)." (3:22) That this is what he is driving at is confirmed in that in the following verse in Romans he concludes: "... for I have already charged that all (*pantas*), both Jews and Greeks, are *under sin* (*hyph' hamartian*)."[2] (3:9)

Vv. 9-31 ⁹ Τί οὖν; προεχόμεθα; οὐ πάντως· προῃτιασάμεθα γὰρ Ἰουδαίους τε καὶ Ἕλληνας πάντας ὑφ' ἁμαρτίαν εἶναι, ¹⁰ καθὼς γέγραπται ὅτι οὐκ ἔστιν δίκαιος οὐδὲ εἷς, ¹¹ οὐκ ἔστιν ὁ συνίων, οὐκ ἔστιν ὁ ἐκζητῶν τὸν θεόν. ¹² πάντες ἐξέκλιναν ἅμα ἠχρεώθησαν· οὐκ ἔστιν ὁ ποιῶν χρηστότητα, [οὐκ ἔστιν] ἕως ἑνός. ¹³ τάφος ἀνεῳγμένος ὁ λάρυγξ αὐτῶν, ταῖς γλώσσαις αὐτῶν ἐδολιοῦσαν, ἰὸς ἀσπίδων ὑπὸ τὰ χείλη αὐτῶν· ¹⁴ ὧν τὸ στόμα ἀρᾶς καὶ πικρίας γέμει, ¹⁵ ὀξεῖς οἱ πόδες αὐτῶν ἐκχέαι αἷμα, ¹⁶ σύντριμμα καὶ ταλαιπωρία ἐν ταῖς ὁδοῖς αὐτῶν, ¹⁷ καὶ ὁδὸν εἰρήνης οὐκ ἔγνωσαν. ¹⁸ οὐκ ἔστιν φόβος θεοῦ ἀπέναντι τῶν ὀφθαλμῶν αὐτῶν. ¹⁹ οἴδαμεν δὲ ὅτι ὅσα ὁ νόμος λέγει τοῖς ἐν τῷ νόμῳ λαλεῖ, ἵνα πᾶν στόμα φραγῇ καὶ ὑπόδικος γένηται πᾶς ὁ κόσμος τῷ θεῷ· ²⁰ διότι ἐξ ἔργων νόμου οὐ δικαιωθήσεται πᾶσα σὰρξ ἐνώπιον αὐτοῦ, διὰ γὰρ νόμου ἐπίγνωσις ἁμαρτίας. ²¹ Νυνὶ δὲ χωρὶς νόμου δικαιοσύνη θεοῦ πεφανέρωται μαρτυρουμένη ὑπὸ τοῦ νόμου καὶ τῶν προφητῶν, ²² δικαιοσύνη δὲ θεοῦ διὰ πίστεως Ἰησοῦ Χριστοῦ εἰς πάντας τοὺς πιστεύοντας. οὐ γάρ ἐστιν διαστολή, ²³ πάντες γὰρ ἥμαρτον καὶ ὑστεροῦνται τῆς δόξης

---

[2] *ta panta* in Gal 3:22 means actually "both Jews and Gentiles" as I explained in *Gal* 156-9. *hyph* is a contraction of *hypo*.

τοῦ θεοῦ ²⁴ δικαιούμενοι δωρεὰν τῇ αὐτοῦ χάριτι διὰ τῆς
ἀπολυτρώσεως τῆς ἐν Χριστῷ Ἰησοῦ· ²⁵ ὃν προέθετο ὁ θεὸς
ἱλαστήριον διὰ [τῆς] πίστεως ἐν τῷ αὐτοῦ αἵματι εἰς
ἔνδειξιν τῆς δικαιοσύνης αὐτοῦ διὰ τὴν πάρεσιν τῶν
προγεγονότων ἁμαρτημάτων ²⁶ ἐν τῇ ἀνοχῇ τοῦ θεοῦ, πρὸς
τὴν ἔνδειξιν τῆς δικαιοσύνης αὐτοῦ ἐν τῷ νῦν καιρῷ, εἰς τὸ
εἶναι αὐτὸν δίκαιον καὶ δικαιοῦντα τὸν ἐκ πίστεως Ἰησοῦ.
²⁷ Ποῦ οὖν ἡ καύχησις; ἐξεκλείσθη. διὰ ποίου νόμου; τῶν
ἔργων; οὐχί, ἀλλὰ διὰ νόμου πίστεως. ²⁸ λογιζόμεθα γὰρ
δικαιοῦσθαι πίστει ἄνθρωπον χωρὶς ἔργων νόμου. ²⁹ ἢ
Ἰουδαίων ὁ θεὸς μόνον; οὐχὶ καὶ ἐθνῶν; ναὶ καὶ ἐθνῶν, ³⁰
εἴπερ εἷς ὁ θεὸς ὃς δικαιώσει περιτομὴν ἐκ πίστεως καὶ
ἀκροβυστίαν διὰ τῆς πίστεως. ³¹ νόμον οὖν καταργοῦμεν διὰ
τῆς πίστεως; μὴ γένοιτο· ἀλλὰ νόμον ἱστάνομεν.

⁹What then? Are we Jews any better off? No, not at all; for I
have already charged that all men, both Jews and Greeks, are
under the power of sin, ¹⁰as it is written: "None is righteous, no,
not one; ¹¹no one understands, no one seeks for God. ¹²All have
turned aside, together they have gone wrong; no one does good,
not even one." ¹³ "Their throat is an open grave, they use their
tongues to deceive." "The venom of asps is under their lips."
¹⁴"Their mouth is full of curses and bitterness." ¹⁵"Their feet are
swift to shed blood, ¹⁶in their paths are ruin and misery, ¹⁷and
the way of peace they do not know." ¹⁸"There is no fear of God
before their eyes." ¹⁹Now we know that whatever the law says it
speaks to those who are under the law, so that every mouth may
be stopped, and the whole world may be held accountable to
God. ²⁰For no human being will be justified in his sight by
works of the law, since through the law comes knowledge of sin.
²¹But now the righteousness of God has been manifested apart
from law, although the law and the prophets bear witness to it,
²²the righteousness of God through faith in Jesus Christ for all
who believe. For there is no distinction; ²³since all have sinned
and fall short of the glory of God, ²⁴they are justified by his grace

as a gift, through the redemption which is in Christ Jesus,
[25]whom God put forward as an expiation by his blood, to be
received by faith. This was to show God's righteousness, because
in his divine forbearance he had passed over former sins; [26]it was
to prove at the present time that he himself is righteous and that
he justifies him who has faith in Jesus. [27]Then what becomes of
our boasting? It is excluded. On what principle? On the
principle of works? No, but on the principle of faith. [28]For we
hold that a man is justified by faith apart from works of law.
[29]Or is God the God of Jews only? Is he not the God of Gentiles
also? Yes, of Gentiles also, [30]since God is one; and he will justify
the circumcised on the ground of their faith and the
uncircumcised through their faith. [31]Do we then overthrow the
law by this faith? By no means! On the contrary, we uphold the
law.

That Paul here is following the lead of Galatians is further
evidenced in his use of the first person plural to speak of himself
and his colleagues as he does in Galatians. After the passage
where he reminisces of the incident at Antioch (Gal 2:11-14),
Paul shifts to the first person plural in the following vv.15-17
quoted above. In Romans, the passage 3:9-20 that starts with
"Are we better off (*proekhometha*; found to be ahead)" (v.9) is
dealing specifically with the Jews. Indeed, after a series of
quotations from scripture accusing each and all of having sinned
time and again (vv.10-18), he writes: "Now we know that
whatever the law says it speaks to those who are within (the
domain of) the law (*en tō nomō*)."[3] (v.19) The scriptural
quotations are purposely selected from the Prophets and the
Book of Psalms in order to bring home the point that the Law's

---

[3] This is the same expression he used earlier in 2:12 (*en nomō*) to speak of the Jews in
contradistinction to the nations that are *anomōs*.

instructions were not followed throughout the pedigree of scriptural Israel. But if all the references are from outside the Law, how can one understand that Paul says that it is the Law that is speaking these words in v.19? A digression is in order here to elucidate a matter that will help dispel many misunderstandings concerning Romans, the worst of which being that Paul is confused and thus confusing what the term *nomos* (Law) entails, and that he seems to be using it with different meanings.

In literature there is the well known phenomenon of *pars pro toto*, mentioning the part as a stand-in for the totality. A classic example is found in the Letters of Ignatius where we hear of "the bishop," "the bishop and the presbyters," and "the bishop, the presbyters, and the deacons." One should not imagine that these are three different instances, since the Ignatian general theme is the unity *around* the bishop *qua* bishop, that is, as head of the church of God. Actually the Greek for bishop is *episkopos*, overseer, the one who sits at the head of the table and looks over the good order of the gathering.[4] The last formula, "the bishop, the presbyters, and the deacons," is the most extended one and includes all those involved in running the gathering. The second formula, "bishop and presbyters," is a shortened form that refers to the "council of elders" presided over by the bishop, but without excluding the deacons who are the table servants and without whom the gathering does not follow its good course; it is a *pars pro toto* formula. The first formula is the most concentrated *pars pro toto*, similar to the president who presides over a board of directors or the speaker who presides over the House of Representatives. The president is the one who *is presiding*, as the *President of the (gathered) Board* and the speaker

---

[4] See my comments on Phil 1:2 in *C-Phil* 59-68.

is the *Speaker of the (gathered) House.* Thus, the *pars* that
functions *pro toto* is always the "senior" or "primary" part.
Whereas the first part "bishop" can function exclusively as well
as inclusively, the second part "presbyters" or the third part
"deacons," refer exclusively to that specific part. The same
applies to the Law, the Prophets, and the Writings. The "Law"
can be all-inclusive of scripture as well as an exclusive reference
to the Pentateuch. "The Law and the Prophets" is as all-inclusive
as "the Law, the Prophets, and the Writings."[5] The equivalence
between "Law" and "Law and Prophets" is actually evident in the
Romans text itself where Paul moves from the first to the second
without a blink of an eye or further explication:

> Now we know that whatever *the law* says it speaks to those who
> are under the law, so that every mouth may be stopped, and the
> whole world may be held accountable to God. For no human
> being will be justified in his sight by works of the law, since
> through the law comes knowledge of sin. But now the
> righteousness of God has been manifested apart from law, this
> being witnessed to by *the law and the prophets*, the righteousness of
> God through faith in Jesus Christ for all who believe. (3:19-22)

The same equivalence is found in Matthew:

> Think not that I have come to abolish *the law and the prophets*; I
> have come not to abolish but to fulfill. For truly, I say to you, till
> heaven and earth pass away, not an iota, not a dot, will pass from
> *the law* until all is accomplished. (5:17-18)

There is, however, a further specific meaning to the term
nomos (Law) besides its reference to the Pentateuch or the entire
scripture, as is evident in the preceding text of Romans where the

---

[5] See Luke 24:44 where Psalms function as all inclusive of the Writings.

phrase "works of the law" has in mind the specific instructions of the Mosaic Law. This "technical" connotation is reflected in the Judaic tradition where the legal texts are put in a category apart when it comes to exegesis. The interpretation of the legal texts is known as *halakah* from the Hebrew verb *halak* meaning "walk," which is used profusely in those texts. Thus the legal passages are binding on the Jew who must "walk" according to their instruction, and if he does, he will be granted life, and if he does not, he will be under curse (Lev 26; Deut 28). The interpretation of all other texts, including the non-legal texts of the "Law," in essence the five books of Moses, the Pentateuch, is called *haggadah* from the Hebrew verb *higgid* meaning "tell, recount, relay." The connotation is that these texts are edifying stories of individuals whose examples of conduct the hearers are to follow or, conversely, to avoid. It is then only when one bears in mind these different functions of *nomos* that one is able to follow Paul's argument with respect and not with condescension toward his "confusion." If Paul is confused, then the more so is Ezekiel and if the latter, the father of scripture, is confused, then neither Jew nor Gentile has any hope since hope cannot be but that which is woven with the words of scripture as it stands. One is to submit to scripture, not judge it, since it is, for all practical purposes, *equivalent* to God himself.

If the indictments of Romans 3:10-18 are meant specifically to the Jews (v.19), then these are liable to God's judgment (*hypodikos*), as are the rest of mankind. Thus *the whole world* is liable to that judgment and no one is excusable (v.20). And, based on the deeds required by the Law, every human being (*pasa sarx*) fails the muster, and thus cannot be declared righteous (v.21a). This accusation is not to be understood as a philosophical statement such as, "No one is perfect." Indeed, it is a scriptural *quotation* whose meaning is, "As I indicated earlier in my discussion of Romans 1:18-2:16, in the scriptural story we find no one that is fully righteous."[6] Consequently, in retrospect, one can see that, through the Law, the realization grew that sin is actually ruling man (3:20b). This topic will be further explicated in Romans 5:12-14. Still, Paul can make this sweeping conclusion since he discussed the matter at length in Galatians 3:15-25.[7]

But the good news is that scripture also gives us hope by speaking of God's merciful intervention to get us out the quagmire. Indeed the Law and the Prophets, i.e., scripture, witness that, at the end, God's righteousness will be made manifest in spite of the fact that men did not prove to be worthy of this righteousness by being themselves righteous. Indeed, the Law prescribes that one is declared righteous when one's sin is expiated through the prescribed offering, and one is given the chance to start anew on this path of acquired righteousness.[8] The quintessential example of such is the animal sacrifice on the Day of Atonement, which is done on behalf of the high priest, all the people and even the temple (Lev 16). Given that the people kept sinning, they created a vicious cycle that made God look laughable before the nations and their deities:

> Has a nation changed its gods, even though they are no gods? But my people have changed their glory for that which does not profit. (Jer 2:11)

---

[6] Such applies even to Noah the "righteous and blameless, in his generation" (Gen 6:9). Though saved from the flood through God's mercy, Noah gets drunk giving the opportunity to his son Ham to commit the sin of impiety (9:20-27).

[7] See *Gal* 138-164.

[8] The verb "expiate/atone" and the noun "expiation/atonement" are ubiquitous in the Books of Exodus, Leviticus and Numbers.

For you are not sent to a people of foreign speech and a hard language, but to the house of Israel—not to many peoples of foreign speech and a hard language, whose words you cannot understand. Surely, if I sent you to such, they would listen to you. But the house of Israel will not listen to you; for they are not willing to listen to me; because all the house of Israel are of a hard forehead and of a stubborn heart. (Ezek 3:5-7)

Earlier Paul brought up that point when he wrote: "The name of God is blasphemed among the Gentiles because of you." (Rom 2:24)

Yet scripture witnesses to an obedient servant who will hearken fully to the goodwill of God, even at the cost of being made the sacrificial lamb for the sins of men (Is 53). There is no need for him to fulfill each and every instruction of the Law. These instructions are, after all, a means to test the people's obedience to God. In his unconditional obedience to the "voice" of God, this servant will implement what the Lord himself said through Jeremiah:

Thus says the Lord of hosts, the God of Israel: "Add your burnt offerings to your sacrifices, and eat the flesh. For in the day that I brought them out of the land of Egypt, I did not speak to your fathers or command them concerning burnt offerings and sacrifices. But this command I gave them, '*Obey my voice, and I will be your God, and you shall be my people*; and walk in all the way that I command you, that it may be well with you.'" (7:21-23)

Then Jeremiah spoke to all the princes and all the people, saying, "The Lord sent me to prophesy against this house and this city all the words you have heard. Now therefore amend your ways and your doings, and *obey the voice of the Lord your God, and the Lord will repent of the evil which he has pronounced against you."* (26:12-13)

Through that servant's obedience unto a death of shame (He had no form or comeliness that we should look at him, and no beauty that we should desire him. He was despised and rejected by men; Is 53:2-3), we are ransomed from the Law's curse (Gal 3:15) and thus declared righteous and get another chance to abide by God's will and have life:[9] "Through his knowledge (of God's will) shall the righteous one, my servant, make many to be accounted righteous." (Is 53:11). In spite of all the curse laid upon him (Gal 3:15) he nevertheless obeyed God, the one whose "goodwill was to bruise him," trusting that that same God's "goodwill shall prosper in his hand" (Is 53:10). In this sense "the righteousness of God was manifested through the trust of Jesus Christ" (Rom 3:22a). In turn, since this unfathomable action of God required trust on the part of Jesus, God's Christ, we, the recipients of this graceful declaration of righteousness, are to trust that we were made righteous: trust in God, in imitation of Jesus Christ's trusting obedience toward the same God. Put otherwise, we are to "trust in Christ Jesus" (Gal 2:16), who made the right choice even though this choice is difficult for us to fathom. And since, in Isaiah, the servant is God's emissary to Gentiles as well as to the Jews (42:1-7; 49:6), Paul announces that his statement is true "unto all those who trust" without any "distinction (between Jew and Gentile)" (Rom 3:22b; also 10:12). For "all have sinned and fall short of the glory of God" (3:23) as he elucidated in Romans 1-2.

The acquired righteousness is granted to all "freely" (*dōrean*) as God's "gift" (*khariti*; grace) through the redemption

---

[9] This thought will be detailed in Rom 5:15-6:23.

(*apolytrōseōs*) which God performed through Jesus Christ (3:24) whom he pre-established (in the prophecy of Isaiah) as a sacrifice of expiation (*hilastērion*), assuming both Jesus' trust and ours in God (*dia pisteōs*) (v.25). The addition "by his blood" is intended to underscore the aspect of sacrificial offering corresponding to the Isaianic lamb. However, the real point of the matter is twofold. First, God shows forth his righteousness by overlooking the sins we have committed *up to his forgiveness* (vv.25-26). Thus, he shows himself to be righteous (*dikaion*; just) by justifying (*dikaiounta*; declaring righteous) anyone who is a member of the community of those "out (on the basis) of the trust of (and in) Jesus" (*ek pisteōs Iēsou*).[10] The repetition of this idea in vv.25-26 underscores its importance for Paul. On the other hand, it is the second point which is the more important since it lies at the center of this repetition. We were given this opportunity ultimately and only due to God's forbearance (*anokhē*; v.26), which he used during the period between our previous sinfulness and the sending of Jesus Christ. Without this divine forbearance, which kept God from condemning us to a deserved death, even the sending of Jesus would have been to no avail. This is precisely what Paul stressed earlier in speaking of the sins of the Jew: "Do you suppose, O man, that when you judge those who do such things and yet do them yourself, you will escape the judgment of God? Or do you presume upon the riches of his kindness and forbearance (*anokhēs*) and patience?" (2:3-4a) Still, one is to remember that such forbearance had the Jew's repentance as its goal: "Do you not know that God's kindness is meant to lead you to repentance? But by your hard and impenitent heart you are storing up wrath for yourself on the day of wrath when God's righteous judgment will be

---

[10] Regarding Paul's coining of the phrase "those out of trust" (*hoi ex pisteōs*) see my detailed discussion of Gal 3:7 in *Gal* 110-13.

revealed." (vv.4b-5) If then the grace lies in granting us the extra time necessary for us to repent, this rule applies the more so with the new and final grace granted to us through God's final emissary, as Paul will illustrate extensively in Romans 6. It would behoove us to equate divine grace with the invitation to repent and return to God. Nevertheless, we do not have indefinite time to do this, since the Lord is coming, and thus *at all times* "salvation is nearer to us now than when we first believed; the night is far gone, the day is at hand" (Rom 13:11-12).

Boasting is understandable if one has accomplished what one is supposed to do. But, since "no human being will be justified in his sight by works of the law" (3:20) and since righteousness is granted through the faith of Jesus Christ and our trusting in his faith (v.21), then any boasting is prohibited (*exekleisthē*; shut out; v.27). We are now under a new law, the law of trust in what God accomplished through Jesus Christ, which later will be referred to as "the law of the spirit of life" (8:2). And since this new law is based on trust, then it applies to any man (3:28). Otherwise God would be the God of the Jews only, which is a ridiculous proposition from the perspective of scripture that holds that there is one God of both the Jews and the nations (v.29). And this God *will justify* both the circumcised and the uncircumcised on the basis of their trust in what he did (v.30). The future tense used here is very important: the final and official declaration of our righteousness will not take place until judgment day. That is why, for the time being, we can only accept the apostolic "consideration" (*logizometha*) that any man trusting in the apostolic message is justified, and we maintain that stand *on hope* until this apostolic surmise is officially validated: "For through the Spirit, by faith, *we wait for the hope of righteousness.*" (Gal 5:5;[11] see also Rom 5:1-2; 8:18-25)

One would expect Paul to conclude that the Law is obsolete, yet he does just the opposite in Romans 3:31, and prepares the hearers for this when he speaks of "the law of faith (trust)" in v.27. For Paul "the law is holy, and the commandment is holy and just and good" (7:12). Hence his conclusion: "Do we then overthrow the law by this faith? By no means! On the contrary, we uphold the law." (3:31)

---

[11] See details in *Gal* 271-6.

Chapter 4

Vv. 1-12 ¹Τί οὖν ἐροῦμεν εὑρηκέναι Ἀβραὰμ τὸν προπάτορα ἡμῶν κατὰ σάρκα; ² εἰ γὰρ Ἀβραὰμ ἐξ ἔργων ἐδικαιώθη, ἔχει καύχημα, ἀλλ' οὐ πρὸς θεόν. ³ τί γὰρ ἡ γραφὴ λέγει; ἐπίστευσεν δὲ Ἀβραὰμ τῷ θεῷ καὶ ἐλογίσθη αὐτῷ εἰς δικαιοσύνην. ⁴ τῷ δὲ ἐργαζομένῳ ὁ μισθὸς οὐ λογίζεται κατὰ χάριν ἀλλὰ κατὰ ὀφείλημα, ⁵ τῷ δὲ μὴ ἐργαζομένῳ πιστεύοντι δὲ ἐπὶ τὸν δικαιοῦντα τὸν ἀσεβῆ λογίζεται ἡ πίστις αὐτοῦ εἰς δικαιοσύνην· ⁶ καθάπερ καὶ Δαυὶδ λέγει τὸν μακαρισμὸν τοῦ ἀνθρώπου ᾧ ὁ θεὸς λογίζεται δικαιοσύνην χωρὶς ἔργων· ⁷ μακάριοι ὧν ἀφέθησαν αἱ ἀνομίαι καὶ ὧν ἐπεκαλύφθησαν αἱ ἁμαρτίαι· ⁸ μακάριος ἀνὴρ οὗ οὐ μὴ λογίσηται κύριος ἁμαρτίαν. ⁹ Ὁ μακαρισμὸς οὖν οὗτος ἐπὶ τὴν περιτομὴν ἢ καὶ ἐπὶ τὴν ἀκροβυστίαν; λέγομεν γάρ· ἐλογίσθη τῷ Ἀβραὰμ ἡ πίστις εἰς δικαιοσύνην. ¹⁰ πῶς οὖν ἐλογίσθη; ἐν περιτομῇ ὄντι ἢ ἐν ἀκροβυστίᾳ; οὐκ ἐν περιτομῇ ἀλλ' ἐν ἀκροβυστίᾳ· ¹¹ καὶ σημεῖον ἔλαβεν περιτομῆς σφραγῖδα τῆς δικαιοσύνης τῆς πίστεως τῆς ἐν τῇ ἀκροβυστίᾳ, εἰς τὸ εἶναι αὐτὸν πατέρα πάντων τῶν πιστευόντων δι' ἀκροβυστίας, εἰς τὸ λογισθῆναι [καὶ] αὐτοῖς [τὴν] δικαιοσύνην, ¹² καὶ πατέρα περιτομῆς τοῖς οὐκ ἐκ περιτομῆς μόνον ἀλλὰ καὶ τοῖς στοιχοῦσιν τοῖς ἴχνεσιν τῆς ἐν ἀκροβυστίᾳ πίστεως τοῦ πατρὸς ἡμῶν Ἀβραάμ.

¹*What then shall we say about Abraham, our forefather according to the flesh?* ²*For if Abraham was justified by works, he has something to boast about, but not before God.* ³*For what does the scripture say?* "Abraham believed God, and it was reckoned to him as righteousness."⁴*Now to one who works, his wages are not reckoned as a gift but as his due.* ⁵*And to one who does not work but trusts him who justifies the ungodly, his faith is reckoned as righteousness.* ⁶*So also David pronounces a blessing upon the man to whom God reckons righteousness apart from works:* ⁷"Blessed are those whose iniquities are forgiven, and whose sins are covered; ⁸blessed is the man against whom*

the Lord will not reckon his sin." [9]Is this blessing pronounced only upon the circumcised, or also upon the uncircumcised? We say that faith was reckoned to Abraham as righteousness. [10]How then was it reckoned to him? Was it before or after he had been circumcised? It was not after, but before he was circumcised. [11]He received circumcision as a sign or seal of the righteousness which he had by faith while he was still uncircumcised. The purpose was to make him the father of all who believe without being circumcised and who thus have righteousness reckoned to them, [12]and likewise the father of the circumcised who are not merely circumcised but also follow the example of the faith which our father Abraham had before he was circumcised.

Having established that God's promised righteousness through his Christ was bestowed freely, as *witnessed* in scripture, Paul proceeds to show in detail how this testimony is found not only in the Prophets, but even in the Law. As usual, Paul is not an innovator, but simply a correct exegete of scripture. That is why he follows the lead of Isaiah who clearly speaks of that promise in terms of Abraham and Sarah:

Therefore thus says the Lord, who redeemed Abraham, concerning the house of Jacob: "Jacob shall no more be ashamed, no more shall his face grow pale. For when he sees his children, the work of my hands, in his midst, they will sanctify my name; they will sanctify the Holy One of Jacob, and will stand in awe of the God of Israel. And those who err in spirit will come to understanding, and those who murmur will accept instruction." (Is 29:22-24)

But you, Israel, my servant, Jacob, whom I have chosen, the offspring of Abraham, my friend; you whom I took from the ends of the earth, and called from its farthest corners, saying to you, You are my servant, I have chosen you and not cast you off; fear not, for I am with you, be not dismayed, for I am your God; I will strengthen you, I will help you, I will uphold you with my victorious right hand. (41:8-10)

Hearken to me, you who pursue deliverance, you who seek the Lord; look to the rock from which you were hewn, and to the quarry from which you were digged. Look to Abraham your father and to Sarah who bore you; for when he was but one I called him, and I blessed him and made him many. For the Lord will comfort Zion; he will comfort all her waste places, and will make her wilderness like Eden, her desert like the garden of the Lord; joy and gladness will be found in her, thanksgiving and the voice of song. (51:1-3)

Consequently, Paul starts his argumentation by asking the rhetorical question as to what scripture is saying, "What then shall we (especially Jews) say regarding how (as hearers of the Law [Pentateuch]) we (shall) have found (*hevrēkenai*) Abraham, our forefather according to the flesh?" (Rom 4:1) The answer is obvious. Even if Abraham boasts that his righteousness was secured through works (v.2a), his boast has no merit before God (v.2b). As Paul has just shown in Romans 3, God ultimately justifies human beings on the basis of "the law (rule) of trust (faith)" (v.27). Indeed, scripture itself says: "Abraham believed (put his trust in) God, and it (this trust) was reckoned to him as righteousness." (4:3; Gen 15:6).[1] Legally speaking, in God's court of justice, anyone who will have *done* (what he is supposed to do) earns his wages (*misthos*) as his due and not as a gift (Rom 4:4). As for Abraham, he is someone who *does not do* but rather trusts in the one who has declared (as only a judge would) the wicked (*asebē*) as righteous, and it is his trust (in God) that is reckoned to him as righteousness (v.5). What is stunning in this verse is that Abraham is referred to as "wicked" which is,

---

[1] In Rom 4 Paul elucidates in more detail his argument of Gal 3.

technically speaking, a word used to speak of Gentiles (1:18).
And this is precisely Paul's intention since he will clarify in 4:10
that the reckoning unto righteousness took place before
Abraham was circumcised, that is, when he was, scripturally
speaking, a mere Gentile—not yet a "Jew."

However, before bringing up that point, Paul digresses to bring
into the picture two quotations about divine reckoning from the
Book of Psalms. The reason is twofold. First of all, throughout
Romans, Paul is keen to show that the message and teaching he
is propounding is pervasive of the entire "holy scriptures" (1:2).
That is why earlier, after having discussed in detail the function
of the Law in Romans 1 and 2, he adduces a series of quotations
from the Prophets and, more so, from Psalms, the book that is
representative of the Writings, the third component of
scripture.[2] Secondly, as I detailed elsewhere,[3] the Book of Psalms
is devised in a way that it relates the shattering story of the
punishment of destruction and the exile of the inhabitants of
sinful Jerusalem, under David and Solomon, followed by the
promise of its reinstatement as the heavenly Zion as written in
the Prophets. Since the scriptural quotations in Romans 3:10-18
concerning the sinful "works" of Israel are mainly taken from
Psalms, here Paul quotes that same book as "looking ahead" for
the same "righteousness without works" (4:7-8) spoken of in the
Law and in the Prophets (3:21). Thus, the intention is to say
that not only does the Law make this statement, but "*also* David[4]
pronounces a blessing upon the man to whom God reckons
righteousness apart from works" (4:6). Hence the deft choice of a

---

[2] See Lk 24:44 (These are my words which I spoke to you, while I was still with you,
that everything written about me in the law of Moses and the prophets and the psalms
must be fulfilled).

[3] *OTI₃* 99-104.

[4] David is the assumed author of Psalms.

quotation that uses the same verb "reckon" of Genesis 15:6: "Blessed are those whose iniquities are forgiven, and whose sins are covered; blessed is the man against whom the Lord will not *reckon (logisētai)* his sin." (Rom 4:7-8; Ps 32:1-2)

After this digression to include the Writings, Paul returns to the main line of his argument. Since the Psalms quotation refers to an unqualified plural "those" as well as an unqualified "man,"[5] Paul raises the question, "Is this blessing pronounced only upon the circumcised, or also upon the uncircumcised?" (Rom 4:9) In order to find the right answer, Paul reverts to the original question with which he started his debate, "How do we find (in the Law) Abraham, the one who was *actually* reckoned righteous?" And Paul surmises, "Did this reckoning take place when Abraham was in the state of circumcision or uncircumcision?" (v.10a) The answer is unequivocal: "While he was uncircumcised" (v.10b) and thus, technically speaking, "wicked" (v.5). Moreover, and more importantly, what really matters is the reckoned righteousness, with circumcision being merely an "external sign" (*sēmeion*), a "visible seal" (*sphragida*) of the righteousness based on trust that was granted while Abraham was "in the state of uncircumcision" (v.11a). This clarification goes hand in hand with what Paul pointed out earlier that, "he is not a real Jew who is one outwardly, nor is true circumcision something external and physical. He is a Jew who is one inwardly, and real circumcision is a matter of the heart" (2:28-29). Consequently, Abraham is the father of both uncircumcised and circumcised. His uncircumcised "children" are to be fully similar to him: though uncircumcised, they are to put their trust in God's promise, which trust is the basis for their being reckoned righteous (4:11b). Abraham's circumcised children are

---

[5] The Greek *anēr* translates the Hebrew *'adam*.

bound to remember that they are to follow closely, as in an army line (*stoikhousin*), in his footsteps (*ikhnesin*) and mirror the trust he exhibited while he was still uncircumcised. Thus the faith of Abraham *as uncircumcised* is the rallying point around which all his children are united, the circumcised as well as the uncircumcised. Indeed, as Paul wrote earlier, "there is no distinction" (3:22). Both parties are ultimately bound to be in the image of their father Abraham to whom the promise was made while uncircumcised.

Now the promise to Abraham and his entire "offspring," that they would inherit the world, was not done through the Law, but rather through the righteousness that is the fruit of the trust he put in God (4:13; Gen 15:1-6). RSV renders Romans 4:13 as "The promise to Abraham and his descendants, that they should inherit the world, did not come through the law but through the righteousness of faith." However, the original Greek sounds thus: "The promise to Abraham *or* (*ē*) to his offspring (descendants), that *he/it* (*avton*) should be the heir (*klēronomon*; inheritor) of the world, did not come through the law but through the righteousness of faith."[6] The pronoun *avton* as well as the noun *klēronomon* are both in the singular and both apply in the original to either Abraham or the seed. This syntax is obviously intentional. What applies to Abraham applies also and *independently* to his offspring, meaning that each generation of that offspring is challenged to the same Abrahamic response of trust. Such is clearly the case of the first "heir" Isaac (Gen 15:4) to whom the Abrahamic blessing was conveyed (I will multiply your descendants as the stars of heaven, and will give to your

---

[6] Although the argument line is following that in Galatians 3:16, one should be careful not to read Galatians, which has "Abraham *and* his seed," into Romans which has "Abraham *or* his seed."

descendants all these lands; and by your descendants all the nations of the earth shall bless themselves; 26:4) *after* Abraham's death (25:8-10). Furthermore, Isaac was reminded that he was granted the Abrahamic promise "*because Abraham obeyed my voice* and kept my charge, my commandments, my statutes, and my laws" (26:5). Indeed, the original promise of Genesis 12:3 and 15:5 was iterated to Abraham in conjunction with his obedience to God's command that he sacrifice Isaac:

> By myself I have sworn, says the Lord, because you have done this, and have not withheld your son, your only son, I will indeed bless you, and I will multiply your descendants as the stars of heaven and as the sand which is on the seashore. And your descendants shall possess the gate of their enemies, and by your descendants shall all the nations of the earth bless themselves, *because you have obeyed my voice.* (22:16-18)

One is to express one's trust in God *in deed* and not only in word. This point will be picked up in Romans 8, at the conclusion of the lengthy argumentation (chs. 1-7) when Paul will refer to "the *law* of the spirit of life" (8:2) that the believers are to follow (vv.3-10).

Vv. 13-25 ¹³ Οὐ γὰρ διὰ νόμου ἡ ἐπαγγελία τῷ Ἀβραὰμ ἢ τῷ σπέρματι αὐτοῦ, τὸ κληρονόμον αὐτὸν εἶναι κόσμου, ἀλλὰ διὰ δικαιοσύνης πίστεως. ¹⁴ εἰ γὰρ οἱ ἐκ νόμου κληρονόμοι, κεκένωται ἡ πίστις καὶ κατήργηται ἡ ἐπαγγελία· ¹⁵ ὁ γὰρ νόμος ὀργὴν κατεργάζεται· οὗ δὲ οὐκ ἔστιν νόμος οὐδὲ παράβασις. ¹⁶ Διὰ τοῦτο ἐκ πίστεως, ἵνα κατὰ χάριν, εἰς τὸ εἶναι βεβαίαν τὴν ἐπαγγελίαν παντὶ τῷ σπέρματι, οὐ τῷ ἐκ τοῦ νόμου μόνον ἀλλὰ καὶ τῷ ἐκ πίστεως Ἀβραάμ, ὅς ἐστιν πατὴρ πάντων ἡμῶν, ¹⁷ καθὼς γέγραπται ὅτι πατέρα πολλῶν ἐθνῶν τέθεικά σε, κατέναντι οὗ ἐπίστευσεν θεοῦ τοῦ ζῳοποιοῦντος τοὺς νεκροὺς καὶ καλοῦντος τὰ μὴ ὄντα ὡς ὄντα. ¹⁸ Ὃς παρ' ἐλπίδα ἐπ' ἐλπίδι ἐπίστευσεν εἰς τὸ γενέσθαι αὐτὸν πατέρα πολλῶν ἐθνῶν κατὰ τὸ εἰρημένον·

οὕτως ἔσται τὸ σπέρμα σου, ¹⁹ καὶ μὴ ἀσθενήσας τῇ πίστει
κατενόησεν τὸ ἑαυτοῦ σῶμα [ἤδη] νενεκρωμένον,
ἑκατονταετής που ὑπάρχων, καὶ τὴν νέκρωσιν τῆς μήτρας
Σάρρας· ²⁰ εἰς δὲ τὴν ἐπαγγελίαν τοῦ θεοῦ οὐ διεκρίθη τῇ
ἀπιστίᾳ ἀλλ' ἐνεδυναμώθη τῇ πίστει, δοὺς δόξαν τῷ θεῷ ²¹
καὶ πληροφορηθεὶς ὅτι ὃ ἐπήγγελται δυνατός ἐστιν καὶ
ποιῆσαι. ²² διὸ [καὶ] ἐλογίσθη αὐτῷ εἰς δικαιοσύνην. ²³ Οὐκ
ἐγράφη δὲ δι' αὐτὸν μόνον ὅτι ἐλογίσθη αὐτῷ ²⁴ ἀλλὰ καὶ δι'
ἡμᾶς, οἷς μέλλει λογίζεσθαι, τοῖς πιστεύουσιν ἐπὶ τὸν
ἐγείραντα Ἰησοῦν τὸν κύριον ἡμῶν ἐκ νεκρῶν, ²⁵ ὃς
παρεδόθη διὰ τὰ παραπτώματα ἡμῶν καὶ ἠγέρθη διὰ τὴν
δικαίωσιν ἡμῶν.

¹³ *The promise to Abraham and his descendants, that they should
inherit the world, did not come through the law but through the
righteousness of faith.* ¹⁴ *If it is the adherents of the law who are
to be the heirs, faith is null and the promise is void.* ¹⁵ *For the
law brings wrath, but where there is no law there is no
transgression.* ¹⁶ *That is why it depends on faith, in order that
the promise may rest on grace and be guaranteed to all his
descendants—not only to the adherents of the law but also to
those who share the faith of Abraham, for he is the father of us
all,* ¹⁷ *as it is written, "I have made you the father of many
nations"—in the presence of the God in whom he believed, who
gives life to the dead and calls into existence the things that do
not exist.* ¹⁸ *In hope he believed against hope, that he should
become the father of many nations; as he had been told, "So
shall your descendants be."* ¹⁹ *He did not weaken in faith when
he considered his own body, which was as good as dead because
he was about a hundred years old, or when he considered the
barrenness of Sarah's womb.* ²⁰ *No distrust made him waver
concerning the promise of God, but he grew strong in his faith as
he gave glory to God,* ²¹ *fully convinced that God was able to do
what he had promised.* ²² *That is why his faith was "reckoned to
him as righteousness."* ²³ *But the words, "it was reckoned to*

him," were written not for his sake alone, [24] but for ours also. It will be reckoned to us who believe in him that raised from the dead Jesus our Lord, [25] who was put to death for our trespasses and raised for our justification.

That the offspring who is heir (Rom 4:13) does not refer only to Isaac is corroborated in the plural "heirs" that opens the explication of v.14, "For if it is (only) the adherents of the law (*hoi ek nomou*) who are (to be) heirs."[7] Isaac is only the prototype heir and all of us are invited to follow his lead and become the offspring of Abraham. Earlier, in Galatians, Paul wrote: "And if you are Christ's, then you are Abraham's offspring, heirs according to promise (*kat' epangelian*)" (3:29); "Now you,[8] brethren, according to (after the manner of) Isaac (*kata Isaak*), are children of promise." (4:28) Actually, Isaac was not a product of the flesh as Ishmael was, but the result of God's promise that both Abraham and Sarah laughed at (Gen 17:17; 18:12).[9] Isaac was indeed, scripturally speaking, the child of God's promise, as Paul underscored in Galatians:

Tell me, you who desire to be under law, do you not hear the law? For it is written that Abraham had two sons, one by a slave and one by a free woman. But the son of the slave was born according to the flesh, the son of the free woman through promise. (4:21-23)

To this status everyone one is invited on the condition that one put one's trust in God's promise. Otherwise, "faith (trust) is nullified" and, more importantly, "the promise (of God) is void." And if the latter, then no one has any hope, since the alternative is to go the way of the Law. Due to our consistent

---

[7] *hoi ek nomou* is an abbreviated form of *hosoi ex ergōn nomou eisin* (Gal 3:10).
[8] Some manuscripts have "we."
[9] Whereas Abraham is said to have slept with Hagar according to Sarah's will (Gen 16:3-4), scripture at no point says that Abraham lay with Sarah after God's promise.

contravening of it, the Law ends up implementing the curse instead of the blessing as prescribed in the Law itself (Lev 26; Deut 28). The reason is simple: unless there is a law there cannot be transgression (Rom 4:15b) and, where there is no transgression, there is no indictment and wrath (4:15a).

That is why (*dia touto*) the divine promise was established *before the Law* and required one's trust (*ek pisteōs*) in that promise. In this way, the promise stems exclusively from God's gracefulness (*kata kharin*) and thus depends on God's faithfulness rather than on the faith of our undependable selves (3:3). This promise is extended to *all* the offspring (*panti tō spermati*) and not only to the Jews on the basis of the Law, but, as was stated in 4:11-12 and reiterated here, to the entire offspring through the trust of Abraham, who is the father of *all* believers. This was established by scripture itself (I have made you the father of many nations; Gen 17:5 [Rom 4:17a]) in conjunction with the establishment of the covenant of circumcision (Gen 17:7-14). At this point, terminology wise, Paul prepares for the application of this principle to his addressees. In referring to God in whom Abraham trusted, Paul qualifies this God as "the one who gives life to the dead (*nekrous*) and the one who calls (*tou kalountos*) as existing (*ōs onta*) the things that do not exist (*ta mē onta*)" (Rom 4:17b). Since Abraham is the subject of the phrase that starts with "trusted" (*epistevsen*), the reference is obviously to what God did to him. Indeed, this is made clear in v.19 where we hear that Abraham's body was "dead" (*nenekrōmenon*) and the womb of Sarah was in a state of barrenness (*nekrōsin*; death). At the same time, this terminology looks ahead to the Roman addressees who "put their trust (*tois pistevousin*) in him that raised from the dead (*nekrōn*) Jesus our Lord" (v.24). It is clear from 1 Corinthians 1:26-29 that the phrase *ta mē onta* (the things that do not exist; v.28) refers to the Gentiles in the sense that they are, scripturally speaking, of no value and yet God *chose* them, just as he had previously chosen Israel. Paul uses this terminology to put to shame both the Jews and the Roman patricians who view themselves as "powerful" (v.28) and "wise" (v.28; Rom 1:14). This reading of the text is corroborated in the choice of the participle *kalountos* (who calls; Rom 4:17) as an epithet of God, which is the appellative Paul uses when speaking of God's calling in conjunction with the preaching of the gospel (Gal 1:6, 15; 5:8; 1 Thess 2:12; 5:24; 2 Tim 1:9).[10]

Magisterially, then, Paul is literarily casting Abraham into "the father of many nations." Notice indeed how this phrase is recalled in Rom 4:17 together with "(Abraham) trusted" (*epistevsen*) in order to include Abraham's offspring with a quotation in v.18 from Genesis 15:5 (So shall your offspring [descendants] be), the verse immediately preceding "And he believed the Lord; and he reckoned it to him as righteousness" (Gen 15:6). This looking ahead of Abraham's trust in God that "many nations" will be part of his offspring, is underscored in the use of the verb "believed" together with the noun "hope" to describe his trustful response: "In hope he believed against hope." (Rom 4:18a) Paul's intent is carried on in the following verses (19-21) where, besides the reference to the root *nekr*— (death), he refers to Abraham as having not "weakened" (*asthenēsas*) but rather "grew strong" (*edynamōthē*) in his trust in God who is "able" (*dynatos*; strong) not only to issue a promise but also to realize it. This terminology corroborates the

---

[10] The same applies to the noun "call(ing)" (*klēsin*) used in the same context (1 Cor 1:26). See Rom 11:29; 1 Cor 7:20; Eph 1:18; 4:1, 4; Phil 3:14; 2 Thess 1:11; 2 Tim 1:9; Heb 3:1; 2 Pet 1:10.

parallelism between Romans 4:16-25 and 1 Corinthians 1:22-29
that reads:

> For Jews demand signs and Greeks seek wisdom, but we preach
> Christ crucified, a stumbling block to Jews and folly to Gentiles,
> but to those who are called (*klētois*), both Jews and Greeks, Christ
> the power (*dynamin*) of God and the wisdom of God. For the
> foolishness of God is wiser than men, and the weakness (*to
> asthēnes*) of God is stronger (*iskhyroteron*) than men. For consider
> your call (*klēsin*), brethren; not many of you were wise according
> to worldly standards, not many were powerful (*dynatoi*), not many
> were of noble birth; God chose what is foolish in the world to
> shame the wise, God chose what is weak (*ta asthēnē*) in the world
> to shame the strong (*ta iskhyra*), God chose what is low and
> despised in the world, even things that are not (*ta mē onta*), to
> bring to nothing things that are (*ta onta*) so that no human being
> might boast in the presence of God.

With this kind of trust Abraham "gave glory to God" (Rom
4:20), thus inviting his children from among the Gentiles to do
the same; this is in contrast with what they were doing before
they were called: "Claiming to be wise, they became fools, and
exchanged the glory of the immortal God for images resembling
mortal man or birds or animals or reptiles." (1:22-23)

Both Jews and Gentiles are potentially able to follow in
Abraham's footsteps because "the reckoning of his trust as
righteousness (Gen 15:6) was not written in view of him alone
(*di' avton monon*) but also in view of us (*di' hēmas*) who trust in
him that raised from the dead Jesus our Lord who was put to
death for our trespasses and raised for our justification" (Rom
4:23-25). As was the case with Abraham, trust cannot but be in
conjunction with a promise that is to be realized in the future.
Abraham had to trust in the promise that God would "raise" a

seed to Abraham in spite of his "as good as dead" body and of
Sarah's necrotic womb (v.19), which is tantamount to God's
"giving life to the dead and calling into existence the things that
do not exist" (v.17). In so doing, God vindicated (justified;
proved to be righteous) Abraham in his trust. Similarly, "we" are
to trust that God who "raised from the dead Jesus the Lord who
was put to death for our trespasses" (vv.24-25) did so in view of
our justification (declaring us righteous) as promised in Isaiah
(53:4-6, 10-12). In other words, we are to trust (believe) in the
message of God delivered through his prophets and consigned in
the scriptures (Rom 1:2). We are to put our trust in the teaching
found in the Law (the five books of Moses) where we hear of
Abraham's trust in the Lord's promise that was realized in the
birth of Isaac. Then, following the lead of Abraham whose
example is set forth in Isaiah 51:2 (Look to Abraham your father
and to Sarah who bore you; for when he was but one I called
him, and I blessed him and made him many) in order to
introduce God's promise two chapters later (Is 53), the hearers of
the Prophets are challenged to trust in that promise. Thus, the
righteousness of God is revealed in scripture *ek pisteōs eis pistin*
(beginning with trust [as described in the Law] and ending in
trust [as required in the Prophets]) (Rom 1:17).

Chapter 5

Vv. 1-11 [1] Δικαιωθέντες οὖν ἐκ πίστεως εἰρήνην ἔχομεν πρὸς τὸν θεὸν διὰ τοῦ κυρίου ἡμῶν Ἰησοῦ Χριστοῦ [2] δι᾽ οὗ καὶ τὴν προσαγωγὴν ἐσχήκαμεν [τῇ πίστει] εἰς τὴν χάριν ταύτην ἐν ᾗ ἑστήκαμεν καὶ καυχώμεθα ἐπ᾽ ἐλπίδι τῆς δόξης τοῦ θεοῦ. [3] οὐ μόνον δέ, ἀλλὰ καὶ καυχώμεθα ἐν ταῖς θλίψεσιν, εἰδότες ὅτι ἡ θλῖψις ὑπομονὴν κατεργάζεται, [4] ἡ δὲ ὑπομονὴ δοκιμήν, ἡ δὲ δοκιμὴ ἐλπίδα. [5] ἡ δὲ ἐλπὶς οὐ καταισχύνει, ὅτι ἡ ἀγάπη τοῦ θεοῦ ἐκκέχυται ἐν ταῖς καρδίαις ἡμῶν διὰ πνεύματος ἁγίου τοῦ δοθέντος ἡμῖν. [6] Ἔτι γὰρ Χριστὸς ὄντων ἡμῶν ἀσθενῶν ἔτι κατὰ καιρὸν ὑπὲρ ἀσεβῶν ἀπέθανεν. [7] μόλις γὰρ ὑπὲρ δικαίου τις ἀποθανεῖται· ὑπὲρ γὰρ τοῦ ἀγαθοῦ τάχα τις καὶ τολμᾷ ἀποθανεῖν· [8] συνίστησιν δὲ τὴν ἑαυτοῦ ἀγάπην εἰς ἡμᾶς ὁ θεός, ὅτι ἔτι ἁμαρτωλῶν ὄντων ἡμῶν Χριστὸς ὑπὲρ ἡμῶν ἀπέθανεν. [9] πολλῷ οὖν μᾶλλον δικαιωθέντες νῦν ἐν τῷ αἵματι αὐτοῦ σωθησόμεθα δι᾽ αὐτοῦ ἀπὸ τῆς ὀργῆς. [10] εἰ γὰρ ἐχθροὶ ὄντες κατηλλάγημεν τῷ θεῷ διὰ τοῦ θανάτου τοῦ υἱοῦ αὐτοῦ, πολλῷ μᾶλλον καταλλαγέντες σωθησόμεθα ἐν τῇ ζωῇ αὐτοῦ· [11] οὐ μόνον δέ, ἀλλὰ καὶ καυχώμενοι ἐν τῷ θεῷ διὰ τοῦ κυρίου ἡμῶν Ἰησοῦ Χριστοῦ δι᾽ οὗ νῦν τὴν καταλλαγὴν ἐλάβομεν.

[1] *Therefore, since we are justified by faith, we have peace with God through our Lord Jesus Christ.* [2] *Through him we have obtained access to this grace in which we stand, and we rejoice in our hope of sharing the glory of God.* [3] *More than that, we rejoice in our sufferings, knowing that suffering produces endurance,* [4] *and endurance produces character, and character produces hope,* [5] *and hope does not disappoint us, because God's love has been poured into our hearts through the Holy Spirit which has been given to us.* [6] *While we were still weak, at the right time Christ died for the ungodly.* [7] *Why, one will hardly die for a righteous man—through perhaps for a good man one will dare even to die.* [8] *But God shows his love for us in that while we were yet sinners Christ died for us.* [9] *Since, therefore, we are now*

justified by his blood, much more shall we be saved by him from the wrath of God. [10]For if while we were enemies we were reconciled to God by the death of his Son, much more, now that we are reconciled, shall we be saved by his life. [11]Not only so, but we also rejoice in God through our Lord Jesus Christ, through whom we have now received our reconciliation.

Since God is the judge, anyone who contravenes his will expressed in his law is his enemy (Rom 5:10) and thus liable to his judgment (Rom 1:18-2:16). Therefore, having been declared righteous *ek pisteōs*, that is, after the manner of Abraham, we have peace, instead of enmity, with God, our judge, through our Lord Jesus Christ, as described in Isaiah 53:4-6, 10-12. However, divine peace will not materialize except in God's coming heavenly Zion. In order to include all those who will be justified from the coming generations of human beings, we have actually only *prosagōgēn* (approach, access, progress) on the way to that peace. As Paul detailed in Philippians 1:3-7,[1] our standing on the way to the eschatological peace is an act of graciousness (*kharin*; grace) on God's part. The intent, however, is that we reach the end of that way. Our boasting (*kavkhōmetha*) is on the hope (Rom 5:2)[2] that we shall attain God's glory, which we are seeking *with patience* (*kath' hypomonēn*) and in well-doing (2:7), after having lost the way to it (1:23). Our trust in God is to be tested, just as Abraham's trust was tested. And this test through afflictions (*thlipsesin*) is part and parcel of the gospel message, as Paul indicated in 1 Thessalonians:

---

[1] See my comments in *C-Phil* 71-6.
[2] Compare with Gal 5:6 (For through the Spirit, by faith, we wait for the hope of righteousness).

> Therefore when we could bear it no longer, we were willing to be
> left behind at Athens alone, and we sent Timothy, our brother and
> God's servant in the gospel of Christ, to establish you in your faith
> and to exhort you, that no one be moved by these afflictions. You
> yourselves know that this is to be our lot. For when we were with
> you, we told you beforehand that we were to suffer affliction; just
> as it has come to pass, and as you know. (3:1-4)

Consequently, these afflictions are a reason for boasting, just as is
our hope to share in God's peace and glory. Indeed, the hope
produced by afflictions is intrinsically linked to *hypomonēn*
(patience, endurance),[3] which is to be continually tested (*dokimē*)
in preparation for the ultimate test of God's judgment (Rom
2:16). Thus patience (endurance) until the end is the real test of
our hope. The reason is that true hope does not disappoint since
it is anchored in the love God has already graciously exhibited
toward us by pouring into our hearts the same Spirit through
which he raised Jesus the Lord for our justification (1:4; 4:25).
Since the provision is that we be obedient to his will (1:5), our
test ultimately lies in persevering in such obedience, as we shall
see in Romans 6.

In order to underscore the aspect of absolute grace, without
any merit on our part, Paul proceeds to expand on God's sheer
love toward us. While we were utterly weak, God exhibited his
power (1:4). Even more, while we were "wicked (ungodly;
asebōn)" and sinners, Christ, the righteous one, died for us (5:6-
8). This manner of justification, beyond any stretch of
imagination, functions as a guarantee that, should we proceed in
our obedience to God, we surely shall be saved from his wrath on
judgment day. Indeed, if while his enemies we were reconciled to
him through Christ's death, now that we are reconciled, we have

---

[3] See my comments in *1 Thess* 39-41.

much more, since we shall be saved unto the life God bestowed upon Christ. However, lest the hearers imagine that they have already attained life eternal, Paul brings them back to their actual reality, that is the status of being reconciled and merely, albeit surely, *on the way* to life. He does so by using, in reference to our having received reconciliation, the same "being boastful" (*kavkhōmenoi*) that he used earlier to speak of our hope *in and through tribulations* to share in God's glory (v.2).

Vv. 12 - 21 ¹²Διὰ τοῦτο ὥσπερ δι᾽ ἑνὸς ἀνθρώπου ἡ ἁμαρτία εἰς τὸν κόσμον εἰσῆλθεν καὶ διὰ τῆς ἁμαρτίας ὁ θάνατος, καὶ οὕτως εἰς πάντας ἀνθρώπους ὁ θάνατος διῆλθεν, ἐφ᾽ ᾧ πάντες ἥμαρτον· ¹³ἄχρι γὰρ νόμου ἁμαρτία ἦν ἐν κόσμῳ, ἁμαρτία δὲ οὐκ ἐλλογεῖται μὴ ὄντος νόμου, ¹⁴ἀλλὰ ἐβασίλευσεν ὁ θάνατος ἀπὸ Ἀδὰμ μέχρι Μωϋσέως καὶ ἐπὶ τοὺς μὴ ἁμαρτήσαντας ἐπὶ τῷ ὁμοιώματι τῆς παραβάσεως Ἀδὰμ ὅς ἐστιν τύπος τοῦ μέλλοντος. ¹⁵Ἀλλ᾽ οὐχ ὡς τὸ παράπτωμα, οὕτως καὶ τὸ χάρισμα· εἰ γὰρ τῷ τοῦ ἑνὸς παραπτώματι οἱ πολλοὶ ἀπέθανον, πολλῷ μᾶλλον ἡ χάρις τοῦ θεοῦ καὶ ἡ δωρεὰ ἐν χάριτι τῇ τοῦ ἑνὸς ἀνθρώπου Ἰησοῦ Χριστοῦ εἰς τοὺς πολλοὺς ἐπερίσσευσεν. ¹⁶καὶ οὐχ ὡς δι᾽ ἑνὸς ἁμαρτήσαντος τὸ δώρημα· τὸ μὲν γὰρ κρίμα ἐξ ἑνὸς εἰς κατάκριμα, τὸ δὲ χάρισμα ἐκ πολλῶν παραπτωμάτων εἰς δικαίωμα. ¹⁷εἰ γὰρ τῷ τοῦ ἑνὸς παραπτώματι ὁ θάνατος ἐβασίλευσεν διὰ τοῦ ἑνός, πολλῷ μᾶλλον οἱ τὴν περισσείαν τῆς χάριτος καὶ τῆς δωρεᾶς τῆς δικαιοσύνης λαμβάνοντες ἐν ζωῇ βασιλεύσουσιν διὰ τοῦ ἑνὸς Ἰησοῦ Χριστοῦ. ¹⁸Ἄρα οὖν ὡς δι᾽ ἑνὸς παραπτώματος εἰς πάντας ἀνθρώπους εἰς κατάκριμα, οὕτως καὶ δι᾽ ἑνὸς δικαιώματος εἰς πάντας ἀνθρώπους εἰς δικαίωσιν ζωῆς· ¹⁹ὥσπερ γὰρ διὰ τῆς παρακοῆς τοῦ ἑνὸς ἀνθρώπου ἁμαρτωλοὶ κατεστάθησαν οἱ πολλοί, οὕτως καὶ διὰ τῆς ὑπακοῆς τοῦ ἑνὸς δίκαιοι κατασταθήσονται οἱ πολλοί. ²⁰νόμος δὲ παρεισῆλθεν, ἵνα πλεονάσῃ τὸ παράπτωμα· οὗ δὲ ἐπλεόνασεν ἡ ἁμαρτία, ὑπερεπερίσσευσεν ἡ χάρις, ²¹ἵνα ὥσπερ ἐβασίλευσεν ἡ ἁμαρτία ἐν τῷ θανάτῳ, οὕτως καὶ ἡ χάρις βασιλεύσῃ διὰ δικαιοσύνης εἰς ζωὴν αἰώνιον διὰ Ἰησοῦ Χριστοῦ τοῦ κυρίου ἡμῶν.

¹²Therefore as sin came into the world through one man and death through sin, and so death spread to all men because all men sinned—¹³sin indeed was in the world before the law was given, but sin is not counted where there is no law. ¹⁴Yet death reigned from Adam to Moses, even over those whose sins were not like the transgression of Adam, who was a type of the one who was to come. ¹⁵But the free gift is not like the trespass. For if many died through one man's trespass, much more have the grace of God and the free gift in the grace of that one man Jesus Christ abounded for many. ¹⁶And the free gift is not like the effect of that one man's sin. For the judgment following one trespass brought condemnation, but the free gift following many trespasses brings justification. ¹⁷If, because of one man's trespass, death reigned through that one man, much more will those who receive the abundance of grace and the free gift of righteousness reign in life through the one man Jesus Christ. ¹⁸Then as one man's trespass led to condemnation for all men, so one man's act of righteousness leads to acquittal and life for all men. ¹⁹For as by one man's disobedience many were made sinners, so by one man's obedience many will be made righteous. ²⁰Law came in, to increase the trespass; but where sin increased, grace abounded all the more, ²¹so that, as sin reigned in death, grace also might reign through righteousness to eternal life through Jesus Christ our Lord.

Through the consistent use of the first person plural pronoun in Romans 5:1-11 Paul is underscoring that this hope while we are *on the way* applies to all, to the Gentiles and also to the Jews who are as "wicked" (v.6) as their forefather Abraham (4:5) when he was asked to trust in God's promise to grant him a seed. Still, in preparation for our passage (5:12-21) Paul introduces the term "sinners" (*hamartolōn*) as a parallel to "wicked" (*asebōn*; ungodly): "While we were still weak, at the right time Christ died for the ungodly (*asebōn*) ... But God shows his love for us in that while we were yet sinners (*hamartolōn*) Christ died for us." (vv.6-8) In doing so, Paul prepares for the encompassing scriptural notion of "sin" (*hamartia*), which applies to all human beings starting with Adam and which, he charges, we all are under (3:9). He will deal with this extensively in the following chapters. The introduction of Adam in the discussion allows him to underscore that the matter of unrighteousness and sin concerns all human beings, and to point out that the salvation brought about by the new Adam concerns the entire humankind as well.

Romans 5:12 is a prime example of how a simple and straightforward scriptural statement can be dragged into endless philosophico-theological sophistries that were strictly forbidden by the Apostle: "See to it that no one makes a prey of you by philosophy and empty deceit, according to human tradition, according to the elemental spirits of the universe, and not according to Christ." (Col 2:8) In Romans 5:12 Paul is merely referring to the first chapters of Genesis. In order to understand what he is saying, one is to remember that, in scripture, natural death is not an issue, since every human being is mortal. Rather, scripture is concerned with death as punishment for disobedience to God's will, that is, as a divine verdict that cuts short the natural course of human life. The corollary is that life is a gift of God which he may discontinue when man does not abide by his will. Adam was "granted" to live by eating from the tree of life, whose fruit was not forbidden to him at the beginning. Adam sinned by contravening God's express command to abstain from eating from the tree of the knowledge of good and evil (Gen 2:16-17; 3:6). Hence, Paul's statement that "sin came into the world through one man and death (as a divine verdict of punishment) [came into the world] *through* sin." Death did not spread automatically or magically to *all* men because of Adam's sin, but rather since (because)[4] *all* sinned just as Adam did, beginning with Cain (Gen 4) and including all men after him (6:5-7), whether Gentiles (11:1-9) or sons of Jacob (Gen 35-50). As Ezekiel makes repeatedly clear, everyone is responsible for one's sin (14:12-23; 18:1-32; 33:1-20). So, until the Law (Exodus through Deuteronomy), sin was in the world as described in Genesis, although sin was not charged (considered) as such since there was no law.

In order to understand what Paul is saying, the following example may be helpful. Before a speed limit sign is posted, those who drive at an exorbitant speed might end up seriously injured, if not dead, but no speeding ticket would be issued. With the advent of a speed limit sign, the contravener might be injured, or even die, *and also* be "ticketed."[5] However, the "reign" (rule) of death was effective even before the speed limit era. So Paul says here that although sin was not accounted as such before the Law, it still reigned from Adam to Moses, even over those who committed sins different than the sin of Adam. This corroborates my earlier explanation of Romans 5:12. Actually the precise phraseology of v.14 confirms that Paul was reading Genesis throughout Romans 5:12-14. Adam sinned by contravening an express *command* of God (Gen 2:16-17). So when speaking of the "sin" of Adam, Paul uses the noun "transgression" (*parabaseōs*), which is a legal term. By introducing *parabasis,* Paul prepares for his ensuing discussion (Rom 5:15-21) where he uses profusely *paraptōma*, a term with a

---

[4] This is the meaning of the Greek *eph' hō* (Acts 7:33; 2 Cor 5:4; Phil 3:12; 4:10).
[5] See earlier my comments on Rom 3:19-20.

similar meaning as *parabasis*,[6] in conjunction with the sins committed between Moses and Jesus Christ. Here in Romans, Paul plays on the oneness of Adam as a type to explain the uniqueness of Jesus Christ as the medium through whom God implements his salvation to *all*. This is similar to what Paul does in 1 Corinthians: "For as by a man came death, by a man has come also the resurrection of the dead. For as in Adam all die, so also in Christ shall all be made alive." (15:21-22) In scripture, Adam actually functions as the antitype of Christ, the one who is to come (Rom 5:14) according to the scriptural promise (Gal 3:19, 24).[7] Starting with Romans 5:15 it is made clear that the typological correspondence between Adam and Christ is one of opposition: "But the free gift is *not like* the trespass (*oukh hōs... houtōs kai...*)." The actual opposition lies in that, on Adam's end, the trespass (*paraptōma;* falling [away]) is *his* doing; whereas, on Christ's end, the doing is not his but rather God's through him; hence, the introduction of *kharisma* (free gift) which is the outcome or result of the divine *kharis* (grace, gracefulness). Put otherwise, in Adam's case, the "deed" (*ergon*) is his; in Christ's case, the "deed" is God's. This depiction prepares for the conclusion of Romans 5:15-21 which will contrast Christ's obedience and submission to God's will against Adam's disobedience to that same will (v.19). Whereas Adam ends up following his own desire, Christ ends up implementing God's volition.

---

[6] *paraptōma* is from the verb *parapiptō* (fall to the side of the main path and thus err) whereas *parabasis* is from the verb *parabainō* (step aside of the main path and thus take a wrong step).

[7] Type here is a generic term which can refer to either similarity (prototype, blueprint) or opposition (antitype). The context militates here for the latter understanding, just as it does in 1 Cor 15:21-22 and 45-49. In the New Testament, Adam and Christ are antitypes.

Romans 5:15-21 is a quintessential example of the fact that scripture is meant to be heard, not read. The "much more" of the free grace and the life it bestows, in contradistinction with death resulting from sin and transgression, can be "heard" through the large number of words used to describe that grace granted by God through Christ when compared to the scarcity of words to speak of the Adamic transgression and its aftermath:

> For if many died through one man's trespass, much more have the grace of God and the free gift in the grace of that one man Jesus Christ abounded for many. (v.15)

> If, because of one man's trespass, death reigned through that one man, much more will those who receive the abundance of grace and the free gift of righteousness reign in life through the one man Jesus Christ. (v.17)

> ... so that, as sin reigned in death, grace also might reign through righteousness to eternal life through Jesus Christ our Lord. (v.21)

Furthermore, the thrice intonation of the same message underscores the assuredness that it is indeed so. Consequently, the hearer does not need to analyze the meaning of each word. Rather, the meaning lies in the totality of the *heard* passage whereby the new life granted freely by God through Christ's obedience overwhelmingly surpasses the penalty of death introduced by Adam's disobedience. However, eternal life is ensured through a daily life of righteousness, which is precisely the point that will be developed in the following chapter.

The sufficiency of the action of Jesus Christ, one man, for the entire humanity is anchored in the oneness of Adam who brought about the calamity of death over the same entire humanity. This death is clearly not the natural death, but that of condemnation (*katakrima*) through divine just judgment (*krima*) (v.16b). That is why the same just judge can issue a judgment of righteousness and innocence (*dikaiōma*) (v.16c) when he so pleases as long as he has a reason to do so, which is precisely what he had in Jesus Christ (Is 53:10-12). Through him, God invited his like, the other human beings, to accede to the same righteousness through the same path of obedience, after they deservedly received the penalty of death by following in the path of Adam's disobedience (Rom 5:19). Indeed, the effect of the action of the one man, whether Adam or Jesus Christ, is not magical. It is rather exemplary as is clear from vv.12 and 14 regarding the disobedient human beings of the scriptural story. As for those who are subsequent to Christ, their reward is in the future to the extent to which they will have proceeded on the way of obedience trodden by Christ himself:

> If, because of one man's trespass, death reigned (*ebasilevsen*) through that one man, much more *will* those who receive the abundance of grace and the free gift of righteousness *reign* (*basilevsousin*) in life through the one man Jesus Christ. Then as one man's trespass *led* (*eis*) to condemnation for all men, so one man's act of righteousness *leads* (*eis*) to acquittal and life for all men. For as by one man's disobedience many *were made* (*katestathēsan*) sinners, so by one man's obedience many *will be made* (*katastathēsontai*) righteous. (vv.17-19)

Magic is nowhere in the purview of this passage. Rather it underscores divine judgment at the end over those who are after Christ, just as it points out the same divine judgment, witnessed to in scripture, over those who preceded him.

At this point, and in view of 7:12 (So the law is holy, and the commandment is holy and just and good) and 8:2 (For the law of the Spirit of life in Christ Jesus has set me free from the law of sin and death), Paul digresses to speak of the function of the

Mosaic law as he did in 3:20 and even earlier in Galatians 3:19-22. The Law's basic intention is to bestow life and blessings (Lev 25:3-13; Deut 28:1-14) by pointing out sin through a set of commandments and statutes, and thus inviting the hearers to avoid perpetrating sin that brings about the penalty of death. In so doing, the Law did not increase sin, but rather identified and instituted the trespass (*paraptōma*) and, by the same token, multiplied it (Rom 5:20a).[8] By contravening God's statutes one incurs the same curses (Lev 26:14-45; Deut 28:15-46) that culminate in exile (Lev 26:36-40; Deut 28:36-37, 47-68; 29:21-28). However, God, out of sheer gracefulness, will remember his covenant with the forefathers and will redeem those whom he had punished (Lev 26:42, 44-45; Deut 30:1-5), by offering them a second chance to follow his law, which will lead to life and prosperity (Deut 30:6-20). It is through his obedient servant that God will realize this plan of salvation for the many sinners (Is 53:10-12). In this sense, "where sin increased, grace abounded all the more, so that, as sin reigned in death, grace also might reign through righteousness to eternal life through Jesus Christ our Lord" (Rom 5:20b-21).

---

[8] See my comments on Gal 3:19 in *Gal* 146-52.

Chapter 6

Vv. 1-14 ¹ Τί οὖν ἐροῦμεν; ἐπιμένωμεν τῇ ἁμαρτίᾳ, ἵνα ἡ χάρις πλεονάσῃ; ² μὴ γένοιτο. οἵτινες ἀπεθάνομεν τῇ ἁμαρτίᾳ, πῶς ἔτι ζήσομεν ἐν αὐτῇ; ³ ἢ ἀγνοεῖτε ὅτι, ὅσοι ἐβαπτίσθημεν εἰς Χριστὸν Ἰησοῦν, εἰς τὸν θάνατον αὐτοῦ ἐβαπτίσθημεν; ⁴ συνετάφημεν οὖν αὐτῷ διὰ τοῦ βαπτίσματος εἰς τὸν θάνατον, ἵνα ὥσπερ ἠγέρθη Χριστὸς ἐκ νεκρῶν διὰ τῆς δόξης τοῦ πατρός, οὕτως καὶ ἡμεῖς ἐν καινότητι ζωῆς περιπατήσωμεν. ⁵ εἰ γὰρ σύμφυτοι γεγόναμεν τῷ ὁμοιώματι τοῦ θανάτου αὐτοῦ, ἀλλὰ καὶ τῆς ἀναστάσεως ἐσόμεθα· ⁶ τοῦτο γινώσκοντες ὅτι ὁ παλαιὸς ἡμῶν ἄνθρωπος συνεσταυρώθη, ἵνα καταργηθῇ τὸ σῶμα τῆς ἁμαρτίας, τοῦ μηκέτι δουλεύειν ἡμᾶς τῇ ἁμαρτίᾳ· ⁷ ὁ γὰρ ἀποθανὼν δεδικαίωται ἀπὸ τῆς ἁμαρτίας. ⁸ εἰ δὲ ἀπεθάνομεν σὺν Χριστῷ, πιστεύομεν ὅτι καὶ συζήσομεν αὐτῷ, ⁹ εἰδότες ὅτι Χριστὸς ἐγερθεὶς ἐκ νεκρῶν οὐκέτι ἀποθνῄσκει, θάνατος αὐτοῦ οὐκέτι κυριεύει. ¹⁰ ὃ γὰρ ἀπέθανεν, τῇ ἁμαρτίᾳ ἀπέθανεν ἐφάπαξ· ὃ δὲ ζῇ, ζῇ τῷ θεῷ. ¹¹ οὕτως καὶ ὑμεῖς λογίζεσθε ἑαυτοὺς [εἶναι] νεκροὺς μὲν τῇ ἁμαρτίᾳ ζῶντας δὲ τῷ θεῷ ἐν Χριστῷ Ἰησοῦ. ¹² Μὴ οὖν βασιλευέτω ἡ ἁμαρτία ἐν τῷ θνητῷ ὑμῶν σώματι εἰς τὸ ὑπακούειν ταῖς ἐπιθυμίαις αὐτοῦ, ¹³ μηδὲ παριστάνετε τὰ μέλη ὑμῶν ὅπλα ἀδικίας τῇ ἁμαρτίᾳ, ἀλλὰ παραστήσατε ἑαυτοὺς τῷ θεῷ ὡσεὶ ἐκ νεκρῶν ζῶντας καὶ τὰ μέλη ὑμῶν ὅπλα δικαιοσύνης τῷ θεῷ. ¹⁴ ἁμαρτία γὰρ ὑμῶν οὐ κυριεύσει· οὐ γάρ ἐστε ὑπὸ νόμον ἀλλὰ ὑπὸ χάριν.

¹*What shall we say then? Are we to continue in sin that grace may abound?* ²*By no means! How can we who died to sin still live in it?* ³*Do you not know that all of us who have been baptized into Christ Jesus were baptized into his death?* ⁴*We were buried therefore with him by baptism into death, so that as Christ was raised from the dead by the glory of the Father, we too might walk in newness of life.* ⁵*For if we have been united with him in a death like his, we shall certainly be united with*

him in a resurrection like his. ⁶We know that our old self was crucified with him so that the sinful body might be destroyed, and we might no longer be enslaved to sin. ⁷For he who has died is freed from sin. ⁸But if we have died with Christ, we believe that we shall also live with him. ⁹For we know that Christ being raised from the dead will never die again; death no longer has dominion over him. ¹⁰The death he died he died to sin, once for all, but the life he lives he lives to God. ¹¹So you also must consider yourselves dead to sin and alive to God in Christ Jesus. ¹²Let not sin therefore reign in your mortal bodies, to make you obey their passions. ¹³Do not yield your members to sin as instruments of wickedness, but yield yourselves to God as men who have been brought from death to life, and your members to God as instruments of righteousness. ¹⁴For sin will have no dominion over you, since you are not under law but under grace.

Just as was the case in Galatians 3:25-29, this graceful intervention on God's part is done through what Paul refers to as baptism. After the first part of his argument (where sin increased, grace abounded all the more; Rom 5:20b), he asks the rhetorical question: "What shall we say then? Are we to continue in sin that grace may abound?" (6:1) His answer is based on the second part of the argument (so that, as sin reigned in death, grace also might reign through righteousness to eternal life through Jesus Christ our Lord; 5:21): "By no means! How can we who died to sin still live in it?" (6:2) Then he refers to baptism as a case in point that his addressees as well as he have died to sin. The believers' death symbolized in baptism is actually a sharing in the death of the messiah Jesus (v.3). The Greek verb *baptizō* means "immerse (in water)"[1] and although

---

[1] See my detailed discussion of the verb *baptizō* in *Gal* 171-2.

the action is intended for cleansing, the baptized still runs the risk of suffocating and dying. The action of baptism has the potential ending as that of being buried under ground. However, if one is "baptized into Christ['s death]" (Gal 3:27; Rom 6:3), one has the potential of sharing in Christ's having been raised by God. Consequently, baptism functions as an invitation to the believer to trust in God's power of vindicating the righteous just as he did Jesus Christ (Rom 4:24-25; 5:18).

However, whereas Jesus Christ was raised unto life without death because he was found righteous, in order for us to join him in that kind of resurrection, we are to have led a righteous life. That is why, the symbolic death of baptism, followed by the symbolic raising out of the waters, opens for us the opportunity of another chance to lead a righteous life after the life of unrighteousness we have led up until baptism. Indeed, our raising out of the baptismal waters is not unto life without death, but rather "so that ... we too might *walk in newness of life*" (6:4). As for life eternal, which is an "already" for Jesus, it is still ahead of us (v.5). Given the invitation to a post-baptismal new kind of life, Paul refers to the pre-baptismal person as "our old person (*ho palaios hēmōn anthrōpos*; v.6) and uses, in conjunction with that person, the same terminology found in Galatians 5:24 (And those who belong to Christ Jesus have crucified the flesh with its passions and desires): "We know that our old self was crucified with him so that the sinful body might be destroyed, and we might no longer be enslaved to sin." (Rom 6:6) And this is only logical, since the person who (symbolically) dies (in baptism) as punishment for sin (so that the sinful body might be destroyed) has been acquitted (*dedikaiōtai*) from sin, that is, has paid his dues for the sin he had lived in. Any sin he would commit after baptism will be imputed to him, and thus his actual future death will be unto eternal divine wrath rather than eternal life (2:6-8).

Hence Paul's invitation, "But if we have died with Christ, we trust that we shall also live with him" (6:8). In other words, in baptism, we look both behind and ahead: behind toward the death of Christ and ahead toward the life eternal in which he reigns and which shall be bestowed upon us should we follow in a path of righteousness similar to his (vv.9-10). At this point Paul introduces the verb "reckon," which he used in conjunction with the example of Abraham who trusted in the God who promises, and can give life beyond the threat of death (4:20-25): "So you also, reckon yourselves dead to sin and alive to God in Christ Jesus." (6:11) Baptism, then, is not a magical event, but an invitation for us to *decide* to turn away from disobedience and live a new kind of life, a life of obedience to the will of God similar to the obedience of Jesus (5:19-21): "Let not sin therefore reign in your mortal bodies, to make you obey their passions." (6:12) This decision on our part is reflected in the three imperatives and the one jussive[2] Paul uses in vv.11-13 in tandem with inviting us to a life of righteousness:

> So you also, *reckon* yourselves dead to sin and alive to God in Christ Jesus. *Let not* sin therefore *reign* in your mortal bodies, to make you obey their passions. *Do not yield* your members to sin as instruments of wickedness, but *yield* yourselves to God as men who have been brought from death to life, and your members to God as instruments of righteousness.

Vv. 15-23 [15] Τί οὖν; ἁμαρτήσωμεν, ὅτι οὐκ ἐσμὲν ὑπὸ νόμον ἀλλὰ ὑπὸ χάριν; μὴ γένοιτο. [16] οὐκ οἴδατε ὅτι ᾧ παριστάνετε ἑαυτοὺς δούλους εἰς ὑπακοήν, δοῦλοί ἐστε ᾧ ὑπακούετε, ἤτοι ἁμαρτίας εἰς θάνατον ἢ ὑπακοῆς εἰς δικαιοσύνην; [17] χάρις δὲ τῷ θεῷ ὅτι ἦτε δοῦλοι τῆς ἁμαρτίας ὑπηκούσατε δὲ ἐκ καρδίας εἰς ὃν παρεδόθητε τύπον διδαχῆς, [18] ἐλευθερωθέντες δὲ ἀπὸ τῆς ἁμαρτίας ἐδουλώθητε

---

[2] Jussive is the form that expresses an order given to a third party.

τῇ δικαιοσύνῃ. ¹⁹ Ἀνθρώπινον λέγω διὰ τὴν ἀσθένειαν τῆς σαρκὸς ὑμῶν. ὥσπερ γὰρ παρεστήσατε τὰ μέλη ὑμῶν δοῦλα τῇ ἀκαθαρσίᾳ καὶ τῇ ἀνομίᾳ εἰς τὴν ἀνομίαν, οὕτως νῦν παραστήσατε τὰ μέλη ὑμῶν δοῦλα τῇ δικαιοσύνῃ εἰς ἁγιασμόν. ²⁰ ὅτε γὰρ δοῦλοι ἦτε τῆς ἁμαρτίας, ἐλεύθεροι ἦτε τῇ δικαιοσύνῃ. ²¹ τίνα οὖν καρπὸν εἴχετε τότε; ἐφ᾽ οἷς νῦν ἐπαισχύνεσθε, τὸ γὰρ τέλος ἐκείνων θάνατος. ²² νυνὶ δὲ ἐλευθερωθέντες ἀπὸ τῆς ἁμαρτίας δουλωθέντες δὲ τῷ θεῷ ἔχετε τὸν καρπὸν ὑμῶν εἰς ἁγιασμόν, τὸ δὲ τέλος ζωὴν αἰώνιον. ²³ τὰ γὰρ ὀψώνια τῆς ἁμαρτίας θάνατος, τὸ δὲ χάρισμα τοῦ θεοῦ ζωὴ αἰώνιος ἐν Χριστῷ Ἰησοῦ τῷ κυρίῳ ἡμῶν.

¹⁵*What then? Are we to sin because we are not under law but under grace? By no means!* ¹⁶*Do you not know that if you yield yourselves to any one as obedient slaves, you are slaves of the one whom you obey, either of sin, which leads to death, or of obedience, which leads to righteousness?* ¹⁷*But thanks be to God, that you who were once slaves of sin have become obedient from the heart to the standard of teaching to which you were committed,* ¹⁸*and, having been set free from sin, have become slaves of righteousness.* ¹⁹*I am speaking in human terms, because of your natural limitations. For just as you once yielded your members to impurity and to greater and greater iniquity, so now yield your members to righteousness for sanctification.* ²⁰*When you were slaves of sin, you were free in regard to righteousness.* ²¹*But then what return did you get from the things of which you are now ashamed? The end of those things is death.* ²²*But now that you have been set free from sin and have become slaves of God, the return you get is sanctification and its end, eternal life.* ²³*For the wages of sin is death, but the free gift of God is eternal life in Christ Jesus our Lord.*

In this passage Paul reprises his argument to make sure that his hearers have understood that the life offered them after baptism is not yet eternal life, which is only promised, but rather the continuation of their own lives. This time, however, they are to lead their lives in righteousness through unequivocal obedience to God, in the way Roman slaves obey their master.[3] This point is already evident in the terminology of the opening verse, "For sin will *have* no *dominion* (*kyrievsei*; lord as a master [lord; *kyrios*] does) over you, since *you are* not under law but *under grace*." Thus, the matter is not one of a new freedom versus a past slavery, but actually freedom from an enslaving lord to submissive slavery to a new lord who wants our good and treats us as his own children. This thought is carried throughout the entire passage. In v.15 we are told that sinning while we are *under* (the dominion of) grace is a contradiction in terms. Then v.16 explains: "Do you not know that if you yield yourselves to any one as obedient slaves, you are slaves of the one whom you obey, either of sin, which leads to death, or of obedience, which leads to righteousness?" Yet, this obedient submission, which gives life instead of death, is the outcome of God's gracefulness that materialized in the type of teaching propagated by Paul among the Gentiles (v.17). V.18 corroborates what was said earlier regarding freedom from an enslaving lordship toward a liberating slavery: "... having been set free from (domineering) sin, [you] have become *slaves of righteousness*" (see also v.20). Considering the harshness of this statement, Paul hurries to say that he is speaking in human metaphor (v.19a) taken from his contemporary Roman social life where a slave remained a slave— at best sometimes a freedman, but never a free citizen—moving from one household to another. The pre-baptismal master is impurity (*akatharsia*; uncleanness), the trademark of the behavior of all men, mainly the Gentiles (1:24), which leads to

---

[3] In Philippians Paul makes it clear that the obedience of Jesus himself to God was one of a slave to his master (2:6-11). See my comments in *C-Phil* 106-33.

iniquity (*anomia*; lawlessness, 2:12). The post-baptismal master is righteousness that leads to sanctification (*hagiasmon*; holiness, 6:22), which is God's calling for us: "For God has not called us for uncleanness (*akatharsia*), but in holiness (*hagiasmō*)." (1 Thess 4:7)

The post-baptismal new master is referred to as "righteousness" (Rom 6:18, 20). This is obviously a metaphor for the life that the baptized is supposed to lead, away from sin that would end in condemnation (v.16). The actual new master is God himself as is clear when one compares vv.18 and 22: "... having been set free from sin, have become slaves of righteousness"; "... now, having been set free from sin and having become slaves of God." Elsewhere, Paul refers to the baptized as "those who are of the household (*oikeious*) of the (community of) faith" (Gal 6:10) and "members of the household (*oikeioi*) of God" (Eph 2:19). This corroborates my contention that Paul is using the imagery of the Roman society where house slaves were members of a Roman patrician's household. This, in turn, binds them to their master's will to which they are to be obedient (Rom 6:16-17). This obedience is to specific orders and thus tangible or visible. A slave cannot fake obedience as though it was a state of mind; hence Paul uses "fruit" to speak of the slave's obedient response (v.22). For the believers, such fruit is to correspond to God's will, which is living a life of holiness (sanctification) that ultimately leads to life eternal (v.22). One is to remember that, for Paul, the believers are, by definition, "saints."[4] One is also to remember that the slave's life, in Roman society as well as in scripture, is at the mercy of his master. Any member of God's

---

[4] See e.g. 2 Cor 1:1; Eph 1:1; Phil 1:1; Col 1:1.

people who does not abide by God's law is excised out of the community unto death.[5]

However, in order to make sure that his hearers understand that while their life is always a gift of God's mercy toward them, they earn the verdict of their death when they are disobedient to God, Paul writes: "For the *wages* (*opsōnia*) of sin is death, but the *free gift* (*kharisma*) of God is eternal life in Christ Jesus our Lord." (v.23) Indeed, had God not sent Paul to preach to the Gentiles what was accomplished through Jesus Christ, they would have remained in their life of impurity and lawlessness, which would lead to their death by divine verdict. God's decision to send Paul to preach was a mere act of his goodwill (*evdokēsen*, Gal 1:15; see also Eph 1:5, 9). Thus the believers are to live and act according to that goodwill (*evdokia*, Phil 2:13).

---

[5] See e.g. Ex 12:15, 19; 30:33, 38; 31:14.

Chapter 7

Vv. 1-6 [1] *"Η ἀγνοεῖτε, ἀδελφοί, γινώσκουσιν γὰρ νόμον λαλῶ, ὅτι ὁ νόμος κυριεύει τοῦ ἀνθρώπου ἐφ' ὅσον χρόνον ζῇ;* [2] *ἡ γὰρ ὕπανδρος γυνὴ τῷ ζῶντι ἀνδρὶ δέδεται νόμῳ· ἐὰν δὲ ἀποθάνῃ ὁ ἀνήρ, κατήργηται ἀπὸ τοῦ νόμου τοῦ ἀνδρός.* [3] *ἄρα οὖν ζῶντος τοῦ ἀνδρὸς μοιχαλὶς χρηματίσει ἐὰν γένηται ἀνδρὶ ἑτέρῳ· ἐὰν δὲ ἀποθάνῃ ὁ ἀνήρ, ἐλευθέρα ἐστὶν ἀπὸ τοῦ νόμου, τοῦ μὴ εἶναι αὐτὴν μοιχαλίδα γενομένην ἀνδρὶ ἑτέρῳ.* [4] *ὥστε, ἀδελφοί μου, καὶ ὑμεῖς ἐθανατώθητε τῷ νόμῳ διὰ τοῦ σώματος τοῦ Χριστοῦ, εἰς τὸ γενέσθαι ὑμᾶς ἑτέρῳ, τῷ ἐκ νεκρῶν ἐγερθέντι, ἵνα καρποφορήσωμεν τῷ θεῷ.* [5] *ὅτε γὰρ ἦμεν ἐν τῇ σαρκί, τὰ παθήματα τῶν ἁμαρτιῶν τὰ διὰ τοῦ νόμου ἐνηργεῖτο ἐν τοῖς μέλεσιν ἡμῶν, εἰς τὸ καρποφορῆσαι τῷ θανάτῳ·* [6] *νυνὶ δὲ κατηργήθημεν ἀπὸ τοῦ νόμου ἀποθανόντες ἐν ᾧ κατειχόμεθα, ὥστε δουλεύειν ἡμᾶς ἐν καινότητι πνεύματος καὶ οὐ παλαιότητι γράμματος.*

[1]*Do you not know, brethren – for I am speaking to those who know the law – that the law is binding on a person only during his life?* [2]*Thus a married woman is bound by law to her husband as long as he lives; but if her husband dies she is discharged from the law concerning the husband.* [3]*Accordingly, she will be called an adulteress if she lives with another man while her husband is alive. But if her husband dies she is free from that law, and if she marries another man she is not an adulteress.* [4]*Likewise, my brethren, you have died to the law through the body of Christ, so that you may belong to another, to him who has been raised from the dead in order that we may bear fruit for God.* [5]*While we were living in the flesh, our sinful passions, aroused by the law, were at work in our members to bear fruit for death.* [6]*But now we are discharged from the law, dead to that which held us captive, so that we serve not under the old written code but in the new life of the Spirit.*

In order to understand correctly this often mishandled chapter of Romans, one is to read it with the view that Romans is, by and large, an elaboration of Galatians, meaning that the lines of thought in both letters run parallel. In Galatians, Paul makes it amply clear that whenever the Mosaic Law is understood as being self-standing and not within the movement of the entire biblical story, it ends up functioning for the Jews the same way pagan deities and their laws function for the Gentiles (Gal 3:1-4:11).[1] It is only when the Mosaic Law is read as part of the Law of scripture that it is understood correctly. That is to say, it is only when the entire "Moses"—that is the scriptural Pentateuch, the five books of Moses—is read as scripture, that "Moses" (the [five books of the] Law) is understood correctly. In Galatians, a *short* letter, Paul writes *at length* to explain that the Mosaic Law functions within the purview of the divine *promise* of *inheritance* (*klēronomia*) to Abraham to the extent that Jesus, as Messiah, is spoken of as "the offspring to whom the promise had been made" (Gal 3:19; see also vv.23-25). Thus, it is insofar as we are Christ's that we are "Abraham's offspring, heirs (*klēronomoi*) according to *promise*" (3:29; see also 4:1-7). What is important to realize is that, in Galatians, all the discussion about the function of the Mosaic Law is to lead Paul's hearers to the understanding that God's purpose in freeing us through Christ is not to lead us into a freedom of lawlessness, but rather to have us submit to God's law (5:13-26) which he terms "the law of Christ" (6:2).

So similarly here, in Romans, in preparation for the centrality of the divine Law which he terms "the law of the Spirit of life in Christ Jesus" (Rom 8:2), Paul digresses to deal with the function of the Mosaic Law as it appears in scripture. He starts his

---

[1] See my detailed comments on Gal 3:24-25; 4:2-3; and 4:9 in *Gal.*

argument by pointing out that he is addressing himself specifically to the "brethren" as people who "know (are knowledgeable in) the law" (7:1a). Furthermore, on purpose, he is using an example that fits Roman law as well as scriptural Law. One is bound to the rule (lordship) of the law (*ho nomos kyrievei*) of one's household so long as one—be it the master or the slave—is alive, that is, living in that household (v.1b). In vv.2-3, Paul deals with the eventual death of the master. However, in v.4, he moves to the case of the eventual death of the slave. This is more in line with his train of thought in chapter 6, as is clear from 7:4 where he reverts to the terminology of 6:1-10. In that case, obviously, the slave is "free" from his master's lordship. However, the death in baptism (6:4) is not an actual death, but a reality we have to reckon as ours (v.11). It is a death to the rule of sin (6:11; 7:4) through our having been integrated into the body of Christ, that is, into the community of both Jews and Gentiles around Jesus Christ, the Messiah and Lord. Paul makes this abundantly clear in 1 Corinthians 6 and 12, and it will be reiterated again in Romans 14. The ultimate intention of this reckoning is to produce fruit to the new master, God (7:4), as already stated in 6:22. Then Paul will sum up his argument concerning the function of the Law in verses 7:5-6. When we were still in the flesh, that is, doing our own will, the passions of sins were aroused by the Law's prohibitions, and worked in our members to bear fruit unto death. Indeed, the Law was given unto blessing and life, but entailed the eventuality of curse and death if we did not abide by it (Lev 26 and Deut 28). Yet, now, through baptism, we are released from the Law in the sense that we have paid with the penalty of death, as prescribed by the Law, for our sins, as Paul explained earlier (Rom 6:7), in order (*hōste*; so that, in view of) for us to serve God, our new master. This new kind of life is under the Spirit's control and not according to

our old way of life that is controlled by the written prescriptions
of the Law (7:6). This last statement is to be understood in the
light of 6:4. The idea is not that we are free to do as we please.
Rather, as Paul explained in detail in Galatians 5:13-26, we are
to submit unconditionally to the will of God's spirit in order to
secure the life promised in the Law, should we abide by God's
will. The alternative is to go back to our old way of life, debating
at every step whether it behooves us to follow God's directives.
This way of life brought us under the curse of death which we
incurred because now and then we opted to disobey God. The
invitation for us now is to submit unconditionally to the
leadership of the Spirit, as described by the verb *stikhōmen* (Gal
5:25), whose literal meaning is "let us march in line." Thus we
are to submit the way soldiers in the army do under the orders of
their superior. Just as in Galatians Paul taught we had been
called to freedom in order to serve (be enslaved to) one another
(5:13), here also he points out repeatedly that the reason behind
our freedom is to be slaves of God (Rom 6:22) and to serve him
as a Roman household slave would serve (7:6), unconditionally,
without following, as we did before baptism, our own desires
and preferences (Gal 5:16-17).

Vv. 7-25 ⁷ Τί οὖν ἐροῦμεν; ὁ νόμος ἁμαρτία; μὴ γένοιτο·
ἀλλὰ τὴν ἁμαρτίαν οὐκ ἔγνων εἰ μὴ διὰ νόμου· τήν τε γὰρ
ἐπιθυμίαν οὐκ ᾔδειν εἰ μὴ ὁ νόμος ἔλεγεν· οὐκ ἐπιθυμήσεις.
⁸ ἀφορμὴν δὲ λαβοῦσα ἡ ἁμαρτία διὰ τῆς ἐντολῆς
κατειργάσατο ἐν ἐμοὶ πᾶσαν ἐπιθυμίαν· χωρὶς γὰρ νόμου
ἁμαρτία νεκρά. ⁹ ἐγὼ δὲ ἔζων χωρὶς νόμου ποτέ, ἐλθούσης δὲ
τῆς ἐντολῆς ἡ ἁμαρτία ἀνέζησεν, ¹⁰ ἐγὼ δὲ ἀπέθανον καὶ
εὑρέθη μοι ἡ ἐντολὴ ἡ εἰς ζωήν, αὕτη εἰς θάνατον· ¹¹ ἡ γὰρ
ἁμαρτία ἀφορμὴν λαβοῦσα διὰ τῆς ἐντολῆς ἐξηπάτησέν με καὶ
δι' αὐτῆς ἀπέκτεινεν. ¹² ὥστε ὁ μὲν νόμος ἅγιος καὶ ἡ
ἐντολὴ ἁγία καὶ δικαία καὶ ἀγαθή. ¹³ Τὸ οὖν ἀγαθὸν ἐμοὶ
ἐγένετο θάνατος; μὴ γένοιτο· ἀλλὰ ἡ ἁμαρτία, ἵνα φανῇ

ἁμαρτία, διὰ τοῦ ἀγαθοῦ μοι κατεργαζομένη θάνατον, ἵνα
γένηται καθ᾽ ὑπερβολὴν ἁμαρτωλὸς ἡ ἁμαρτία διὰ τῆς
ἐντολῆς. ¹⁴ Οἴδαμεν γὰρ ὅτι ὁ νόμος πνευματικός ἐστιν, ἐγὼ
δὲ σάρκινός εἰμι πεπραμένος ὑπὸ τὴν ἁμαρτίαν. ¹⁵ ὃ γὰρ
κατεργάζομαι οὐ γινώσκω· οὐ γὰρ ὃ θέλω τοῦτο πράσσω,
ἀλλ᾽ ὃ μισῶ τοῦτο ποιῶ. ¹⁶ εἰ δὲ ὃ οὐ θέλω τοῦτο ποιῶ,
σύμφημι τῷ νόμῳ ὅτι καλός. ¹⁷ νυνὶ δὲ οὐκέτι ἐγὼ
κατεργάζομαι αὐτὸ ἀλλὰ ἡ οἰκοῦσα ἐν ἐμοὶ ἁμαρτία. ¹⁸ Οἶδα
γὰρ ὅτι οὐκ οἰκεῖ ἐν ἐμοί, τοῦτ᾽ ἔστιν ἐν τῇ σαρκί μου,
ἀγαθόν· τὸ γὰρ θέλειν παράκειταί μοι, τὸ δὲ κατεργάζεσθαι
τὸ καλὸν οὔ· ¹⁹ οὐ γὰρ ὃ θέλω ποιῶ ἀγαθόν, ἀλλὰ ὃ οὐ θέλω
κακὸν τοῦτο πράσσω. ²⁰ εἰ δὲ ὃ οὐ θέλω [ἐγὼ] τοῦτο ποιῶ,
οὐκέτι ἐγὼ κατεργάζομαι αὐτὸ ἀλλὰ ἡ οἰκοῦσα ἐν ἐμοὶ
ἁμαρτία. ²¹ εὑρίσκω ἄρα τὸν νόμον, τῷ θέλοντι ἐμοὶ ποιεῖν
τὸ καλόν, ὅτι ἐμοὶ τὸ κακὸν παράκειται· ²² συνήδομαι γὰρ
τῷ νόμῳ τοῦ θεοῦ κατὰ τὸν ἔσω ἄνθρωπον, ²³ βλέπω δὲ
ἕτερον νόμον ἐν τοῖς μέλεσίν μου ἀντιστρατευόμενον τῷ
νόμῳ τοῦ νοός μου καὶ αἰχμαλωτίζοντά με ἐν τῷ νόμῳ τῆς
ἁμαρτίας τῷ ὄντι ἐν τοῖς μέλεσίν μου. ²⁴ Ταλαίπωρος ἐγὼ
ἄνθρωπος· τίς με ῥύσεται ἐκ τοῦ σώματος τοῦ θανάτου
τούτου; ²⁵ χάρις δὲ τῷ θεῷ διὰ Ἰησοῦ Χριστοῦ τοῦ κυρίου
ἡμῶν. Ἄρα οὖν αὐτὸς ἐγὼ τῷ μὲν νοῒ δουλεύω νόμῳ θεοῦ
τῇ δὲ σαρκὶ νόμῳ ἁμαρτίας.

⁷*What then shall we say? That the law is sin? By no means! Yet, if it had not been for the law, I should not have known sin. I should not have known what it is to covet if the law had not said, "You shall not covet."* ⁸*But sin, finding opportunity in the commandment, wrought in me all kinds of covetousness. Apart from the law sin lies dead.* ⁹*I was once alive apart from the law, but when the commandment came, sin revived and I died;* ¹⁰*the very commandment which promised life proved to be death to me.* ¹¹*For sin, finding opportunity in the commandment, deceived me and by it killed me.* ¹²*So the law is holy, and the commandment is holy and just and good.* ¹³*Did that which is good, then, bring death to me? By no means! It was sin, working death in me through what is good, in order that sin might be*

shown to be sin, and through the commandment might become sinful beyond measure. [14]We know that the law is spiritual; but I am carnal, sold under sin. [15]I do not understand my own actions. For I do not do what I want, but I do the very thing I hate. [16]Now if I do what I do not want, I agree that the law is good. [17]So then it is no longer I that do it, but sin which dwells within me. [18]For I know that nothing good dwells within me, that is, in my flesh. I can will what is right, but I cannot do it. [19]For I do not do the good I want, but the evil I do not want is what I do. [20]Now if I do what I do not want, it is no longer I that do it, but sin which dwells within me. [21]So I find it to be a law that when I want to do right, evil lies close at hand. [22]For I delight in the law of God, in my inmost self, [23]but I see in my members another law at war with the law of my mind and making me captive to the law of sin which dwells in my members. [24]Wretched man that I am! Who will deliver me from this body of death? [25]Thanks be to God through Jesus Christ our Lord! So then, I of myself serve the law of God with my mind, but with my flesh I serve the law of sin.

In order to make sure that, after baptism, the Gentile as well as the Jew not revert to their pre-baptismal way of life, Paul uses the rest of Romans 7 to explain in detail the mechanism by which matters in scripture went wrong. The reason behind our having ended in a state of slavery, with wages being death, is not a flaw inherent in God's law. Indeed, how could that be since "the law is holy, and the commandment is holy and just and good" (v.12) and God's final aim "in Christ Jesus" is to harness us to "the *law* of the Spirit of life" (8:2)? So Paul begins by asking the rhetorical question, "What then shall we say? That the law is sin?" to which he replies with the equally rhetorical and unequivocal "By no means!" (7:7). He then revisits the statement he made earlier in the letter (through the law comes the knowledge of sin; 3:20) and explicates: "if it had not been for the law, I should not have known sin. I should not have known what it is to covet (*epithymian*) if the law had not said, 'You shall not covet (*epithymēseis*).'" (7:7) It is important to notice that, out of the entire Decalogue, Paul chose the prohibition of *epithymia*, which is the term he uses in Galatians in conjunction with the desires of the flesh, that is to say, the human wishes against the Spirit's will (5:16-17) *after* the believers have been called to freedom (v.13). The intention is clearly to underscore that sinning after baptism is actually reverting to doing what one was previously doing and thus nullifying the work of God. And such behavior, according to Paul, is inconceivable: "What shall we say then? Are we to continue in sin that grace may abound? By no means! How can we who died to sin still live in it?" (Rom 6:1-2)

Before engaging into a detailed discussion of the function of the Law and our response to it, Paul splits one human person in two—into our actual self, on the one hand, and "our old man (being)" or "the (our) sinful body," on the other hand. Here, in contrast to Romans 6:6, he goes a step further by personalizing our pre-baptismal being, our "sinful body," into the self-standing entity of sin. It is as though sin is an outlandish reality that pervades our being. We speak of a cancerous tumor much in the same way today. The tumor is made of our own cells, yet, in order for us to be healed, the physicians treat it as though it were an opponent or a foreign element that invaded our body and became part of our reality. In so doing, the physicians make it psychologically easier on us to put up a real fight *against* the tumor which is an integral part of us. Similarly, in order to invite us to discard our sinful behavior and follow a new way of life, Paul personalizes sinful behavior into "sin." In doing so, he puts pressure on us to put up a fight *against* our sinning selves, so to speak: "But sin, finding opportunity in the commandment, wrought in me all kinds of covetousness. Apart from the law sin lies dead." (7:8). Paul does something similar, in another setting, when he considers his own "body" as the opponent he needs to subdue:

> Do you not know that in a race all the runners compete, but only one receives the prize? So run that you may obtain it. Every athlete exercises self-control in all things. They do it to receive a perishable wreath, but we an imperishable. Well, I do not run aimlessly, I do not box as one beating the air; but I pommel *my body* and subdue it, lest after preaching to others *I myself* should be disqualified. (1 Cor 9:24-27)

In Romans 7:8b-10 Paul is following the scriptural story line. He reprises his argument of Romans 5:12-13 where he says that, before the Law, sin was not "counted" as such and thus dormant, practically "dead" (7:8b), yet ready to attack. We heard this early in Genesis: "So Cain was very angry, and his countenance fell. The Lord said to Cain, 'Why are you angry, and why has your countenance fallen? If you do well, will you not be accepted? And if you do not do well, sin is couching at the door; its desire is for you, but you must master it.'" (4:5b-7) So, before the Law, people were living without knowing the threat of the just punishment. To make them aware of such punishment, God issued the Law to guide them on the right way. However, instead of choosing the right way unto the blessing of life, human beings opted for contravening the divine injunctions. This led to the curse of exile and death. Consequently, "the very commandment which promised life proved to be death to me" (Rom 7:10), as foreseen in the Law (Lev 26 and Deut 28). If thus it is (my) sin that "deceived me and killed me" (Rom 7:11), then "the law (issued by God) is holy, and the commandment (of God) is holy and just and good" (v.12).

So, as in the case of Adam in the garden, "it was sin, working death in me through what is good, in order that sin might be shown to be sin, and through the commandment might become sinful beyond measure" (v.13). This statement reflects the highest level of personalization of sin. That is why, in order to make sure that human beings not be "off the hook," Paul hurries to put the blame on them: "We know that the law is spiritual; but *I* am carnal (*sarkinos*; fleshly), sold under sin." (v.14) By the same token he is preparing for his conclusion in Rom 8:1-8 where the Law is that of the Spirit (of God) and, if so, then we are no longer to behave "fleshly" (*kata sarka*; according to the flesh, v.4). And in order to give hope *in God's law* to his hearers who are living the dilemma of disobeying the will of God whose intention is gracious toward them, Paul uses the verb "know" (*ginōskō*) to describe our act of contravening God's will: "I do not know (*ginōskō*) what I am accomplishing.[2] For I do not do what I want, but I do the very thing I hate. Now if I do what I do not want, I agree that the law is good." (7:15-16) Paul can come to this reasoning since, as a rule, the Law in the Old Testament is the object of knowledge.[3] Furthermore, the Law, being good, is worthy of knowledge.

The logical outcome then for Paul is to put up a fight against the opponent, sin, which "dwells within me" (v.17), that is to say, which behaviorally is "an integral part of me." This is clear from v.18, "dwells within me, that is, in my flesh." The flesh is

---

[2] RSV misses the point by translating the Greek into "I do not understand my own actions," making it sound as a psychological bewilderment.

[3] See earlier Paul's statement: "But if you call yourself a Jew and *rely upon the law* and boast in God and *know his will* and approve what is excellent, because you are *instructed in the law...*" (2:17-18). The intentionality behind the use of *ginōskō* on Paul's part is put in relief by the occurrence of the verb *oidamen/oida* (we are/ I am aware) both before and after (vv.14 and 18).

the expression of human will, as opposed to the spirit, which is the expression of God's will. More importantly, sin is (the) *evil* (enemy) *because* it is prohibited by the *good* Law. Again, in order not to let us "off the hook," Paul introduces another metaphor to describe our sin of disobedience. By contravening God's law, we are de facto instituting a "law" of our own (vv.21-23) that we obey, and thus end up its "captive of war" (v.23),[4] or are "bound to it" as a slave (see earlier Romans 6). And a captive of war is an exile who will eventually end up dead and buried in a strange land, as the condemned Adam and Israel did. The wretchedness of this is that it works as a maze that is hard to get out of (7:24a). The only possible rescue can come from God himself by his intervention through his Messiah Jesus (v.25a), as Paul explained in Romans 5:1-11. And since that action is one of sheer grace(fullness) (v.2), our reaction can be only one of acknowledging that grace(fullness): "Thanks[5] be to God through Jesus Christ our Lord!" (7:25a)

The ending of Romans 7 (v.25b) is magisterial for two reasons. First, it concludes the entire discussion of the chapter without allowing the positive note of vv.24a-25b to be the last word in the matter. The real fully positive conclusion is deferred to the end of Romans 8 where absolutely nothing, "will be able to separate us from the love of God in Christ Jesus our Lord" (v.39). Secondly, Paul introduces into the discussion the term "mind" (*nous*; 7:23, 25), which has not appeared since 1:28. He does so in order to underscore our responsibility when we choose to act against God's law. On the one hand, our mind tells us to submit to the divine law; that is why "the law of sin" is said to be

---

[4] Paul's use of *aikhmalōtizonta me* (making me a captive of war) is again intentional since it reflects the reality of warring (enmity) between sin and us, as is already evident in the parallel *antistratevomenon* (at war with).

[5] The Greek is powerful: "Grace (*kharis*) be to God through Jesus Christ our Lord!"

opposed to "the law of my mind" (7:23), which is the counterpart of "my delight in the law of God" (v.22). Then, in v.25 we are told that "I of myself serve the law of God with my mind, but with my flesh I serve the law of sin." Consequently, the "mind" is the center of our deliberative and responsible decision[6] when compared to the "flesh" which is ruled by desire (*epithymia*).[7] Paul is evidently preparing for the following chapter where he will pin down our flesh against our *phronēma* (thought/thinking) as opposite sources of our decision to walk or not to walk on God's way. In other words, Paul is preparing to invite his hearers to "use their mind" this time around, since they were given a second chance through baptism; and, as he stressed in Romans 6, it is their last chance.

---

[6] See 1 Cor 14:14-15, 18-19 (For if I pray in a tongue, my spirit prays but my mind is unfruitful. What am I to do? I will pray with the spirit and I will pray with the mind also; I will sing with the spirit and I will sing with the mind also ... I thank God that I speak in tongues more than you all; nevertheless, in church I would rather speak five words with my mind, in order to instruct others, than ten thousand words in a tongue.)

[7] The Greek *epithymia* is from the same root as *thymos* (thymus) which is the gland that was considered as behind our non-reflective (re)actions (so-called "gut reactions").

Chapter 8

Vv. 1-18 ¹ Οὐδὲν ἄρα νῦν κατάκριμα τοῖς ἐν Χριστῷ Ἰησοῦ. ² ὁ γὰρ νόμος τοῦ πνεύματος τῆς ζωῆς ἐν Χριστῷ Ἰησοῦ ἠλευθέρωσέν σε ἀπὸ τοῦ νόμου τῆς ἁμαρτίας καὶ τοῦ θανάτου. ³ Τὸ γὰρ ἀδύνατον τοῦ νόμου ἐν ᾧ ἠσθένει διὰ τῆς σαρκός, ὁ θεὸς τὸν ἑαυτοῦ υἱὸν πέμψας ἐν ὁμοιώματι σαρκὸς ἁμαρτίας καὶ περὶ ἁμαρτίας κατέκρινεν τὴν ἁμαρτίαν ἐν τῇ σαρκί, ⁴ ἵνα τὸ δικαίωμα τοῦ νόμου πληρωθῇ ἐν ἡμῖν τοῖς μὴ κατὰ σάρκα περιπατοῦσιν ἀλλὰ κατὰ πνεῦμα. ⁵ οἱ γὰρ κατὰ σάρκα ὄντες τὰ τῆς σαρκὸς φρονοῦσιν, οἱ δὲ κατὰ πνεῦμα τὰ τοῦ πνεύματος. ⁶ τὸ γὰρ φρόνημα τῆς σαρκὸς θάνατος, τὸ δὲ φρόνημα τοῦ πνεύματος ζωὴ καὶ εἰρήνη· ⁷ διότι τὸ φρόνημα τῆς σαρκὸς ἔχθρα εἰς θεόν, τῷ γὰρ νόμῳ τοῦ θεοῦ οὐχ ὑποτάσσεται, οὐδὲ γὰρ δύναται· ⁸ οἱ δὲ ἐν σαρκὶ ὄντες θεῷ ἀρέσαι οὐ δύνανται. ⁹ ὑμεῖς δὲ οὐκ ἐστὲ ἐν σαρκὶ ἀλλὰ ἐν πνεύματι, εἴπερ πνεῦμα θεοῦ οἰκεῖ ἐν ὑμῖν. εἰ δέ τις πνεῦμα Χριστοῦ οὐκ ἔχει, οὗτος οὐκ ἔστιν αὐτοῦ. ¹⁰ εἰ δὲ Χριστὸς ἐν ὑμῖν, τὸ μὲν σῶμα νεκρὸν διὰ ἁμαρτίαν τὸ δὲ πνεῦμα ζωὴ διὰ δικαιοσύνην. ¹¹ εἰ δὲ τὸ πνεῦμα τοῦ ἐγείραντος τὸν Ἰησοῦν ἐκ νεκρῶν οἰκεῖ ἐν ὑμῖν, ὁ ἐγείρας Χριστὸν ἐκ νεκρῶν ζῳοποιήσει καὶ τὰ θνητὰ σώματα ὑμῶν διὰ τοῦ ἐνοικοῦντος αὐτοῦ πνεύματος ἐν ὑμῖν. ¹² Ἄρα οὖν, ἀδελφοί, ὀφειλέται ἐσμὲν οὐ τῇ σαρκὶ τοῦ κατὰ σάρκα ζῆν, ¹³ εἰ γὰρ κατὰ σάρκα ζῆτε, μέλλετε ἀποθνῄσκειν· εἰ δὲ πνεύματι τὰς πράξεις τοῦ σώματος θανατοῦτε, ζήσεσθε. ¹⁴ ὅσοι γὰρ πνεύματι θεοῦ ἄγονται, οὗτοι υἱοὶ θεοῦ εἰσιν. ¹⁵ οὐ γὰρ ἐλάβετε πνεῦμα δουλείας πάλιν εἰς φόβον ἀλλὰ ἐλάβετε πνεῦμα υἱοθεσίας ἐν ᾧ κράζομεν· αββα ὁ πατήρ. ¹⁶ αὐτὸ τὸ πνεῦμα συμμαρτυρεῖ τῷ πνεύματι ἡμῶν ὅτι ἐσμὲν τέκνα θεοῦ. ¹⁷ εἰ δὲ τέκνα, καὶ κληρονόμοι· κληρονόμοι μὲν θεοῦ, συγκληρονόμοι δὲ Χριστοῦ, εἴπερ συμπάσχομεν ἵνα καὶ συνδοξασθῶμεν. ¹⁸ Λογίζομαι γὰρ ὅτι οὐκ ἄξια τὰ παθήματα τοῦ νῦν καιροῦ πρὸς τὴν μέλλουσαν δόξαν ἀποκαλυφθῆναι εἰς ἡμᾶς.

¹There is therefore now no condemnation for those who are in Christ Jesus. ²For the law of the Spirit of life in Christ Jesus has set me free from the law of sin and death. ³For God has done what the law, weakened by the flesh, could not do: sending his own Son in the likeness of sinful flesh and for sin, he condemned sin in the flesh, ⁴in order that the just requirement of the law might be fulfilled in us, who walk not according to the flesh but according to the Spirit. ⁵For those who live according to the flesh set their minds on the things of the flesh, but those who live according to the Spirit set their minds on the things of the Spirit. ⁶To set the mind on the flesh is death, but to set the mind on the Spirit is life and peace. ⁷For the mind that is set on the flesh is hostile to God; it does not submit to God's law, indeed it cannot; ⁸and those who are in the flesh cannot please God. ⁹But you are not in the flesh, you are in the Spirit, if in fact the Spirit of God dwells in you. Any one who does not have the Spirit of Christ does not belong to him. ¹⁰But if Christ is in you, although your bodies are dead because of sin, your spirits are alive because of righteousness. ¹¹If the Spirit of him who raised Jesus from the dead dwells in you, he who raised Christ Jesus from the dead will give life to your mortal bodies also through his Spirit which dwells in you. ¹²So then, brethren, we are debtors, not to the flesh, to live according to the flesh— ¹³for if you live according to the flesh you will die, but if by the Spirit you put to death the deeds of the body you will live. ¹⁴For all who are led by the Spirit of God are sons of God. ¹⁵For you did not receive the spirit of slavery to fall back into fear, but you have received the spirit of sonship. When we cry, "Abba! Father!" ¹⁶it is the Spirit himself bearing witness with our spirit that we are children of God, ¹⁷and if children, then heirs, heirs of God and fellow heirs with Christ, provided we suffer with him in order that we may also be glorified with him. ¹⁸I consider that the sufferings of this present time are not worth comparing with the glory that is to be revealed to us.

If then one is in Christ Jesus, that is to say, a member of the household of God where his will rules (Romans 6), that one cannot possibly succumb under divine condemnation (Rom 8:1) since God himself is the judge and "if he is for us, who is (could possibly be) against us?" (v.31). However, membership in that household entails following the law that governs it, which is the law of God's spirit that leads to life, and not the law of our own will, which leads to sin and death and from which law we were freed (v.2), as Paul explained in the previous two chapters.

Yet instead of obeying God's law in order to attain the blessing of life promised in that Law, we opted for disobedience that led to the curse of death. This happened because we chose to follow our own mind. In order to secure that we not repeat the same mistake, God yoked us to obeying his law under the leadership of his spirit. To explain how this happened, Paul coins his magisterial statement in vv.3-4 where he brings together key words that he used earlier to sum up the entire scriptural story. Since the original Greek is densely written, I shall try to explain it by relegating the details to the footnotes for those readers who would want to make the effort to follow the line of thought in the original text.

In scripture in general, and in the Pauline letters in particular, the most important facet of the Spirit is power (*dynamis*),[1] which is the opposite of weakness (*asthenia*). The Israelites were brought out of the land of slavery and death and were granted the Law to ensure their freedom and life in Canaan. However,

---

[1] This is readily understandable in Hebrew since *ruaḥ* means "wind."

since God is the just judge, the Law also entailed the curse of exile and death. In the biblical story, whenever the people would opt to disobey the Law and, consequently, would be punished by God, it sounds as though God (or the Law) is unable (does not have the power)[2] to implement his original plan and thus looks weak.[3] It is as though God gives in. Such was the case in 1 Samuel 8 when God asks Samuel to give in to the request of the people to have a king, in order to show the people the destructive outcome of their misguided choice. Ultimately, God proves to have the upper hand by condemning the people with exile and death for their sin. But subsequently, through his special elect one, he implements his original promise to save not only his people, but also all the nations since all are his people (Is 42:1-7; Is 49:6; 52:13-53:12).[4] Hence Paul's statement in Romans 8:3-4:[5] "For whatever was not able (had no power) to be done through (or by) the Law, due to the fact that God (or the Law) was being weakened (put in the position of not being able) due to the (counter-stance of) the flesh (human will), by sending his son in the likeness of the flesh of sin and for the sake

---

[2] In Greek the verb *dynamai* (be able to, have power) is from the same root as *dynamis* (power) and *to adynaton* (the not being able, the powerlessness) which is used in Rom 8:3.

[3] Considering that the original meaning of faith (belief) is trust in God's word of promise, the most pertinent example for my readers is Mk 6:5-6a (And he could not [*ouk ēdynato*; was not able to] do any mighty work there, except that he laid his hands upon a few sick people and healed them. And he marveled because of their unbelief [*apistian*; lack of faith, lack of trust]).

[4] Notice how the overture of Second-Isaiah (40-55) reflects God's implementation of his original plan as well as his educational punishment: "*Comfort, comfort* my people, says your God. *Speak tenderly* to Jerusalem, and cry to her that her warfare is ended, that her iniquity is pardoned, that *she has received from the Lord's hand double for all her sins.*" (40:1-2)

[5] I am rendering the original as closely as possible: "*To gar adynaton tou nomou, en hō esthenei dia tēs sarkos, ho Theos ton heavtou hyion pempsas en omoiōmati sarkos hamartias katekrinen tēn hamartian en tē sarki, hina to dikaiōma tou nomou plērōthē en hēmin, tois mē kata sarka peripatousin, alla kata pnevma.*"

(because) of sin,[6] God condemned (was able to condemn) sin in the flesh, in order that the right decree of the law might be fulfilled among us, who walk not according to the flesh but according to the Spirit." The main point in this statement is that, now the verdict of condemnation has been issued not against us, but against someone else for our sake. As in the case of the sacrificial lamb (Is 53:5-7), we are to take this opportunity to realize that, this time around, we are to "walk" (behave) according to the will of the spirit (of God), as expressed in God's law, and not according to our own will, the will of the flesh.

To underscore that such has to be a conscious decision on our part, Paul introduces the Greek terminology of *phroneō* (think; take a mental stance) which corresponds to the Greek *nous* (mind) he has just brought into the picture (7:23, 25). His intention is to "translate" the scriptural Semitic terminology into Greek verbiage in the same way the Septuagint did before him. The scriptural "walking" is not done with one's feet. Rather, it is a way of life that one has to decide for with one's mind. The other classical example of such terminology is "turning (around), returning" (Hebrew *šub*) which is rendered in the Septuagint and the New Testament as *metanoia* (changing of mind)[7] as well as *hypostrephein* (return, turn around).[8] So, immediately after saying "who walk not according to the flesh but according to the Spirit" (Rom 8:4) he writes: "For those who are according to the flesh set their minds (*phronousin*) on the things of the flesh, but those who (are) according to the Spirit (set their minds) on the things of the Spirit." (v.5) And, immediately thereafter, in order to

---

[6] Recall Paul's statement in Galatians "Christ redeemed us from the curse of the law, *having become a curse for us.*" (3:13) See my comments in *Gal* 129-33.

[7] *(meta)noia* is from the root *nous.*

[8] Another example is the use of the Aramaic *'abba* together with the Greek *ho patēr* in order to say "Father!" (Mk 14:36; Rom 8:15; Gal 4:6).

prepare for the summation of his teaching up to this point, he concludes with terminology he used in the earlier chapters and verses: "To set the mind on the flesh[9] (*to phronēma tēs sarkos*) is death,[10] but to set the mind on the Spirit[11] is life[12] and peace.[13] For the mind that is set on the flesh[14] is hostile (enemy)[15] to God; it does not submit[16] to God's law, indeed it cannot (*oude dynatai*)."[17] (vv.6-7) Then he adds v.8 as a codicil, using terminology that looks ahead as well as backwards, thus functioning as a link between the preceding and the following: "and those who are in the flesh (*en sarki*)[18] cannot (*ou dynatai*)[19] please[20] God."

Then, in order not to allow his hearers any vacillation or give them even the slightest illusion that they have a choice, Paul immediately and unequivocally counteracts by saying: "But you are not in the flesh, you are in the Spirit,[21] if in fact[22] the Spirit of God dwells (*oikei*) among you." (v.9a) Instead of sin dwelling

---

[9] See Rom 8:5.

[10] See Rom 6.

[11] See Rom 8:5.

[12] See Rom 2:7; 5:10, 17, 18, 21; 6:4, 10, 13, 22, 23.

[13] See Rom 2:10; 5:1.

[14] See Rom 8:5.

[15] See Rom 5:10.

[16] The verb *hypotassō* (submit) has the same connotation as the verb *hypakouō* (obey; Rom 6:12, 16) and *hypakoē* (obedience; Rom 1:5; 5:19; 6:16 [twice]).

[17] Rom 8:3. See also 1:4, 16, 20; 4:21.

[18] See Rom 8:5 where we have the corresponding "according to the flesh (*kata sarka*)."

[19] See Rom 8:7.

[20] See Rom 12:1 and 2 (*evarestos*; acceptable, pleasing; from the same root as *aresai* in 8:8); 14:18 (*evarestos*); 15:1 and 2.

[21] Corresponding to "according to the Spirit" of v.5.

[22] This "if in fact" (*eiper*) does not reflect a doubt on Paul's part but rather puts pressure on his hearers to make of their new status a reality in their daily lives, as will also be the case in Rom 8:17 and as is the case in 1 Cor 15:1-2.

in me[23] (7:17, 18, 29, 23), it is now the Spirit who dwells (ought to be dwelling) among the believers and leads (ought to be leading) them as an army superior would lead those under his command (Gal 5:25). This imagery of God's spirit making his building (*oikodomia*)[24] out of (dwelling in) the church community is developed in 1 Corinthians 3:9-17 where Paul uses the same phrase "the Spirit of God dwells among you" (v.16).[25] Since the imagery goes back to Galatians 6:10 where the believers are referred to as "members of a household" (*oikoious*), a caveat is in order here. Very often, the dwelling of the Spirit is understood as being in each of us individually. Such does not fit the household background of the metaphor. Sin is an individual action and responsibility,[26] whereas the leadership of the paterfamilias is as communitarian as the dwelling of the deity (or the monarch) among its people. To consider God (or his spirit) as having many residences or temples is, scripturally speaking, blasphemous since it contradicts Deuteronomy (12:10-27; 14:23-25; 16:1-17). This was the dilemma of the Transjordanian tribes in Joshua 22. When gathering the scattered bones of the Israelites, the function of the Spirit was not to raise up individuals back to individual lives, but to reinstate the Israelites as his *people* Israel:

> Then he said to me, "Son of man, these bones are the *whole house of Israel*. Behold, they say, 'Our bones are dried up, and our hope is lost; we are clean cut off.' Therefore prophesy, and say to them, Thus says the Lord God: Behold, I will open your graves, and raise

---

[23] In the sense, as I explained earlier, of my having opted to contravene God's will expressed in his law.

[24] The noun *oikodomē* (building, house) is from the same root as *oikei* (dwells as in a house).

[25] The ubiquity of this important metaphor is evident from its use in 1 Cor 14:3-4, 12, 17, 26; Eph 2:19-22.

[26] See e.g. Gen 4:7 and Ezek 18.

you from your graves, O my people; and I will bring you home into the land of Israel. And you shall know that I am the Lord, when I open your graves, and raise you from your graves, O my people. And I will put my Spirit within you, and you shall live, and I will place you in your own land; then you shall know that I, the Lord, have spoken, and I have done it, says the Lord." (Ezek 37:11-14; see also vv.21, 23, 27)

However, the responsibility to keep alive the new reality pertaining to Christ's messianic community falls on each and every one of the members: "Any one who does not have the Spirit of Christ does not belong to him." (Rom 8:9b) Then, in vv.11-13, Paul recalls his teaching in Romans 6 concerning baptism: the new life granted us can still be unto ultimate death if we do not renew our ways according to the will of the Spirit. Life eternal promised us is not one that is already here, but one that lies at the end of the "way of living righteously" by putting to death our sinful deeds. Moreover, we are "indebted" to live righteously since we were not entitled to that second chance given to us. In other words, we are to be "led" by the Spirit of God (v.14a) as Paul earlier wrote in Galatians 5:18. He reiterates here his appeal in Galatians regarding adoption as children: "For all who are led by the Spirit of God are sons of God." (Rom 8:14)

At this point, Paul appeals to the argument of adoption he used in Galatians 4:1-7 and expands it along the lines of Romans 5. In Galatians he was concentrating on Abraham only (Gal 3) and thus the adoption and heirship passage (Gal 4:1-7) was linked to the argument ending in 3:29 (And if you are Christ's, then you are Abraham's offspring, heirs according to promise). Since in Romans Paul expanded the discussion on Abraham (ch.4) to include Adam (ch.5), here in chapter 8 he includes the scriptural "Adamic" story within the purview of his discussion on adoption and heirship.

"For you did not receive the spirit of slavery to fall back (*palin*; again) into fear, but you have received the spirit of sonship" (8:15) sounds awkward after the previous talk about our having become slaves of God. The verse is to be heard against the background of the Roman household. As I explained earlier in chapter 6, the paterfamilias was the sole master (lord) of all members of his household, children as well as slaves. It is only his behavior that made the difference. His own children could be treated harshly and feel as "slaves." Conversely, his treatment of his household slaves could be considerate and even affectionate to the extent that they and members of their families would actually feel as "children." That is why Paul qualified the element "fear" with "again" (*palin*). By moving from a harsh household to another household ruled by a loving paterfamilias, the slaves, though still slaves, do not experience "again" what they experienced in their previous household. In the new household, they have no need to fear their master since they are *treated* as children by him. Consequently, *slaves* may call him Father, just as his own children would. So, in Romans 8:25 we are as adopted children. This imagery of adoption is very forceful in the ears of Paul's hearers. The reason is that, according to Roman law, even the biological progeny of a paterfamilias are not legally his children unless they are officially adopted by him, becoming thus his genuine children.[27] Adoption is a fatherly prerogative, and God decided, by a sheer graceful decision on his part, to reckon us, his enemies, as his children (5:1-11).

---

[27] The term "genuine" is originally more legal than meets the eye. Unless and until a child was held by his father on the latter's knee (Latin *genu*)—or lap or bosom—the child was not considered genuine.

As to the Aramaic *'abba* followed by the Greek *ho patēr* (the Father) is the exact same phrase which is found in Galatians 4:6.[28] It is intended to underscore the fact that the scriptural God is at the same time and in the same capacity the God of Gentiles as well as Jews, as Paul earlier emphatically asserted: "Or is God the God of Jews only? Is he not the God of Gentiles also? Yes, of Gentiles also, since God is one; and he will justify the circumcised on the ground of their faith and the uncircumcised through their faith." (Rom 3:29-30) The basis for that full equality has its root in that it is the Spirit, which is the spirit of sonship, that allows both to say "Father" when addressing God (8:15). It is thus the witness borne by that Spirit that sustains each one of us in the confession that God is our Father and we are his children (v.16). Otherwise, such boldness on our part would be an impertinence, since God is essentially "the God and Father of our Lord Jesus Christ" (15:6; see also 2 Cor 1:3; Eph 1:3; Col 1:3; 1 Pet 1:3), not ours. As in Galatians 4:1-7, the ultimate goal of adoption is to become not just someone's child, but actually an heir, since the child, according to Roman law, does not necessarily end as an heir. That is why Paul immediately adds "and if children, then heirs, namely heirs of God" (Rom 8:17). However, since the Lord Jesus Christ is the only one who, through his having been raised from the dead, was granted officially the title "Son of God" (1:3-4), we accede to heirship by sharing in the inheritance of Jesus Christ: "on the one hand, heirs of God, on the other hand, co-heirs (fellow heirs) with Christ." (8:17) Still, as Paul explained earlier, there is the other condition of joining Christ in a death similar to his, that is, suffering for the sake of the others out of obedience to God, since it is only then that we shall share in the glory

---

[28] *Gal* 206-16.

bestowed upon him (6:3-11). Hence the full statement sounds thus: "and if children, then heirs, heirs of God and fellow heirs with Christ, *provided* we suffer with him *in order that* we may also be glorified with him." (8:17) And, as usual, in order to preempt any mumbling on the part of the hearers regarding the difficulty of the condition, Paul hurries to add, "I reckon (*logizomai*: consider) that the sufferings of this present time are not worth comparing with the glory that is to be revealed to us" (v.18). "Reckon" is the same verb Paul used in chapter 6 to bond us to Christ: "So you also must reckon (*logizesthe*; consider) yourselves dead to sin and alive to God in Christ Jesus." (v.11)

Vv. 19-30 ¹⁹ ἡ γὰρ ἀποκαραδοκία τῆς κτίσεως τὴν ἀποκάλυψιν τῶν υἱῶν τοῦ θεοῦ ἀπεκδέχεται. ²⁰ τῇ γὰρ ματαιότητι ἡ κτίσις ὑπετάγη, οὐχ ἑκοῦσα ἀλλὰ διὰ τὸν ὑποτάξαντα, ἐφ' ἐλπίδι ²¹ ὅτι καὶ αὐτὴ ἡ κτίσις ἐλευθερωθήσεται ἀπὸ τῆς δουλείας τῆς φθορᾶς εἰς τὴν ἐλευθερίαν τῆς δόξης τῶν τέκνων τοῦ θεοῦ. ²² οἴδαμεν γὰρ ὅτι πᾶσα ἡ κτίσις συστενάζει καὶ συνωδίνει ἄχρι τοῦ νῦν· ²³ οὐ μόνον δέ, ἀλλὰ καὶ αὐτοὶ τὴν ἀπαρχὴν τοῦ πνεύματος ἔχοντες, ἡμεῖς καὶ αὐτοὶ ἐν ἑαυτοῖς στενάζομεν υἱοθεσίαν ἀπεκδεχόμενοι, τὴν ἀπολύτρωσιν τοῦ σώματος ἡμῶν. ²⁴ τῇ γὰρ ἐλπίδι ἐσώθημεν· ἐλπὶς δὲ βλεπομένη οὐκ ἔστιν ἐλπίς· ὃ γὰρ βλέπει τίς ἐλπίζει; ²⁵ εἰ δὲ ὃ οὐ βλέπομεν ἐλπίζομεν, δι' ὑπομονῆς ἀπεκδεχόμεθα. ²⁶ Ὡσαύτως δὲ καὶ τὸ πνεῦμα συναντιλαμβάνεται τῇ ἀσθενείᾳ ἡμῶν· τὸ γὰρ τί προσευξώμεθα καθὸ δεῖ οὐκ οἴδαμεν, ἀλλὰ αὐτὸ τὸ πνεῦμα ὑπερεντυγχάνει στεναγμοῖς ἀλαλήτοις· ²⁷ ὁ δὲ ἐραυνῶν τὰς καρδίας οἶδεν τί τὸ φρόνημα τοῦ πνεύματος, ὅτι κατὰ θεὸν ἐντυγχάνει ὑπὲρ ἁγίων. ²⁸ Οἴδαμεν δὲ ὅτι τοῖς ἀγαπῶσιν τὸν θεὸν πάντα συνεργεῖ εἰς ἀγαθόν, τοῖς κατὰ πρόθεσιν κλητοῖς οὖσιν. ²⁹ ὅτι οὓς προέγνω, καὶ προώρισεν συμμόρφους τῆς εἰκόνος τοῦ υἱοῦ αὐτοῦ, εἰς τὸ εἶναι αὐτὸν πρωτότοκον ἐν πολλοῖς ἀδελφοῖς· ³⁰ οὓς δὲ προώρισεν, τούτους καὶ ἐκάλεσεν· καὶ οὓς ἐκάλεσεν, τούτους καὶ ἐδικαίωσεν· οὓς δὲ ἐδικαίωσεν, τούτους καὶ ἐδόξασεν.

[19] For the creation waits with eager longing for the revealing of the sons of God; [20] for the creation was subjected to futility, not of its own will but by the will of him who subjected it in hope; [21] because the creation itself will be set free from its bondage to decay and obtain the glorious liberty of the children of God. [22] We know that the whole creation has been groaning in travail together until now; [23] and not only the creation, but we ourselves, who have the first fruits of the Spirit, groan inwardly as we wait for adoption as sons, the redemption of our bodies. [24] For in this hope we were saved. Now hope that is seen is not hope. For who hopes for what he sees? [25] But if we hope for what we do not see, we wait for it with patience. [26] Likewise the Spirit helps us in our weakness; for we do not know how to pray as we ought, but the Spirit himself intercedes for us with sighs too deep for words. [27] And he who searches the hearts of men knows what is the mind of the Spirit, because the Spirit intercedes for the saints according to the will of God. [28] We know that in everything God works for good with those who love him, who are called according to his purpose. [29] For those whom he foreknew he also predestined to be conformed to the image of his Son, in order that he might be the first-born among many brethren. [30] And those whom he predestined he also called; and those whom he called he also justified; and those whom he justified he also glorified.

As I pointed out earlier, in Romans, in distinction to Galatians, Paul includes Adam in his discussion along with Abraham. So in Romans 8:19-21 he covers the entire span between Adam's sin and the ultimate revelation lying ahead of us at the end of human history, as he did in 5:12-21. Adam was supposed to be a true son of God, obeying his commandment. The creation that was betrayed by Adam is longing for sons of Adam who would be obedient to God's will and thus, at the same time, be sons of God (v.19). Instead of being subjected to *mataiotēti* (futility; vanity; emptiness; nonsense) through Adam's disobedience, the merciful God made it so that creation was, through God's will, "in hope" of one day being set free of the subjection imposed upon it, and would end up reveling in glory instead of being doomed to decay (vv.20-21). The close relation between the fate of human beings and that of the rest of creation is most evident in Genesis:

> And to Adam he said, "Because you have listened to the voice of your wife, and have eaten of the tree of which I commanded you, 'You shall not eat of it,' cursed is the ground because of you; in toil you shall eat of it all the days of your life; thorns and thistles it shall bring forth to you; and you shall eat the plants of the field. In the sweat of your face you shall eat bread till you return to the ground, for out of it you were taken; you are dust, and to dust you shall return." (3:17-19)

> The Lord saw that the wickedness of man was great in the earth, and that every imagination of the thoughts of his heart was only evil continually. And the Lord was sorry that he had made man on the earth, and it grieved him to his heart. So the Lord said, "I will blot out man whom I have created from the face of the ground, man and beast and creeping things and birds of the air, for I am sorry that I have made them." (6:5-7)

That is why Paul follows up by saying that the whole creation groans together (*systenazei*) with us who are groaning (*stenazomen*) (Rom 8:22-23). He even says that the same creation joins in the travail (*synōdinei*) in order to produce the new creation free of "thorns and thistles." Similarly, Paul is in travail with his children: "My little children, with whom I am again in travail (*ōdinō*) until Christ be formed (fully take shape) in you!" (Gal 4:19) That is why, here in Romans, he speaks of the believers as having (only) "the first fruits of the Spirit" and are awaiting full-fledged "adoption as sons" on the day of the "redemption of our bodies (now bound to death because of sin)," which lies ahead of us. This is Paul's way to prompt us to continue walking the road he has put us on, "forgetting what lies behind and straining forward to what lies ahead, and pressing on toward the goal for the prize of the upward call of God in Christ Jesus" (Phil 3:13-14). In so doing, the entire creation for which we are responsible (Gen 1:26, 28) will join us in God's blessing of eternal life.

The reason behind our having to look ahead is that "the hope in which we were saved" requires "patience (forbearance)" (8:24-25). This is an iteration of what he wrote in Romans 5:2-3, at the beginning of his lengthy discussion of God's plan of salvation (chs.5-8). And in this difficult period of "longing, awaiting" (*apekdekh*— 8:19, 23, 25), during which we are tested (5:3-5) and could find ourselves weak in our resolve, we are to rely on God's spirit to help us by leading us in uttering the prayer which we could not utter by ourselves (8:26-27) and under whose behest we call the God and Father of the Lord Jesus Christ *'abba, ho patēr*, that is to say, our own Father (vv.14-16). Ultimately, it is that Father himself who is in control. He knows our "weak" hearts (centers of our will); he also knows the manner of thinking (*phronēma*) of his own spirit and the required behavior linked to that thinking (vv.5-8). In his goodness toward us, he makes sure that "the Spirit intercedes for the saints according to the will of God" (v.27). The result is that "the Spirit himself bears witness with our spirit that we are children of God" (v.16).

In scripture, beginning with the story of Adam (Gen 2-3), God's plan (purpose), rooted in his love for us (Rom 5:8), fails unless we accept to submit to it. In other words, as Paul puts it, "we know (from scripture) that in everything God works for good with those who love him" (8:28). Unless we respond to God with our love for him, the "good" we and God are hoping for is eschewed and supplanted by the evil neither we nor he want (7:12-23). In order to understand why our love for God is equated as submission to his will, one is to understand that the love of a junior toward a senior does not entail the same meaning as the love of a senior toward a junior. Parents' love for their children entails care for them, a care that the children are not able to provide for themselves. Moreover, parents' love toward their children precedes that of their children's love toward them. Assuming we are talking about a normal family setting, children's love for their parents requires an understanding of this reality and of their need for their parents. Thus it behooves the children to obey their parents' instructions which are for the children's benefit. In scripture, love for God is equivalent to love for his law and commandments.[29] That is why, in scripture, everything in God's plan starts with his calling us (1:1, 7). He is, by definition, "the one who calls" (Rom 4:17; 9:11; Gal 1:6, 15; 5:8; 1Thess 2:12; 5:24).

God's plan encompasses all the children of Abraham, Gentiles as well as Jews (Rom 4)—in fact all the children of Adam (ch.5)—who were included even before they were born: "He received circumcision as a sign or seal of the righteousness which he had by faith while he was still uncircumcised. The purpose was to make him the father of all who believe without being circumcised and who thus have righteousness reckoned to them, and likewise the father of the circumcised who are not merely circumcised but also follow the example of the faith which our father Abraham had before he was circumcised." (4:11-12)

---

[29] See e.g. Deut 6:4-9; 10:12-13; 11:1, 13; 30:16; Josh 22:5; Ps 119:47-48, 97, 113, 119, 127, 159, 163, 165, 167; 145:18-20; Is 56:6; Ezek 33:31-32.

Hence, God foreknew us *as children of Abraham* and, consequently, he pre-ordained (*proōrisen* [from the root *horizō*]) us to be conformed to the image of his Son who was ordained (designated; *horisthentos* [from the same root *horizō*]) by God as his Son (1:4), thus making of him the *prōtotokon* (the first in line) among many brethren that join Jesus Christ in calling God "Father" (*'abba, ho patēr*). This plan of including us was carried through Paul, God's assignee (set apart; *aphōrismenos* [from the same root *horizō*]) for this mission, which mission is "according to God's promise in scripture" (1:1-2).

Consequently, God's foreknowledge and pre-ordaining here are not to be equated with what came to be known as "predestination." Rather it is to be understood as God carrying out his plan *as consigned in scripture*. This understanding is confirmed in that, in the following verse (8:30a), Paul picks up the verb "pre-ordained" (*proōrisen*) in order to prepare for reverting to the original verb "called" with which he started. Indeed, it is the calling which is the point at which God encounters each of us to enact his promise, just as he did with the apostle through whom he calls us: "Paul, a servant of Jesus Christ, *called* to be an apostle, *set apart* for the gospel of God ... we have received grace and apostleship to bring about the obedience of faith for the sake of his name among all the nations, including yourselves who are *called* to belong to Jesus Christ." (1:1, 5-6).[30] This gospel (*evangelion*) with which Paul is commissioned is "the gospel of God which *he promised beforehand* through his prophets in the holy scriptures" (1:1-2). Thus, by coupling the verb "pre-ordained" with "called" Paul is

---

[30] Compare with what he writes earlier in Galatians: "But when he who had set me apart (*aphorisas* [from the same root *horizō*]) *before I was born*, and had *called* me through his grace, was pleased to reveal his Son to me, *in order that I might evangelize (evangelizōmai) him among the Gentiles...*" (1:15-16)

recalling the beginning of Romans where his pre-ordained calling (1:1) is in view of the calling of the Gentiles (vv.5-6). On the other hand, the gospel he is preaching is "the power of God for salvation to every one who has faith, to the Jew first and also to the Greek, for in it the righteousness of God is revealed" (vv.16-17); that is why "and those whom he called he also justified (made righteous)" (8:30b). Again, since such righteousness is ultimately the path for glory that can be bestowed only by God (2:7, 10), Paul ends with "and those whom he justified he also glorified" (8:30c).

The case for predestination is very much based on the use of the Greek aorist verbal tense, which is falsely assumed as referring to a past action. Since all the verbs in 8:29-30 are in the aorist and since the first three (foreknew, pre-ordained, called) are arguably connected to an intervention by God in the past, one is tempted to read the last two verbs (justified, glorified) as also referring to a consummated action. Even if that were true of righteousness, it cannot possibly be the case with glory that is the end of the road beyond the final judgment (2:7, 10) and thus is still "to be revealed" (8:18). The solution to this apparent puzzle lies in the function of the Greek aorist tense. Recent studies have shown that approaching the verbs from the classically imposed perspective of time (past, present, and future) distort their function. Verbs are essentially modal, and thus describe an action rather than locate such action in time. Take, for instance, "should or would like," "shall or will have eaten," "were I to do something." The time factor is usually supplied through temporal adverbs (yesterday, now, tomorrow). Thus, the aorist, as its Greek appellation indicates (*aoristos*; undetermined), is modal par excellence.[31] It refers to the fullness or assuredness of the action rather than its time.[32] Consequently, when it refers to something that cannot be realized except in the future, as in "God glorified those whom he called," it means that such glorification is an assured matter "provided we suffer with him in order that we may also be glorified with him" (v.17), which Paul wrote just before mentioning the revelation of that comimg (*mellousan*) glory (v.18).

This understanding is evidenced in the case of justification, as discussed in the passage 5:1-11. Further, in Galatians, Paul makes clear that God's justification of us in Jesus Christ is not so much a past, and thus consummated, action; rather it is a secure matter should we continue on the path of righteousness until the end. Justified by our faith in Christ (Gal 2:17) "by (that same) faith, we wait for the hope of righteousness" (5:5). The reason is that justification, that is to say, the declaration that someone is righteous (innocent) is a legal term that applies to the ultimate verdict of the (divine) court, and this will not take place until the Lord comes.[33] The same understanding is evident in Romans 5 where Paul writes: "Therefore, *since we are justified by faith*, we have peace with God through our Lord Jesus Christ. Through him we have obtained access to this grace in which we stand, and

---

[31] Actually, the aorist completely loses any temporal connotation when used outside the indicative mode.

[32] In the same way as the imperfect (incomplete) tense in the Semitic languages functions. Actually, in the Semitic languages, there are only two basic conjugation forms, the one referring to the completed action and the other, to the still incomplete action. When using proverbs, one may use either form to mean the same thing. Using the incomplete verb form makes of the statement a general one (the one who begets does not die); whereas using the complete form (the one who begat [has begotten] did not [has not] die [died]) is more forceful in that it underscores the assuredness of the matter *whenever it happens*.

[33] See *Gal* 271-6.

we rejoice in our hope of sharing the glory of God." (5:1-2)[34] By the same token, the verbs "foreknew," "pre-ordained," and "called" are also not so much a "past" tense verbs since they describe actions that *look ahead* toward glorification.

Vv. 31-39 ³¹ Τί οὖν ἐροῦμεν πρὸς ταῦτα; εἰ ὁ θεὸς ὑπὲρ ἡμῶν, τίς καθ᾽ ἡμῶν; ³² ὅς γε τοῦ ἰδίου υἱοῦ οὐκ ἐφείσατο ἀλλὰ ὑπὲρ ἡμῶν πάντων παρέδωκεν αὐτόν, πῶς οὐχὶ καὶ σὺν αὐτῷ τὰ πάντα ἡμῖν χαρίσεται; ³³ τίς ἐγκαλέσει κατὰ ἐκλεκτῶν θεοῦ; θεὸς ὁ δικαιῶν· ³⁴ τίς ὁ κατακρινῶν; Χριστὸς [Ἰησοῦς] ὁ ἀποθανών, μᾶλλον δὲ ἐγερθείς, ὃς καί ἐστιν ἐν δεξιᾷ τοῦ θεοῦ, ὃς καὶ ἐντυγχάνει ὑπὲρ ἡμῶν. ³⁵ τίς ἡμᾶς χωρίσει ἀπὸ τῆς ἀγάπης τοῦ Χριστοῦ; θλῖψις ἢ στενοχωρία ἢ διωγμὸς ἢ λιμὸς ἢ γυμνότης ἢ κίνδυνος ἢ μάχαιρα; ³⁶ καθὼς γέγραπται ὅτι ἕνεκεν σοῦ θανατούμεθα ὅλην τὴν ἡμέραν, ἐλογίσθημεν ὡς πρόβατα σφαγῆς. ³⁷ ἀλλ᾽ ἐν τούτοις πᾶσιν ὑπερνικῶμεν διὰ τοῦ ἀγαπήσαντος ἡμᾶς. ³⁸ πέπεισμαι γὰρ ὅτι οὔτε θάνατος οὔτε ζωὴ οὔτε ἄγγελοι οὔτε ἀρχαὶ οὔτε ἐνεστῶτα οὔτε μέλλοντα οὔτε δυνάμεις ³⁹ οὔτε ὕψωμα οὔτε βάθος οὔτε τις κτίσις ἑτέρα δυνήσεται ἡμᾶς χωρίσαι ἀπὸ τῆς ἀγάπης τοῦ θεοῦ τῆς ἐν Χριστῷ Ἰησοῦ τῷ κυρίῳ ἡμῶν.

³¹*What then shall we say to this? If God is for us, who is against us?* ³²*He who did not spare his own Son but gave him up for us all, will he not also give us all things with him?* ³³*Who shall bring any charge against God's elect? It is God who justifies;* ³⁴*who is to condemn? Is it Christ Jesus, who died, yes, who was raised from the dead, who is at the right hand of God, who indeed intercedes for us?* ³⁵*Who shall separate us from the love of Christ? Shall tribulation, or distress, or persecution, or famine, or nakedness, or peril, or sword?* ³⁶*As it is written, "For thy sake we are being killed all the day long; we are regarded as sheep to*

---

[34] Notice how here justification and glory are joined just as they are in 8:30, the verse we are discussing.

be slaughtered." [37]*No, in all these things we are more than conquerors through him who loved us.* [38]*For I am sure that neither death, nor life, nor angels, nor principalities, nor things present, nor things to come, nor powers,* [39]*nor height, nor depth, nor anything else in all creation, will be able to separate us from the love of God in Christ Jesus our Lord.*

Having arrived at the end of his argument Paul offers a doxology of thanksgiving to God who both originated and realized in Jesus Christ the plan of our salvation out of love for us, as the Apostle emphasized in 5:1-11. The background of this doxology reflects the courtroom setting, which corroborates my understanding of the previous verses. Paul asks a series of rhetorical questions concerning God as our judge, instead of Rome, and Jesus Christ as our defense attorney, instead of Caesar. This passage forms an *inclusio* with 1:16-17 where Paul states that he is not ashamed of the gospel for whose cause he would stand trial before the Roman authorities, since the vindication of his righteousness comes from the gospel and not from Rome.

If God, the sole valid judge, is on our side, who could possibly stand against us in his court? If the judge himself did not spare his own son and delivered him to death for our sake while we were his enemies (5:1-11), which a Roman emperor would most probably never do, how much more will he grant us everything, including life beyond death, the way he did for his son (6:1-9)? Who indeed can dare to plead against God's elect, and thus chosen unto justification, when that same God himself is the judge? Who can condemn us when Jesus Christ, who died because of our sins and thus should have functioned as our accuser, is now raised and seated in glory at the judge's right, and is functioning as our intercessor? Looking more closely at the verb *entynkhanei* (8:34) to speak of this action of intercession on the part of the glorified Christ will confirm that such intercession is neither magical nor blind. If so, the divine judgment would be unjust. Rather, Christ's intercession corresponds to that of the Spirit (*entynkhanei*, v.27; *hyperentynkhanei*, v.26) which helps us to correctly pray "Father" (*'abba, ho patēr*) and to understand that we are hereby confessing that God is our new paterfamilias, and we are to abide by his directives (6:19-23). We can do this only insofar as we follow the intercessory urgings of the (law of the) Spirit who leads us on the path that is "according to the will of God" (*kata Theon*, 8:27). Consequently Christ's intercession as our defense attorney amounts to making the case, on judgment day, that we have followed the law of the Spirit. Only then it will be shown indeed that those who will have proven to have been faithfully obedient to the teaching of Paul (6:17-18) will undergo judgment, but not condemnation. This is precisely how he opened his discussion of why and how we shall attain glory: "There is therefore now no condemnation for those who are in Christ Jesus. For the law of the Spirit of life in Christ Jesus has set me free from the law of sin and death." (8:1-2)

And lest the hearers forget that glory is not earned by them, Paul insists that the entire plan was God's. His plan originated in and was carried through the love of Christ (v.35) or, more precisely, the love of God for us in Christ (v.39; see also 5:1-11). If this is so, why would a faithful slave of God and of his Christ be worried about what would be his share of ill within the confines of the Roman empire and especially in the "theater," the arena of death? Tribulation, distress, persecution, and hunger apply generally to all slaves unless they are protected by a paterfamilias; nudity, peril, and ultimately (the Roman) sword (8:35) are specifically applicable to the situation of a gladiator or a slave thrown to the beasts. This is corroborated by Paul's

choice of the scriptural quotation he introduces to back up his
proposition: "For thy sake we are being killed (*thanatoumetha*) all
the day long; we are reckoned (*elogisthēmen*) as sheep to be
slaughtered." (v.36)[35] Notice Paul's choice of a scriptural
quotation using the verb "reckon" (*logizomai*) that pervades
Romans 4, which deals with our being children of Abraham to
whom the promise of life and inheritance was made, and
reappears in 6:11 to describe the challenge posed to us in
baptism which functions as the circumcision in heart: "So you
also must reckon yourselves dead to sin and alive to God in
Christ Jesus." The reason is that the actual result of our victory
will not be revealed until the Lord comes. At that time the
scriptural God will prove to be mightier than the Roman
emperor, just as he proved mightier than Pharaoh. That is why,
in all these hurdles, including death by the (Roman) sword, and
until that day when the Lord comes, we have to trust that we *are*
more than conquerors (*hypernikōmen* is in the present tense),
that is to say, we are conquerors over the conqueror, by
definition the Roman emperor, through the one who loved us
(8:37). At this point, Paul puts all his apostolic weight in giving
the reason behind all his statements: "For I am sure that neither
death, nor life, nor angels, nor principalities, nor things present,
nor things to come, nor powers, nor height, nor depth, nor
anything else in all creation, will be able (*dynēsetai*; will have
power) to separate us from the love of God in Christ Jesus our
Lord." (vv.38-39) To our ears, the statement sounds thus: "As
for me, your apostle who brought you the gospel of truth in
which you are to trust, I myself am fully assured (*pepeismai*), I

---

[35] Notice the similar terminology he uses in 1 Cor 4:11 (To the present hour we
hunger and thirst, we are ill-clad [*gymnitevomen* from the same root as *gymnotēs*—
nudity] and buffeted and homeless) with reference to being "sentenced to death"
(*epithanatious* from the same root as *thanatoumetha*) in the "theater" (*theatron*) (v.9).

am already convinced, that nothing imaginable or beyond imagination will overpower God and separate us from the love God exhibited toward us in sacrificing his messiah, our Lord and Master, for our sake, unworthy though we be. That, o my hearers, patricians of the city of Rome, is something your own emperor would never do for you. He would rather use you for his own glory."

Chapter 9

Vv. 1-5 ¹ Ἀλήθειαν λέγω ἐν Χριστῷ, οὐ ψεύδομαι, συμμαρτυρούσης μοι τῆς συνειδήσεώς μου ἐν πνεύματι ἁγίῳ, ² ὅτι λύπη μοί ἐστιν μεγάλη καὶ ἀδιάλειπτος ὀδύνη τῇ καρδίᾳ μου. ³ ηὐχόμην γὰρ ἀνάθεμα εἶναι αὐτὸς ἐγὼ ἀπὸ τοῦ Χριστοῦ ὑπὲρ τῶν ἀδελφῶν μου τῶν συγγενῶν μου κατὰ σάρκα, ⁴ οἵτινές εἰσιν Ἰσραηλῖται, ὧν ἡ υἱοθεσία καὶ ἡ δόξα καὶ αἱ διαθῆκαι καὶ ἡ νομοθεσία καὶ ἡ λατρεία καὶ αἱ ἐπαγγελίαι, ⁵ ὧν οἱ πατέρες καὶ ἐξ ὧν ὁ Χριστὸς τὸ κατὰ σάρκα, ὁ ὢν ἐπὶ πάντων θεὸς εὐλογητὸς εἰς τοὺς αἰῶνας, ἀμήν.

¹I am speaking the truth in Christ, I am not lying; my conscience bears me witness in the Holy Spirit, ²that I have great sorrow and unceasing anguish in my heart. ³For I could wish that I myself were accursed and cut off from Christ for the sake of my brethren, my kinsmen by race. ⁴They are Israelites, and to them belong the sonship, the glory, the covenants, the giving of the law, the worship, and the promises; ⁵to them belong the patriarchs, and of their race, according to the flesh, is the Christ. God who is over all be blessed for ever. Amen.

In response to Paul's gospel, a Roman patrician might retort, "This is all well and good. But how do you expect *us* to endorse such an incredible proposition when many a Jew, if not the majority of them, has declined to submit to that proposition consigned in their own scriptures?" Paul's response to this thorny, yet valid, criticism is to revisit those same scriptures in Romans 9-11 to show that the Jews' refusal is actually an integral part of the scriptural story. By the same token, Jewish recalcitrance is no excuse for a cheap cop-out by the Romans to refuse the challenge of the gospel proposition, especially since, in that same scriptural story, one hears of many Gentiles who submitted to it, the most prominent case being the Ninevites' repentance in the Book of Jonah.

And in order to forego any contemptuous arrogance toward the Jews on the part of the Romans, Paul, as apostle of God (Rom 1:1) to the Gentiles (11:13), begins by expressing his sorrow and grief (9:2), just as God does "through his prophets in the holy scriptures," over the Israelites' stubbornness. The fact that Paul does so *as apostle* is evident in his use of the phrase "I am not lying" (*ou psevdomai*), which occurs elsewhere in reference to his apostolic mission (2 Cor 11:31; Gal 1:20; 1 Tim 2:7).[1] More importantly, the phraseology of Romans 9:1-2 is reminiscent of that found in Romans 2:15-16 where mention is made of the gospel he was assigned to preach (1:1-2).[2] The noun "gospel" brackets as an *inclusio* Romans 1-11. Indeed, it occurs no less than four times (1:1, 9, 16; 2:16) in Romans 1:1-2:16 only to disappear until its mention in Romans 10:16. Thus, in Romans 1:1-2:16 Paul introduces his thesis that the gospel of God brings salvation only to those, Gentiles as well as Jews, who trust (believe) that God is the judge to whom all human beings are accountable. At the outset of reviewing the scriptural story from the perspective of Israel's recalcitrance, Paul sums up this thesis by using the terminology of Romans 2:15-16, and he includes himself under God's judgment (9:1-2). This is not surprising; not even an apostle is exempt from such judgment (1 Cor 4:1-5). Still, what is important in this matter is not to feel contempt toward those who fail to believe (an attitude that was condemned in Romans 2:1-5), but rather sorrow and grief for

---

[1] In 1 Timothy we have even the full formula found in Rom 9:1 "I am speaking the truth (*alētheian legō*), I am not lying."

[2] Paul's putting himself under judgment is also reflected in that taking an oath that one is saying the truth is ultimately done "before God" as we hear in Gal 1:20: "In what I am writing to you, before God (*enōpion tou theou*), I do not lie!."

them. Being the opposite of joy (*khara*) (2 Cor 2:3), which is ultimately related to the sharing in the kingdom of God (Rom 14:17; Gal 5:21-22), sorrow (*lypē*; pain) is the lack of hope for that kingdom (1 Thess 4:13). Hope is anchored in proceeding on the path toward that kingdom, a path we were called onto through God's grace (Rom 5:1-2; Gal 1:6). Consequently, once we are committed, any change of mind or behavior along the way is punishable by the curse of anathema—being excised from the messianic community (Gal 5:4)—even if one is an apostle (1:8-9). That Paul had Galatians in mind is evident in that the terminology of "being accursed (anathema) from Christ (*anathema apo tou Khristou*)"[3] is a compact formula reminiscent of Galatians:

> But even if we, or an angel from heaven, should preach to you a gospel contrary to that which we preached to you, let him be accursed (*anathema*). As we have said before, so now I say again, If any one is preaching to you a gospel contrary to that which you received, let him be accursed (*anathema*). (Gal 1:8-9) … You are severed from Christ (*apo Khristou*), you who would be justified by the law; you have fallen away from grace. (Gal 5:4)[4]

How could Paul even entertain the wish of being accursed and cut off from the messianic community and thus ultimately from the hope of inheriting the Kingdom, especially when such a prerogative is God's alone? Even more, later in Romans 11:1, he makes the point that God's non-rejection of his people hangs by the thin thread of Paul's faithfulness to the gospel. Usually, the explanation given is that Paul's statement stems from his infinite

---

[3] See my discussion regarding the term "Christ" being referential to the messianic community in *Gal* 138-43, 187-8.

[4] Notice how RSV renders Rom 9:3 into "For I could wish that I myself were accursed and *cut off* from Christ" thus adding "cut off, " which is not in the original, to make sense out of the original Greek.

love for his brethren; however, such an attitude is questionable on two grounds. First, according to 1 Corinthians 13:3 (If I give away all I have, and if I deliver my body to be burned, but have not love, I gain nothing) sacrificing oneself for others is not a guarantee that such is done out of love. On the other hand, his statement is made in conjunction with his preaching the gospel, as I explain in my comments on Romans 11:1. In this regard, it is unimaginable that Paul would have allowed himself to be facetious.   We must look in another direction for the explanation.

The term "Israelite(s)" occurs only three times in the Pauline corpus, in Romans 9:3, Romans 11:1 and 2 Cor 11:22. The third instance reads: "Are they Hebrews? So am I. Are they Israelites? So am I. Are they progeny (*sperma*) of Abraham? So am I." This clearly refers to Paul's colleagues, the "apostles of Christ" whom he dubs "false apostles" (2 Cor 11:13). We see the same terminology of "Israelite" and "progeny of Abraham" in Romans 11:1 where Paul presents himself as another Elijah and thus a plenipotentiary divine messenger (v.2), or put otherwise, as an apostle, which is made clear a few verses later (v.13).[5] Given then that Romans 9:1-5 is an introduction to Paul's following argumentation (9:6-11:32) which revolves around the "progeny (*sperma*) of Abraham" (9:6),[6] it stands to reason that in v.3 the intended "my brethren, my kinsmen according to the flesh" are more specifically Paul's peers, the Jerusalemite Jewish

---

[5] The correspondence between Rom 11:1 and 2 Cor 11:22 is further corroborated in Phil 3:5 (of the nation of Israel, of the tribe of Benjamin, a Hebrew born of Hebrews) which is a cross between Rom 11:1 (an Israelite, of the progeny [*spermatos*] of Abraham, of the tribe of Benjamin) and 2 Cor 11:22 (Are they Hebrews? So am I. Are they Israelites? So am I. Are they progeny [*sperma*] of Abraham? So am I).

[6] The reference to "the forefathers" (*hoi pateres/tous pateras*) brackets the entire argument as an *inclusio* (9:5 and 11:28).

Christian leaders who were opposing his openness to the Gentiles.[7] Indeed, at the end of the letter, Paul mentions his intention of visiting those Jerusalemite leaders with the *koinōnia* (fellowship) for "the poor among the saints at Jerusalem" from "Macedonia and Achaia." Such a visit is the fulfillment of Paul's promise made to his Jerusalemite fellows at the conclusion of their first meeting (Gal 2:1-10): "… and when they perceived the grace that was given to me, James and Cephas and John, who were reputed to be pillars, gave to me and Barnabas the right hand of fellowship (*koinōnias*), that we should go to the Gentiles and they to the circumcised; only they would have us remember the poor, which very thing I was eager to do." (vv.9-10)[8]

Consequently, Paul's intention in Romans 9:3 is simply to say that, for the sake of the gospel, it would have been more expedient if he were the "enemy of God" (11:28) and thus "accursed" (*anathema*) and his opponents were true apostles (such as Peter should have been) or true supporters (such as James should have been) of the gospel *as he actually is*.[9] The

---

[7] The reference to them as *primarily* "brethren" precludes their being merely Jews. That term is exclusively used in the Pauline corpus to refer to the Christian believers. If Paul meant to speak of the Jews in general, he would have written "my kinsmen according to the flesh." Also the RSV rendering of *kata sarka* as "by race" instead of "according to the flesh" is misleading since it is interpretive and forces the text to be understood as referring to the Jews in general. The fallacy of such interpretation is that the other three instances of the term "kinsman/kinsmen" in the New Testament occur in Rom 16 (vv.7, 11, 21) and appear simply so without the addition *kata sarka*. Thus the latter phrase has another function which I will discuss shortly.

[8] See on this entire matter Michael Arbanas, *The Chosen people of God in Paul's epistle to the Romans*, MDiv thesis, St Vladimir's Seminary, 1998.

[9] Besides "for the sake of" the Greek preposition *hyper* (followed by the genitive case) has the meaning of "instead, in the place of" as in 2 Cor 5:14-15 and Philem 13, e.g. It is in this latter sense that the preposition is to be taken in Rom 9:3. Otherwise, Paul would have sounded as saying that his "sacrifice" would function soteriologically (salvifically) for others as that of Christ, which would have been awkward in a letter

reason is that such *casus irrealis* would have entailed the *assurance* that the *koinōnia* of Macedonia and Achaia to the poor among the saints of Jerusalem would be accepted and, consequently, "the fullness of the blessing of Christ" would reach also the western confines of the Roman empire (15:28-29). Were they true apostles or at least true supporters of "the truth of the gospel" (Gal 2:5, 14),[10] Paul's peers would function just as he does, namely as apostles to the Gentiles (Rom 11:13), simply because, *qua* Jews, they have an "advantage" over the Gentiles in that "they were entrusted with the oracles of God" (Rom 3:1-2). Indeed, it is *in the scriptures* that is found the gospel terminology of "sonship, glory, covenants, giving of the law, worship, and promises," (9:4) and especially of "forefathers and Christ (Messiah)" (v.5).[11]

Unfortunately, the RSV translation "to them *belong*" instead of the original "whose (are)" (*'ōn*) (vv.4-5), has reinforced the widespread assumption, especially after the founding of the 21st century state of Israel in 1948, that the Jews *have as their own possession* the above enumerated "gifts" of God. In scripture, the gift is a trust and remains the property of the one who bestows it. Since God is by definition the *melek* (king; owner; possessor), his children may not dispense of their inheritance, including the Law itself, but keep it as a trust to be passed along *as inheritance*. The Israelites, God's children, enjoy the gift which never becomes their possession since, by definition, they remain all along God's children. Actually, whenever they behave as the

---

where, throughout the first eight chapters, Christ has been presented as a unique and "once for all" case.

[10] See also my comments on Rom 1:18, 25; 2:8, 20; 9:1.

[11] Notice especially the plurals "covenants" and "promises" which cannot be explained except as an actual reference to the scriptural texts that speak of several promises as well as covenants.

owners of God's gifts and use them according to their will, God intervenes to put an end to such by dispossessing them of his gifts. The most compelling examples are the land, Jerusalem, and the temple that are all decimated by express divine edict.[12] Not only do the children of Israel not *own* any of God's gifts, but even they themselves *belong* to God, and not he to them: he is theirs as their *melek* (owner) in the sense that they may not even choose any other deity; whereas, he reserves to himself the right to change their status at will:

> When she had weaned Not pitied, she conceived and bore a son. And the Lord said, "Call his name Not my people, for you are not my people and I am not your God." Yet the number of the people of Israel shall be like the sand of the sea, which can be neither measured nor numbered; and in the place where it was said to them, "You are not my people," it shall be said to them, "Sons of the living God." And the people of Judah and the people of Israel shall be gathered together, and they shall appoint for themselves one head; and they shall go up from the land, for great shall be the day of Jezreel. Say to your brother, "My people." (Hos 1:8-2:1)

On purpose, Paul leaves "the promises" until the end in order to prepare for the special mention of "the forefathers and the Christ" (Rom 9:4), who will be specifically discussed in Romans 9-10. On the other hand, these three elements, (the promises, the forefathers, and the Christ) form the axis of Galatians 3 where Paul discusses how Abraham and Christ are related through God's promise in Genesis. This in turn corroborates my

---

[12] See e.g. Deut 4:425-26 where the Israelites are forewarned throughout their generations: "When you beget children and children's children, and have grown old in the land, if you act corruptly by making a graven image in the form of anything, and by doing what is evil in the sight of the Lord your God, so as to provoke him to anger, I call heaven and earth to witness against you this day, that you will soon utterly perish from the land which you are going over the Jordan to possess; you will not live long upon it, but will be utterly destroyed."

reading that Galatians actually forms the background for Paul's argument in Romans 9-10 as well as in the introductory verses Romans 9:1-5.

But what about the strange phraseology of v.5a, "Whose (are) the forefathers and from whom (is) the Christ (when one deals with this subject) according to the flesh (*ho Khristos to kata sarka*)?"[13] In order to understand this awkwardness, one is to start with v.5b which, grammatically, can be either a relative clause qualifying the preceding "the Christ" or an independent clause. In the former case, the verse would read "… and from them is the Christ, the one according to the flesh, who is the God (who is) over all (and) blessed unto the ages, amen." Besides being syntactically overly complicated, the epithet "blessed" occurs in Romans (1:25) and elsewhere in the letters (2 Cor 1:3; 11:31; Eph 1:3; 1 Pet 1:3) only in conjunction with God, and never with Christ. The same occurs in Luke 1:68, where "blessed" is used as an alternate for God himself and in Mark: "Are you the Christ, the Son of the Blessed?" (Mk 14:61) The intentionality of forcing the hearer to understand Romans 9:5b as an independent clause (May God who is over all, be blessed unto the ages. Amen) is actually behind the awkward neuter *to kata sarka* after the masculine *ho Khristos* in v.5a. Still the question remains, "Why did Paul not end with simply 'whose are the forefathers and from whom is the Christ'?"

The addition "according to the flesh" is meant to correspond to the same phrase qualifying Paul's peers and opponents in Romans 9:3. They do not endorse the fullness of the gospel whereby Jesus Christ is not just "of the progeny of David,

---

[13] I indulged in this periphrastic translation because the relative pronoun *to* following "the Christ" is neuter whereas *ho Khristos* is obviously masculine.

according to the flesh" and thus simply a messiah for the Jews, but also "Son of God in power according to the Spirit" and thus "Lord of all, including the Gentiles" (1:3-4). Consequently, the Christ that comes out of their preaching is "from them" and "according to the flesh" and thus cannot reach the Gentiles. And since the gospel is nothing other than the teaching of scripture (1:2), what Paul's opponents are teaching amounts to a "lie" that does not correspond to God's "truth" (1:25a). Consequently it is tantamount to a blasphemy that warrants a counter-blasphemy statement[14] similar to the one at the end of 1:25: "(God) who is blessed unto the ages! Amen." By the same token, this statement at the end of 9:5 functions as a rallying point to go back to the scriptural story that will readily show that "the word of God does not fail" (v.6a), even when God's representatives disappoint him (11:2-4).

Vv. 6-18 ⁶ Οὐχ οἷον δὲ ὅτι ἐκπέπτωκεν ὁ λόγος τοῦ θεοῦ. οὐ γὰρ πάντες οἱ ἐξ Ἰσραὴλ οὗτοι Ἰσραήλ· ⁷ οὐδ' ὅτι εἰσὶν σπέρμα Ἀβραὰμ πάντες τέκνα, ἀλλ· ἐν Ἰσαὰκ κληθήσεταί σοι σπέρμα. ⁸ τοῦτ' ἔστιν, οὐ τὰ τέκνα τῆς σαρκὸς ταῦτα τέκνα τοῦ θεοῦ ἀλλὰ τὰ τέκνα τῆς ἐπαγγελίας λογίζεται εἰς σπέρμα. ⁹ ἐπαγγελίας γὰρ ὁ λόγος οὗτος· κατὰ τὸν καιρὸν τοῦτον ἐλεύσομαι καὶ ἔσται τῇ Σάρρᾳ υἱός. ¹⁰ Οὐ μόνον δέ, ἀλλὰ καὶ Ῥεβέκκα ἐξ ἑνὸς κοίτην ἔχουσα, Ἰσαὰκ τοῦ πατρὸς ἡμῶν· ¹¹ μήπω γὰρ γεννηθέντων μηδὲ πραξάντων τι ἀγαθὸν ἢ φαῦλον, ἵνα ἡ κατ' ἐκλογὴν πρόθεσις τοῦ θεοῦ μένῃ, ¹² οὐκ ἐξ ἔργων ἀλλ' ἐκ τοῦ καλοῦντος, ἐρρέθη αὐτῇ ὅτι ὁ μείζων δουλεύσει τῷ ἐλάσσονι, ¹³ καθὼς γέγραπται· τὸν Ἰακὼβ ἠγάπησα, τὸν δὲ Ἠσαῦ ἐμίσησα. ¹⁴ Τί οὖν ἐροῦμεν; μὴ ἀδικία παρὰ τῷ θεῷ; μὴ γένοιτο. ¹⁵ τῷ Μωϋσεῖ γὰρ λέγει· ἐλεήσω ὃν ἂν ἐλεῶ καὶ οἰκτιρήσω ὃν ἂν οἰκτίρω. ¹⁶ ἄρα οὖν οὐ τοῦ θέλοντος οὐδὲ τοῦ τρέχοντος ἀλλὰ τοῦ

---

[14] Whose function corresponds to that of the oft used *mē genoito* (may it not be so; by no means) that Paul adds after a potentially blasphemous statement (Rom 3:3, 6, 31; 6:2, 15; 7:7, 13; 9:14; 11:1, 11; 1 Cor 6:15; Gal 2:17; 3:21; 6:14).

ἐλεῶντος θεοῦ. ¹⁷ λέγει γὰρ ἡ γραφὴ τῷ Φαραὼ ὅτι εἰς αὐτὸ
τοῦτο ἐξήγειρά σε ὅπως ἐνδείξωμαι ἐν σοὶ τὴν δύναμίν μου
καὶ ὅπως διαγγελῇ τὸ ὄνομά μου ἐν πάσῃ τῇ γῇ. ¹⁸ ἄρα οὖν
ὃν θέλει ἐλεεῖ, ὃν δὲ θέλει σκληρύνει.

> ⁶*But it is not as though the word of God had failed. For not all
> who are descended from Israel belong to Israel,* ⁷*and not all are
> children of Abraham because they are his descendants; but
> "Through Isaac shall your descendants be named."* ⁸*This means
> that it is not the children of the flesh who are the children of
> God, but the children of the promise are reckoned as
> descendants.* ⁹*For this is what the promise said, "About this time
> I will return and Sarah shall have a son."* ¹⁰*And not only so, but
> also when Rebecca had conceived children by one man, our
> forefather Isaac,* ¹¹*though they were not yet born and had done
> nothing either good or bad, in order that God's purpose of
> election might continue, not because of works but because of his
> call,* ¹²*she was told, "The elder will serve the younger."* ¹³*As it is
> written, "Jacob I loved, but Esau I hated."* ¹⁴*What shall we say
> then? Is there injustice on God's part? By no means!* ¹⁵*For he says
> to Moses, "I will have mercy on whom I have mercy, and I will
> have compassion on whom I have compassion."* ¹⁶*So it depends
> not upon man's will or exertion, but upon God's mercy.* ¹⁷*For
> the scripture says to Pharaoh, "I have raised you up for the very
> purpose of showing my power in you, so that my name may be
> proclaimed in all the earth."* ¹⁸*So then he has mercy upon
> whomever he wills, and he hardens the heart of whomever he
> wills.*

One may assume from the previous verses that the word of God,
that is to say the scriptural story beginning with the promise to
the forefathers, did not attain its goal, which is the promised
Messiah, as detailed in Galatians 3:15-19. Since Paul mentions
the forefathers and Christ in the same breath in Romans 9:5a,

this misunderstanding must lie in the phrase "according to the flesh," as I explained earlier. In vv.1-5, Paul was critiquing his peers' misunderstanding of scripture. It stands to reason then that he would embark on explicating to his addressees the true intention and meaning of scripture, which he does in Romans 9:6-10:21 where, as we shall see, he covers, from a bird's eye view, all three parts of the Old Testament.

The word of "the God who is over all and is blessed unto the ages" cannot possibly fail. The reason is that, according to the scriptural story consigned in the Law and the Prophets, not all those who are "out of Israel," descendants of Israel, are indeed Israel, or "the Israel of God" as Paul terms it (Gal 6:16). Put otherwise, the progeny of Israel is not "according to the flesh." This is so right from the beginning. In the Book of Genesis not all those who are "from the forefathers," Abraham and Isaac, end up as Israel. Indeed, in the case of Abraham's progeny, not all are factually "children." However, since Paul had made the case for the believers' being "children of God" (Rom 8:12-25), he uses an interplay between "progeny" and "children" based on scripture itself: "In (through) Isaac a progeny shall be named (raised) for you." (9:7 quoting Gen 21:12) Thus, already in Genesis, the term "progeny," which is eminently "fleshly," is introduced as referring to a reality at another level, namely, the level of the promise of God (Rom 9:8).[15] The corollary is that the progeny is made of two kinds of children, those of the flesh and those of the promise, and only the latter end up being the progeny willed by God. Here Paul purposely uses the verb "reckon," which occurs in scripture in conjunction with Abraham's trust in God's word of promise (4:3, quoting Gen 15:6). Put otherwise, in scripture it is God's "reckoning" that establishes the reality at hand, and

---

[15] Paul here follows the line of thought he developed in Gal 4:21.28.

ROMANS: A COMMENTARY

not human will, which is the product of the flesh. God's will, expressed in his word of promise, makes us his children. Paul's addressees related fully to this reasoning since, according to Roman law, the genuine children were established through the sheer will of the Roman patrician.[16] The idea of promise is further stressed in that it is taken up in the following verse (Rom 9:9) through another quotation from Genesis 18 where its importance is evident through its repetition (vv.10 and 14).

Then Paul moves to cover the progeny of Isaac, the second forefather in Genesis. Having dealt with the terminology of "children" in discussing the "progeny" of Abraham, Paul introduces his terminology of "works" versus God's free call in his discussion of Isaac's descendants. Here also, Paul points out that it is God's sheer will that differentiates between twins (Rom 9:10). The story of the birth of Rebecca's twins is helpful in understanding this matter since a newborn has not had the opportunity to do good or evil. So, God's purpose or plan (*prothesis*) hangs on mere choice (*eklogēn*; election), which one cannot earn through works (personal effort). Everything lies in the decision of God, who issues the call, and we are his elect insofar as we respond to his call. His decision to love Jacob and hate Esau illustrates this. To conclude that there is injustice on the part of God (v.14a) calls for the same reaction made at the conclusion of 3:5: "*mē genoito* (by no means!)." (9:14b) For if God is unjust, how could he be the judge of the world, which he actually is? (3:6) Our hope is in him since he is the sole God. However, Paul goes one step further by saying that God's decision to ultimately exercise his mercy and compassion (9:15) cannot but be to our advantage. By quoting Genesis and then introducing a quotation from the last book of the twelve

---

[16] See ch.8, fn.27.

prophets, Malachi 1:2-3 (Jacob I loved, but Esau I hated; Rom 9:13), Paul is thus, in one stroke of the brush, covering the entire Law and the Prophets, i.e., scripture. The literary shift is clear when one compares the two consecutive quotations which go from negative to positive, then to two positives: "Jacob I loved, but Esau I hated" (Mal 1:2-3) where we have "hate" opposed to "love" (Rom 9:13); and "I will have mercy on whom I have mercy, and I will have compassion on whom I have compassion" (Ex 33:19), where mercy and compassion go hand in hand (Rom 9:15). That it is God's mercy which is stressed is evident from Paul's concluding remark introduced by the double preposition *ara oun* (Thus therefore; So then; So indeed): "So indeed it depends not upon man's will or exertion (racing), but upon God's mercy." (v.16) Consequently, the God who calls (v.12) is the merciful God (v.16). On the other hand, the mention of mercy as God's *ultimate* choice is corroborated by, and prepares for, the conclusion of God's planned odyssey (*prothesis*; v.11) covered in Romans 9-11:

> For the gifts and the call of God are irrevocable. Just as you were once disobedient to God but now have received mercy because of their disobedience, so they have now been disobedient in order that by the mercy shown to you they also may receive mercy. For God has consigned all men to disobedience, that he may have mercy upon all. (11:29-32)

This conclusion is immediately followed by a doxological hymn to the merciful God (vv.33-36), which rejoins the ending of Romans 8 where the only other occurrence of *prothesis* in the letter (v.28) precedes a similar burst of thanksgiving to the inexplicable and unfathomable merciful love of God *the judge* for us (vv.31-39).[17]

Yet, in order to introduce the beginning of the "odyssey" which revolves around Israel's obstinacy, Paul adds another scriptural quotation (9:17) that also concludes with a statement following the double preposition *ara oun* (Thus therefore; So then; So indeed; v.18), but this time, instead of mercy and compassion, we have the coupling of mercy with the hardening of heart. Still, God is the agent of both these actions in order to underscore his "power" against all adversity and to enact his ultimate purpose of having "his name proclaimed in all the earth" (v.17). If Pharaoh himself could not resist God's power that saved Israel from the yoke of slavery, much less can Israel's disobedience resist God's will (v.19) that one day the Gentiles would "call upon the name of the Lord" (10:13). A striking feature of 9:17, which quotes Exodus 9:16, is that "the scripture" is introduced as addressing Pharaoh! Hence the full equivalence between the scriptural God and scripture itself is at its clearest here in 9:17; one is not to differentiate between the two since God has no statue made by the hand of man; his "visible" form is scripture itself.[18] Still the practical purpose of Paul's underscoring this reality at this juncture is to draw the attention of his hearers to the fact that, in the following passages, he is not embarking upon a philosophical-mental discussion about God and his plan, but rather he will be quoting scripture itself to unfold God's plan. In other words, Paul is not improvising or creating his own thoughts about God and his "economy" with the help of outside philosophical or theological input. Rather he

---

[17] See my comments earlier on that passage.
[18] See my comments earlier on Rom 2:20.

is pointing out what God himself has already uttered *in scripture*, as witnessed in the scriptural quotations packed in Romans 9-11.

Vv. 19-29 ¹⁹ Ἐρεῖς μοι οὖν· τί [οὖν] ἔτι μέμφεται; τῷ γὰρ βουλήματι αὐτοῦ τίς ἀνθέστηκεν; ²⁰ ὦ ἄνθρωπε, μενοῦνγε σὺ τίς εἶ ὁ ἀνταποκρινόμενος τῷ θεῷ; μὴ ἐρεῖ τὸ πλάσμα τῷ πλάσαντι· τί με ἐποίησας οὕτως; ²¹ ἢ οὐκ ἔχει ἐξουσίαν ὁ κεραμεὺς τοῦ πηλοῦ ἐκ τοῦ αὐτοῦ φυράματος ποιῆσαι ὃ μὲν εἰς τιμὴν σκεῦος ὃ δὲ εἰς ἀτιμίαν; ²² εἰ δὲ θέλων ὁ θεὸς ἐνδείξασθαι τὴν ὀργὴν καὶ γνωρίσαι τὸ δυνατὸν αὐτοῦ ἤνεγκεν ἐν πολλῇ μακροθυμίᾳ σκεύη ὀργῆς κατηρτισμένα εἰς ἀπώλειαν, ²³ καὶ ἵνα γνωρίσῃ τὸν πλοῦτον τῆς δόξης αὐτοῦ ἐπὶ σκεύη ἐλέους ἃ προητοίμασεν εἰς δόξαν; ²⁴ Οὓς καὶ ἐκάλεσεν ἡμᾶς οὐ μόνον ἐξ Ἰουδαίων ἀλλὰ καὶ ἐξ ἐθνῶν, ²⁵ ὡς καὶ ἐν τῷ Ὡσηὲ λέγει· καλέσω τὸν οὐ λαόν μου λαόν μου καὶ τὴν οὐκ ἠγαπημένην ἠγαπημένην· ²⁶ καὶ ἔσται ἐν τῷ τόπῳ οὗ ἐρρέθη αὐτοῖς· οὐ λαός μου ὑμεῖς, ἐκεῖ κληθήσονται υἱοὶ θεοῦ ζῶντος. ²⁷ Ἡσαΐας δὲ κράζει ὑπὲρ τοῦ Ἰσραήλ· ἐὰν ᾖ ὁ ἀριθμὸς τῶν υἱῶν Ἰσραὴλ ὡς ἡ ἄμμος τῆς θαλάσσης, τὸ ὑπόλειμμα σωθήσεται· ²⁸ λόγον γὰρ συντελῶν καὶ συντέμνων ποιήσει κύριος ἐπὶ τῆς γῆς. ²⁹ καὶ καθὼς προείρηκεν Ἡσαΐας· εἰ μὴ κύριος σαβαὼθ ἐγκατέλιπεν ἡμῖν σπέρμα, ὡς Σόδομα ἂν ἐγενήθημεν καὶ ὡς Γόμορρα ἂν ὡμοιώθημεν.

¹⁹You will say to me then, "Why does he still find fault? For who can resist his will?" ²⁰But who are you, a man, to answer back to God? Will what is molded say to its molder, "Why have you made me thus?" ²¹Has the potter no right over the clay, to make out of the same lump one vessel for beauty and another for menial use? ²²What if God, desiring to show his wrath and to make known his power, has endured with much patience the vessels of wrath made for destruction, ²³in order to make known the riches of his glory for the vessels of mercy, which he has prepared beforehand for glory, ²⁴even us whom he has called, not from the Jews only but also from the Gentiles? ²⁵As indeed he says in Hosea, "Those who were not my people I will call 'my

*people,' and her who was not beloved I will call 'my beloved.'" [26]
"And in the very place where it was said to them, 'You are not
my people,' they will be called 'sons of the living God.'" [27]And
Isaiah cries out concerning Israel: "Though the number of the
sons of Israel be as the sand of the sea, only a remnant of them
will be saved; [28]for the Lord will execute his sentence upon the
earth with rigor and dispatch." [29]And as Isaiah predicted, "If
the Lord of hosts had not left us children, we would have fared
like Sodom and been made like Gomorrah."*

The expected objector to Paul's line of argumentation is the Jew.
Hence Paul's appeal to the same diatribe he used in Romans 2
where he addresses his hearer in the singular, calling him "O
man" (9:20; compare with 2:1). The complaint is along the same
line as that of 9:14. If God is so willful, then there is no basis for
just judgment; his will is imposed regardless of what the human
being does or does not do (v.19). Paul's retort, as usual, is based
on scripture which teaches that God is not only our judge, but
he is our maker, as in the way a potter makes or forms a vessel
from clay. Here again, the result is to our benefit, as it was in
vv.13-16 where the "willful" God ended up exercising his mercy:
we, the clay vessels that God made, end up as "vessels of mercy"
(v.23). And in order to make sure that we do not imagine that
we have *earned* his merciful verdict, Paul reminds his hearers, as
he did in Romans 2:4,[19] that God's wrathful condemnation of
his people, because they disobeyed him (Is 29:1-16), was not
only just, but it took place at the end of a long wait, full of
patience on God's part (Rom 9:22), giving them plenty of time
to repent (2:4), yet they did not. That would have been a sad

---

[19] The correspondence between Rom 2 and 9 is evident in the use of the same
terminology of "honor," "dishonor," "glory," "wrath," "kindness/forbearance
(*makrothymia*)," "richness."

ending for Israel had the same "powerful" and "willful" God not decided to wait patiently for his people's change of heart:

> We have all become like one who is unclean, and all our righteous deeds are like a polluted garment. We all fade like a leaf, and our iniquities, like the wind, take us away. There is no one that calls upon thy name, that bestirs himself to take hold of thee; for thou hast hid thy face from us, and hast delivered us into the hand of our iniquities. Yet, O Lord, thou art our Father; we are the clay, and thou art our potter; we are all the work of thy hand. Be not exceedingly angry, O Lord, and remember not iniquity for ever. Behold, consider, we are all thy people. (Is 64:6-9)

Further, in Isaiah 66, we hear that, together with the reassembling of his scattered people, the scriptural God, who is the God of all, well before the rise of the forefathers (Gen 1-11), will gather the nations from whose midst he will raise even "priests and Levites" (Is 66:20-21). Hence Paul's powerful rhetorical retort to the complaining Jew, and beyond him, to the arrogant Roman:

> What if God, desiring to show his wrath and to make known his power, has endured with much patience the vessels of wrath made for destruction, in order to make known the riches of his glory for the vessels of mercy, which he has prepared beforehand for glory, even us whom he has called, not from the Jews only but also from the Gentiles? (Rom 9:22-24)

Before summing up the Isaianic story (vv.27-29), and in order to ensure that his hearers, including the objecting Jew, be convinced that what he just covered is simply the scriptural story, Paul appeals in vv.25-26 to Hosea, the first volume in the scroll of the Twelve Prophets, to show that what Paul delineated is thoroughly scriptural and not just something specific to one prophet or one book.[20] He actually started this process in Romans 9:21 where he brought into the discussion phraseology from Jeremiah and from the Wisdom of Solomon, a book representative of the Writings, the third part of scripture.[21] In so doing, he covered the Law (Genesis, Exodus, and Deuteronomy), the Prophets (Isaiah and Jeremiah, Hosea and Malachi) and the Writings (Wisdom of Solomon). The quotations from Hosea are well chosen: those who were not my people I will call "my people," and her who was not beloved I will call "my beloved" (2:23); and in the very place where it was said to them, "You are not my people," they will be called "sons of the living God" (1:10). They answer the question, "What if God, desiring to show his wrath and to make known his power, has endured with much patience the vessels of wrath made for destruction, in order to make known the riches of his glory for the vessels of mercy, which he has prepared beforehand for glory, *even us whom he has called, not from the Jews only but also from the Gentiles?*" (Rom 9:22-24) Indeed, since the sinful Israel is as much "not my people" as the Gentiles, by the same token the Gentiles who are submissive to God's will are on an equal footing with repentant Israel.[22] Although Paul bitterly experienced his Jewish contemporaries' recalcitrance toward the gospel message, he finds hope as well as solace in Isaiah's predictions that, at least, a "remnant" (*hypoleimma*) and a "left

---

[20] See earlier my comments on the inclusion of Mal 1:2-3.

[21] Compare Rom 9:21 (Has the potter no right over the clay, to make out of the same lump one vessel for honor and another for dishonor?) to Jer 18:6 (O house of Israel, can I not do with you as this potter has done? says the Lord. Behold, like the clay in the potter's hand, so are you in my hand, O house of Israel) and Wis of Sol 15:7 (For when a potter kneads the soft earth and laboriously molds each vessel for our service, he fashions out of the same clay both the vessels that serve clean uses and those for contrary uses, making all in like manner; but which shall be the use of each of these, the worker in clay is the judge).

[22] God will choose his priests and Levites from both (Is 66:20-21).

over progeny" (*enkatelipen* ... *sperma*) will remain, as Isaiah foresaw (Is 10:22-23 in Rom 9:27-28; and Is 1:9 in Rom 9: 29).²³

Vv. 30-33 ³⁰ *Τί οὖν ἐροῦμεν; ὅτι ἔθνη τὰ μὴ διώκοντα δικαιοσύνην κατέλαβεν δικαιοσύνην, δικαιοσύνην δὲ τὴν ἐκ πίστεως,* ³¹ *Ἰσραὴλ δὲ διώκων νόμον δικαιοσύνης εἰς νόμον οὐκ ἔφθασεν.* ³² *διὰ τί; ὅτι οὐκ ἐκ πίστεως ἀλλ᾽ ὡς ἐξ ἔργων· προσέκοψαν τῷ λίθῳ τοῦ προσκόμματος,* ³³ *καθὼς γέγραπται· ἰδοὺ τίθημι ἐν Σιὼν λίθον προσκόμματος καὶ πέτραν σκανδάλου, καὶ ὁ πιστεύων ἐπ᾽ αὐτῷ οὐ καταισχυνθήσεται.*

10:1-4 ¹ *Ἀδελφοί, ἡ μὲν εὐδοκία τῆς ἐμῆς καρδίας καὶ ἡ δέησις πρὸς τὸν θεὸν ὑπὲρ αὐτῶν εἰς σωτηρίαν.* ² *μαρτυρῶ γὰρ αὐτοῖς ὅτι ζῆλον θεοῦ ἔχουσιν ἀλλ᾽ οὐ κατ᾽ ἐπίγνωσιν·* ³ *ἀγνοοῦντες γὰρ τὴν τοῦ θεοῦ δικαιοσύνην καὶ τὴν ἰδίαν [δικαιοσύνην] ζητοῦντες στῆσαι, τῇ δικαιοσύνῃ τοῦ θεοῦ οὐχ ὑπετάγησαν.* ⁴ *τέλος γὰρ νόμου Χριστὸς εἰς δικαιοσύνην παντὶ τῷ πιστεύοντι.*

³⁰*What shall we say, then? That Gentiles who did not pursue righteousness have attained it, that is, righteousness through faith;* ³¹*but that Israel who pursued the righteousness which is based on law did not succeed in fulfilling that law.* ³²*Why? Because they did not pursue it through faith, but as if it were based on works. They have stumbled over the stumbling stone,* ³³*as it is written, "Behold, I am laying in Zion a stone that will make men stumble, a rock that will make them fall; and he who believes in him will not be put to shame."*

Romans 10 ¹*Brethren, my heart's desire and prayer to God for them is that they may be saved.* ²*I bear them witness that they*

²³ That Paul was "reading" scripture as it stands finds corroboration in that, when quoting Is 1:9 (Rom 9:29) *after* Is 10:22-23 (Rom 9:27-28) he prefaces it with "and as Isaiah *said before* (*proeirēken*) [following KJV; and not "predicted" as RSV and JB]." See my detailed comments in *Gal* 4.

have a zeal for God, but it is not enlightened. ³For, being
ignorant of the righteousness that comes from God, and seeking
to establish their own, they did not submit to God's
righteousness. ⁴For Christ is the end of the law, that every one
who has faith may be justified.

To explain why only a minority of the Jews accepted the
gospel message when Gentiles were doing so, Paul
recapitulates his lengthy argument from earlier chapters,
especially Romans 2:17-3:20. Righteousness is a matter of the
Law, so the "Law-less" Gentiles could not be pursuing such
righteousness. Still they attained that state of righteousness in
God's eyes by trusting in what he did through his Messiah (Rom
9:30; see earlier 3:21-31). On the other hand, Israel realized that
the Law would grant righteousness should one abide by it. The
"Law-full" Israelites kept trying to fulfill the works of that Law,
yet time and again failed to do so and kept breaking its
commandments, as witnessed in scripture. Consequently, they
did not attain the status of being within the requirements of that
Law (9:31). The solution for them would have been to trust in
God's graceful decision to establish their righteousness through
his "servant" (Is 53:10-12); instead, they kept trying to attain it
by abiding by the commandments. In Isaiah's words, they kept
stumbling on the test that God himself established, the test being
whether they would trust in his "graceful" intervention on their
behalf in spite of their unworthiness (Rom 9:33).

Paul iterates his prayer of vv.1-3 that his heart's "goodwill"
(*evdokia*) is to see his "brethren, my kinsmen by race" on the
path to salvation (*eis sōtērian*) (10:1), which is God's own desire:
"For I am not ashamed of the gospel: it is the power of God for
salvation (*eis sōtērian*) to every one who has faith, *to the Jew first*
and also to the Greek." (1:16). It is clear that what triggered the

reference to this statement is the terminology of the last phrase of
the Isaianic quotation in Romans 9:33: "… and he who believes
in him will not be put to shame." Paul is aware that his
colleagues have the zeal to do well, just as he once had (Phil 3:6),
however their zeal was not according to the fullness of
knowledge (*ou kat' epignōsin*) (Rom 10:2). True knowledge lies
in understanding the scriptural teaching that righteousness
cannot be attained through one's endeavors, but by submitting
to the fact that God grants it, as Paul explained earlier in
Romans 3. In Romans 10:4 he sums up his earlier conclusion of
Romans 3:19-31 that the ultimate end of the scriptural story line
lies in Christ who functions unto righteousness for everyone, the
Jew first but also the Gentile, who trusts in what God did
through Christ, as witnessed in scripture.

Chapter 10

Vv. 5-21 ⁵ Μωϋσῆς γὰρ γράφει τὴν δικαιοσύνην τὴν ἐκ [τοῦ] νόμου ὅτι ὁ ποιήσας αὐτὰ ἄνθρωπος ζήσεται ἐν αὐτοῖς. ⁶ ἡ δὲ ἐκ πίστεως δικαιοσύνη οὕτως λέγει· μὴ εἴπῃς ἐν τῇ καρδίᾳ σου· τίς ἀναβήσεται εἰς τὸν οὐρανόν; τοῦτ᾽ ἔστιν Χριστὸν καταγαγεῖν· ⁷ ἤ· τίς καταβήσεται εἰς τὴν ἄβυσσον; τοῦτ᾽ ἔστιν Χριστὸν ἐκ νεκρῶν ἀναγαγεῖν. ⁸ ἀλλὰ τί λέγει; ἐγγύς σου τὸ ῥῆμά ἐστιν ἐν τῷ στόματί σου καὶ ἐν τῇ καρδίᾳ σου, τοῦτ᾽ ἔστιν τὸ ῥῆμα τῆς πίστεως ὃ κηρύσσομεν. ⁹ ὅτι ἐὰν ὁμολογήσῃς ἐν τῷ στόματί σου κύριον Ἰησοῦν καὶ πιστεύσῃς ἐν τῇ καρδίᾳ σου ὅτι ὁ θεὸς αὐτὸν ἤγειρεν ἐκ νεκρῶν, σωθήσῃ· ¹⁰ καρδίᾳ γὰρ πιστεύεται εἰς δικαιοσύνην, στόματι δὲ ὁμολογεῖται εἰς σωτηρίαν. ¹¹ λέγει γὰρ ἡ γραφή· πᾶς ὁ πιστεύων ἐπ᾽ αὐτῷ οὐ καταισχυνθήσεται. ¹² οὐ γάρ ἐστιν διαστολὴ Ἰουδαίου τε καὶ Ἕλληνος, ὁ γὰρ αὐτὸς κύριος πάντων, πλουτῶν εἰς πάντας τοὺς ἐπικαλουμένους αὐτόν· ¹³ πᾶς γὰρ ὃς ἂν ἐπικαλέσηται τὸ ὄνομα κυρίου σωθήσεται. ¹⁴ Πῶς οὖν ἐπικαλέσωνται εἰς ὃν οὐκ ἐπίστευσαν; πῶς δὲ πιστεύσωσιν οὗ οὐκ ἤκουσαν; πῶς δὲ ἀκούσωσιν χωρὶς κηρύσσοντος; ¹⁵ πῶς δὲ κηρύξωσιν ἐὰν μὴ ἀποσταλῶσιν; καθὼς γέγραπται· ὡς ὡραῖοι οἱ πόδες τῶν εὐαγγελιζομένων [τὰ] ἀγαθά. ¹⁶ Ἀλλ᾽ οὐ πάντες ὑπήκουσαν τῷ εὐαγγελίῳ. Ἡσαΐας γὰρ λέγει· κύριε, τίς ἐπίστευσεν τῇ ἀκοῇ ἡμῶν; ¹⁷ ἄρα ἡ πίστις ἐξ ἀκοῆς, ἡ δὲ ἀκοὴ διὰ ῥήματος Χριστοῦ. ¹⁸ ἀλλὰ λέγω, μὴ οὐκ ἤκουσαν; μενοῦνγε· εἰς πᾶσαν τὴν γῆν ἐξῆλθεν ὁ φθόγγος αὐτῶν καὶ εἰς τὰ πέρατα τῆς οἰκουμένης τὰ ῥήματα αὐτῶν. ¹⁹ ἀλλὰ λέγω, μὴ Ἰσραὴλ οὐκ ἔγνω; πρῶτος Μωϋσῆς λέγει· ἐγὼ παραζηλώσω ὑμᾶς ἐπ᾽ οὐκ ἔθνει, ἐπ᾽ ἔθνει ἀσυνέτῳ παροργιῶ ὑμᾶς. ²⁰ Ἡσαΐας δὲ ἀποτολμᾷ καὶ λέγει· εὑρέθην [ἐν] τοῖς ἐμὲ μὴ ζητοῦσιν, ἐμφανὴς ἐγενόμην τοῖς ἐμὲ μὴ ἐπερωτῶσιν. ²¹ πρὸς δὲ τὸν Ἰσραὴλ λέγει· ὅλην τὴν ἡμέραν ἐξεπέτασα τὰς χεῖράς μου πρὸς λαὸν ἀπειθοῦντα καὶ ἀντιλέγοντα.

⁵*Moses writes that the man who practices the righteousness which is based on the law shall live by it.* ⁶*But the righteousness*

based on faith says, Do not say in your heart, "Who will ascend into heaven?" (that is, to bring Christ down) [7]or "Who will descend into the abyss?" (that is, to bring Christ up from the dead). [8]But what does it say? The word is near you, on your lips and in your heart (that is, the word of faith which we preach); [9]because, if you confess with your lips that Jesus is Lord and believe in your heart that God raised him from the dead, you will be saved. [10]For man believes with his heart and so is justified, and he confesses with his lips and so is saved. [11]The scripture says, "No one who believes in him will be put to shame." [12]For there is no distinction between Jew and Greek; the same Lord is Lord of all and bestows his riches upon all who call upon him. [13]For, "every one who calls upon the name of the Lord will be saved." [14]But how are men to call upon him in whom they have not believed? And how are they to believe in him of whom they have never heard? And how are they to hear without a preacher? [15]And how can men preach unless they are sent? As it is written, "How beautiful are the feet of those who preach good news!" [16]But they have not all obeyed the gospel; for Isaiah says, "Lord, who has believed what he has heard from us?" [17]So faith comes from what is heard, and what is heard comes by the preaching of Christ. [18]But I ask, have they not heard? Indeed they have; for "Their voice has gone out to all the earth, and their words to the ends of the world." [19]Again I ask, did Israel not understand? First Moses says, "I will make you jealous of those who are not a nation; with a foolish nation I will make you angry." [20]Then Isaiah is so bold as to say, "I have been found by those who did not seek me; I have shown myself to those who did not ask for me." [21]But of Israel he says, "All day long I have held out my hands to a disobedient and contrary people."

What was succinctly stated in 2:21-22 (But now the righteousness of God has been manifested apart from law, as the Law and the Prophets bear witness to it, the righteousness of God through faith in Jesus Christ for all who believe) is taken up in detail in chapter 10. In order to prove his point, Paul revisits the scriptural story, starting with the Law, more specifically Deuteronomy as its typical representative, and ending with the Prophets, more specifically Isaiah as their typical representative, and the Writings, whose main representation is in the Book of Palms.

In Leviticus, which is half-way between Genesis, where the promise is made to Abraham and his progeny, and Deuteronomy, where the progeny is about to enter the land of that promise, we hear of what Paul refers to as righteousness based on (works of) the Law (*ek tou nomou*) (Rom 10:5): "You shall therefore keep my statutes and my ordinances, by doing which a man shall live." (Lev 18:5) In the Book of Numbers, however, we hear the following:

> And the Lord said to Moses and to Aaron, "How long shall this wicked congregation murmur against me? I have heard the murmurings of the people of Israel, which they murmur against me. Say to them, 'As I live,' says the Lord, 'what you have said in my hearing I will do to you: your dead bodies shall fall in this wilderness; and of all your number, numbered from twenty years old and upward, who have murmured against me, not one shall come into the land where I swore that I would make you dwell, except Caleb the son of Jephunneh and Joshua the son of Nun. But your little ones, who you said would become a prey, I will bring in, and they shall know the land which you have despised. But as for you, your dead bodies shall fall in this wilderness. And your children shall be shepherds in the wilderness forty years, and shall suffer for your faithlessness, until the last of your dead bodies

lies in the wilderness. According to the number of the days in which you spied out the land, forty days, for every day a year, you shall bear your iniquity, forty years, and you shall know my displeasure.' I, the Lord, have spoken; surely this will I do to all this wicked congregation that are gathered together against me: in this wilderness they shall come to a full end, and there they shall die." (14:26-35)

This punishment will be further confirmed in Joshua:

For the people of Israel walked forty years in the wilderness, till all the nation, the men of war that came forth out of Egypt, perished, because they did not hearken to the voice of the Lord; to them the Lord swore that he would not let them see the land which the Lord had sworn to their fathers to give us, a land flowing with milk and honey. So it was their children, whom he raised up in their stead, that Joshua circumcised; for they were uncircumcised, because they had not been circumcised on the way. (5:6-7)

This means that the generation addressed in Leviticus was unable to conform to the requirements of the Law and thus found death instead of life, just as was forewarned at the end of Leviticus 26.

The reissuing of the Law in Deuteronomy did not secure a better future for the second generation born in the wilderness, or for subsequent generations who ultimately were expelled from the land of the promise. Because of this situation, Deuteronomy, not unlike the Ezekelian message, was conceived as a "book" or "scroll" (Deut 30:10; Ezek 2:9-3:3) that could be carried around without need of a city temple to preserve it. To be sure, the king of Jerusalem, high priest of the temple, would have a copy of it and would be subject to its contents. The original, however, was to remain out of his control lest he change it in any way:

And when he sits on the throne of his kingdom, he shall write for himself in a book a copy of this law, from that which is in the charge of the Levitical priests; and it shall be with him, and he shall read in it all the days of his life, that he may learn to fear the Lord his God, by keeping all the words of this law and these statutes, and doing them; that his heart may not be lifted up above his brethren, and that he may not turn aside from the commandment, either to the right hand or to the left; so that he may continue long in his kingdom, he and his children, in Israel. (Deut 17:18-10)

Consequently, one is not to look to the heavens or across the seas (abyss) to locate the message (Deut 30:12-13), let alone the messenger. The message is "not far off" (v.11) but "very near you; it is in your mouth and in your heart, so that you can do it" (v.14). By prefacing this quotation (Rom 10:6c-8) with the words "Do not say in your heart" (v.6b) from Deuteronomy 9:4, Paul is virtually including the entire Book of Deuteronomy and, as *pars pro toto*, the entire Law. More importantly, he is obliquely drawing the attention of his hearers to the words of Deuteronomy 9:4-6:

Do not say in your heart, after the Lord your God has thrust them out before you, "It is because of my righteousness that the Lord has brought me in to possess this land"; whereas it is because of the wickedness of these nations that the Lord is driving them out before you. Not because of your righteousness or the uprightness of your heart are you going in to possess their land; but because of the wickedness of these nations the Lord your God is driving them out from before you, and that he may confirm the word which the Lord swore to your fathers, to Abraham, to Isaac, and to Jacob. Know therefore, that the Lord your God is not giving you this good land to possess because of your righteousness; *for you are a stubborn people.*

Since the assumption is that the new generation and the subsequent ones are as stubborn and disobedient as the one who left Egypt, it stands to reason that righteousness would ultimately lie in God's keeping his promise and implementing his salvation down the road. As I indicated at different points in this discussion of Romans, especially in conjunction with 5:1-11, that plan will materialize through the Isaianic servant whose righteousness will make many to be accounted righteous (Is 53:10-12). That this was Paul's thought here is evident in that in the rest of the chapter he not only quotes extensively from Isaiah but also does so *in sequence*, as though *reading through* the Book of Isaiah: Isaiah 28:16 in Romans 10:11; Isaiah 52:7 in Romans 10:15; Isaiah 53:1 in Romans 10:16; Isaiah 65:1-2 in Romans 10:20-21. Even more, chapter 10 of Romans is actually an explication of Romans 9:30-33 that ended with quoting Isaiah 28:16 (he who trusts in him will not be put to shame) which is iterated again in Romans 10:11 at the start of the Isaiah serial quotations. Thus, Romans 10 looks like a repeat of Romans 9 from another perspective. Whereas chapter 9 deals with how the poor response in Israel toward the call of the gospel is actually "foreseen" in scripture, chapter 10 shows how the stunning response of a large number of Gentiles to that call is equally "foreseen" in that same scripture. The conclusion is that, in spite of all appearances, God is in control, and this is the topic of the following chapter 11.

But how one is to explain the strange construction in Romans 10:6-8 where Paul interpolates additions pertaining to his gospel preaching within the actual text of Deuteronomy? At the outset of the letter, Paul established that God's raising Christ from the dead, *as he understood and preached it*, was the realization of God's promise made "beforehand through his prophets in the holy scriptures" (Rom 1:2). Later in the letter (5:1-11, 8:14-17,

28-30, 32-34), expanding on what he wrote in Galatians 4:1-7, Paul reminds us that sending Christ on that mission was also a graceful action on God's part without any link to our own efforts. Here in Romans 10:6-8 Paul recapitulates his entire teaching regarding this matter, as is evident from the way he ends his statement in v.8b: "*ho kēryssomen*; that which we herald/preach." Paul's heralding as apostle holds together the two sections of chapter 10 (vv.5-13 and 14-21). What he does in vv.6-8 is expand on Deuteronomy 30:12-14 in order to underscore that Christ was not "brought down (*katagagein*) from heaven" nor was he "brought up (*anagagein*) from the dead" by the will of man. Further, the apostolic preaching which brings Christ, "as God's sent," to the hearers, and invites them to accept the message with full trust, has reached the Roman patricians through Paul, another "sent" by God. Thus all is grace.

Can one say more about Romans 10:6-8? I believe one can. The interpolations as well as the rephrasing of the original— changing "Who will go over the sea" (Deut 30:13) into "Who will descend into the abyss?" in Romans 10:7a—are functional within the larger context and prepare for the following vv.9-13. The noun "abyss" is rare in the New Testament; outside the book of Revelation (where it is used seven times), it is found only here in Romans and in Luke 8:31. In Revelation the abyss is the domain of the dragon, God's opponent (9:1, 2, 11; 20:1, 3), but also representative of the Roman emperor (11:7; 17:8). In Luke 8:31, abyss is mentioned in conjunction with the demon whose name is "legion" (v.30), which connects the abyss to the realm of the Roman power.[1] It is safe then to conclude that abyss points to the Roman sea, the domain of Roman power that

---

[1] See my comments on the healing of the Gadarene demoniac (Mk 8:28-34/Lk 8:26-39) in *NTI₁* 165-6 and *NTI₂* 72-3.

executed the Christ of God, "sending him down" into the domain of the dead. Thus the change from "sea" to "abyss" is smoother than it looks, especially that abyss in scripture refers to the deep waters. By the same token, Paul is forbidding the Roman patricians to seek the salvaging of God's Christ from the domain of the dead by appealing to Roman authorities, as did Joseph of Arimathea when he asked for the body of Jesus from Pontius Pilate,[2] who falsely believed that he had power to release, and thus save, Jesus (Jn 19:38). Paul is thus telling the patricians of Rome that, once they accept his preaching, they are to refocus their trust from the Roman emperor to the scriptural God. Such an understanding of Romans 10:8 makes sense since it prepares for what Paul says in vv.9-10: "because, if you confess with your lips that Jesus is Lord and believe in your heart that God raised him from the dead, you will be saved. For man believes with his heart and so is justified, and he confesses with his lips and so is saved." Like Paul (1:16) they are not to be ashamed of the gospel he is preaching to them (10:11). The phraseology is clearly reminiscent of that applying to the gladiators in the arena, who are literally at the mercy of the emperor, their "savior."

However, Paul concludes in vv.12-13 that God's riches (v.12) in kindness (2:4) apply to the Jew as well as the Gentile, actually to the Jew before the Gentile.[3] Neither the Gentile nor the Jew is to submit to the power of Rome, much less "go up" to Jerusalem as though it were the representative of heaven whence God speaks and, consequently, as though his Christ resided there (10:6). This rejoins what Paul said of the "present" Jerusalem as

---

[2] See my comments in *NTI₁* 230-4.

[3] The particle *te* before the conjunction *kai* in the phrase *Ioudaiou te kai Ellēnos* (Jew but also Gentile; Rom 10:12) is reminiscent of what we find in 1:16; 2:9, 10 where we have the adverb *prōton* (first; firstly) after "Jew."

well as of his apostleship in Galatians, the letter that forms the
kernel of Romans:

> But when he who had set me apart before I was born, and had
> called me through his grace, was pleased to reveal his Son to me,
> in order that I might preach him among the Gentiles, I did not
> confer with flesh and blood, nor did I go up to Jerusalem to those
> who were apostles before me, but I went away into Arabia; and
> again I returned to Damascus. (Gal 1:15-17)

> Now Hagar is Mount Sinai in Arabia; she corresponds to the
> present Jerusalem, for she is in slavery with her children. But the
> Jerusalem above is free, and she is our mother. (Gal 4:25-26)

The "word" of God that the citizens of Rome are to abide by is
"near them," within their reach, since it is none other than the
"word of faith" that "we preach" (Rom 10:8). Having established
the scriptural thesis that the "goal of scripture" is righteousness
and, through it, salvation for everyone, Jew and Gentile alike,
who trusts (v.4), "who calls upon the name of the Lord" (v.13),
he asks the series of rhetorical questions: "But how are men to
call upon him in whom they have not believed? And how are
they to believe in him of whom they have never heard? And how
are they to hear without a herald/preacher (*kēryssontos*)? And how
can men herald/preach (*kēryxōsin*) unless they are sent (as
apostles) (*apostalōsin*)?" (vv.14-15a) And, just as he wrote in
Galatians (1:15-17), Paul's commissioning by God to herald the
gospel is not only theoretically necessary (Rom 10:14-15b), but
also actually according to scripture: "*As it is written*, 'How
beautiful are the feet of those who evangelize!'" (v.15b)

At this point, Paul is ready to answer his contemporary Jews'
recalcitrance to accept the gospel promised in their scriptures.
Just as the spreading of the gospel is scriptural, unfortunately so

is its refusal by some. And since it is the central issue discussed here, Paul visits it on two levels, the level of its hearing and that of its acceptance and thus submission to it. On both counts, scripture "foresaw" the outcome: though *all* heard the gospel being preached (Rom 10:18; quoting Ps 19:4/LXX 18:5),[4] yet *not all* believed it and obeyed it (Rom 10:16; quoting Is 53:1).

Ultimately, what counts is that not only has scripture "foreseen" what Paul described as the positive response of the Gentiles and the negative attitude of most of the Jews (Rom 9:30-31), but also scripture has "foreseen" the divine plan for getting the latter on the right track. In his usual way, Paul quotes from the Law and the Prophets: "Again I ask, did Israel not understand? First Moses says, 'I will make you jealous of (*parazēlōsō*; I will make you much more zealous than) those who are not a nation; with a foolish nation I will make you angry' (Deut 32:21). Then Isaiah is so bold as to say, 'I have been found by those who did not seek (*zētousin*) me; I have shown myself to those who did not ask for me' (Is 65:1)." (Rom 10:19-20) The choice of quotations corresponds, terminology wise, to what Paul said earlier regarding Israel's missing the mark: "I bear them witness that they have a zeal (*zēlon*) for God, but it is not enlightened. For, being ignorant of the righteousness that comes from God, and seeking (*zētountes*) to establish their own, they did not submit to God's righteousness." (10:2-3) Thus the intention is not to discard the Jews who oppose the gospel, but to invite them to seek God with a righteous and enlightened zeal so that they turn from a nation that is "not my people" again into "God's people." In this case, the Gentiles who accepted the

---

[4] As I indicated earlier, by quoting from Psalms Paul again uses the entire scripture: the Law, the Prophets, and the Writings.

gospel become the muster for such turning around or repentance.

This joining of the already believing Gentiles and the hopefully repentant Jews is done through a masterful split of the one quotation from Isaiah 65:1-2 that introduces each verse with a comment: "Then Isaiah is so bold as to say, 'I have been found by those who did not seek me; I have shown myself to those who did not ask for me.' But unto[5] Israel he says, 'All day long I have held out my hands to a disobedient and contrary people.'" (Rom 10:20-21) The quoted address to Israel is intentionally ambivalent. When read together with vv.19-20, v.21 sounds as though Israel is bound to remain obstinate. But when the three verses are heard independently as is the intention of the author who prefaced them each with a different introduction, they unfold the scriptural God's plan in three steps. The first step is God's intention to use the Gentiles' acceptance of the gospel to stir the jealousy and zeal of the Jews. He does this by offering his gospel to the Gentiles through Paul. The second step heralds God's success: a good number of Gentiles respond. The third step proves more difficult due to the Jews' obstinacy, yet he keeps the door open *in spite of* their refusal: "*All day long I have held out my hands* to a disobedient and contrary people." Thus the third step is *on hope* that God will have the last word by having a larger number in Israel repent in spite of the resistance of many, as Isaiah actually indicates:

> I spread out my hands all the day to a rebellious people, who walk in a way that is not good, following their own devices; a people who provoke me to my face continually, sacrificing in gardens and burning incense upon bricks; who sit in tombs, and spend the

---

[5] RSV translates *pros* into "of," which misses Paul's point. It gives *pros ton Israēl* in Rom 10:21 the same value as *hyper tou Israēl* (regarding/about/of Israel) in 9:27.

night in secret places; who eat swine's flesh, and broth of abominable things is in their vessels; who say, "Keep to yourself, do not come near me, for I am set apart from you." These are a smoke in my nostrils, a fire that burns all the day. Behold, it is written before me: "I will not keep silent, but I will repay, yea, I will repay into their bosom their iniquities and their fathers' iniquities together, says the Lord; because they burned incense upon the mountains and reviled me upon the hills, I will measure into their bosom payment for their former doings." Thus says the Lord: "As the wine is found in the cluster, and they say, 'Do not destroy it, for there is a blessing in it,' so I will do for my servants' sake, and not destroy them all. I will bring forth descendants from Jacob, and from Judah inheritors of my mountains; my chosen shall inherit it, and my servants shall dwell there. Sharon shall become a pasture for flocks, and the Valley of Achor a place for herds to lie down, for my people who have sought me. But you who forsake the Lord, who forget my holy mountain, who set a table for Fortune and fill cups of mixed wine for Destiny; I will destine you to the sword, and all of you shall bow down to the slaughter; because, when I called, you did not answer, when I spoke, you did not listen, but you did what was evil in my eyes, and chose what I did not delight in." Therefore thus says the Lord God: "Behold, my servants shall eat, but you shall be hungry; behold, my servants shall drink, but you shall be thirsty; behold, my servants shall rejoice, but you shall be put to shame; behold, my servants shall sing for gladness of heart, but you shall cry out for pain of heart, and shall wail for anguish of spirit. You shall leave your name to my chosen for a curse, and the Lord God will slay you; but his servants he will call by a different name. So that he who blesses himself in the land shall bless himself by the God of truth, and he who takes an oath in the land shall swear by the God of truth; because the former troubles are forgotten and are hid from my eyes." (Is 65:2-16)

The ambivalence will be solved in Romans 11 where Paul will take his time developing in detail Isaiah's thought in order to forego any arrogance on the part of the patricians of Rome who are prone to such an attitude. If the non-iconic God is not interested in Jerusalem, much less is he interested in Rome!

Chapter 11

Vv. 1-10 ¹ *Λέγω οὖν, μὴ ἀπώσατο ὁ θεὸς τὸν λαὸν αὐτοῦ; μὴ γένοιτο· καὶ γὰρ ἐγὼ Ἰσραηλίτης εἰμί, ἐκ σπέρματος Ἀβραάμ, φυλῆς Βενιαμίν. ² οὐκ ἀπώσατο ὁ θεὸς τὸν λαὸν αὐτοῦ ὃν προέγνω. ἢ οὐκ οἴδατε ἐν Ἠλίᾳ τί λέγει ἡ γραφή, ὡς ἐντυγχάνει τῷ θεῷ κατὰ τοῦ Ἰσραήλ; ³ κύριε, τοὺς προφήτας σου ἀπέκτειναν, τὰ θυσιαστήριά σου κατέσκαψαν, κἀγὼ ὑπελείφθην μόνος καὶ ζητοῦσιν τὴν ψυχήν μου. ⁴ ἀλλὰ τί λέγει αὐτῷ ὁ χρηματισμός; κατέλιπον ἐμαυτῷ ἑπτακισχιλίους ἄνδρας, οἵτινες οὐκ ἔκαμψαν γόνυ τῇ Βάαλ. ⁵ οὕτως οὖν καὶ ἐν τῷ νῦν καιρῷ λεῖμμα κατ᾿ ἐκλογὴν χάριτος γέγονεν· ⁶ εἰ δὲ χάριτι, οὐκέτι ἐξ ἔργων, ἐπεὶ ἡ χάρις οὐκέτι γίνεται χάρις. ⁷ Τί οὖν; ὃ ἐπιζητεῖ Ἰσραήλ, τοῦτο οὐκ ἐπέτυχεν, ἡ δὲ ἐκλογὴ ἐπέτυχεν· οἱ δὲ λοιποὶ ἐπωρώθησαν, ⁸ καθὼς γέγραπται· ἔδωκεν αὐτοῖς ὁ θεὸς πνεῦμα κατανύξεως, ὀφθαλμοὺς τοῦ μὴ βλέπειν καὶ ὦτα τοῦ μὴ ἀκούειν, ἕως τῆς σήμερον ἡμέρας. ⁹ καὶ Δαυὶδ λέγει· γενηθήτω ἡ τράπεζα αὐτῶν εἰς παγίδα καὶ εἰς θήραν καὶ εἰς σκάνδαλον καὶ εἰς ἀνταπόδομα αὐτοῖς, ¹⁰ σκοτισθήτωσαν οἱ ὀφθαλμοὶ αὐτῶν τοῦ μὴ βλέπειν καὶ τὸν νῶτον αὐτῶν διὰ παντὸς σύγκαμψον.*

¹*I ask, then, has God rejected his people? By no means! I myself am an Israelite, a descendant of Abraham, a member of the tribe of Benjamin.* ²*God has not rejected his people whom he foreknew. Do you not know what the scripture says of Elijah, how he pleads with God against Israel?* ³*"Lord, they have killed thy prophets, they have demolished thy altars, and I alone am left, and they seek my life."* ⁴*But what is God's reply to him? "I have kept for myself seven thousand men who have not bowed the knee to Baal."* ⁵*So too at the present time there is a remnant, chosen by grace.* ⁶*But if it is by grace, it is no longer on the basis of works; otherwise grace would no longer be grace.* ⁷*What then? Israel failed to obtain what it sought. The elect obtained it, but the rest were hardened,* ⁸*as it is written, "God gave them a spirit*

197

*of stupor, eyes that should not see and ears that should not hear,
down to this very day." ⁹And David says, "Let their table
become a snare and a trap, a pitfall and a retribution for them;
¹⁰let their eyes be darkened so that they cannot see, and bend
their backs for ever."*

My understanding of Romans 10:19-21 is corroborated in
11:1 where Paul answers the assumed conclusion that
God has rejected his people due to their obstinate disobedience
with his classic "By no means!" The reason he responds so is
simple. If the Gentiles trusted in the scriptural God unto their
salvation, it is because they were offered that opportunity
through Paul, who was assigned by God to share the gospel with
them. Paul himself is "an Israelite, from the progeny of
Abraham, a member of the tribe of Benjamin (whence was
chosen the first king of Israel, whose name he bears)." The
conclusion is clear: God did not reject his people. Notice how
Paul phrases his question in v.1 to prepare for his appeal to
scripture in v.2: "I ask, then, has God rejected his people? By no
means! ... *God has not rejected his people* (1 Sam 12:22; Ps 94:14)
whom he foreknew." Not only does Paul appeal to scripture—as
is his habit and as he will readily make clear immediately
thereafter (Do you not know what the scripture says of
Elijah?)—but he does so once more by being inclusive, using
quotations from both the Prophets (1 Samuel) and the Writings
(Psalms). What is striking though is the addition "whom he
foreknew." This is exactly the phrase he used to speak about
God's plan for all believers, Jews as well as Gentiles, in Romans
8:29. This corresponds to what he taught about the progeny of
Abraham in Romans 4 and what he will say concerning the
oneness of God's olive tree later in chapter 11.

Yet scripture teaches Paul not to fall in the trap as did his zealous predecessor, Elijah. That prophet interceded (*entynkhanei*) *against* (*kata*) Israel (11:2) to God. It is sheer arrogance if not blasphemy on Elijah's part to assume that he alone, among God's people, is faithful (v.3), and Paul is not going to do the same. He knows his scripture and thus God's retort to Elijah: "I have kept for myself seven thousand men who have not bowed the knee to Baal." (v.4) The number 7000 is metaphorical and refers to all (1000) those, whatever their number, who are for now faithful to God, a number that is known only to him (7).[1] Consequently, if it would have been arrogant on Paul's part to assume that he is the only Jew to have responded to God's call, it would have been more presumptuous of him to assume that he knows the number of those who have responded to God's call. It is enough that he is not alone, and thus the door of repentance for his obstinate colleagues is still wide open. This is precisely what he says in v.5 when he compares his time to that of Elijah and calls those few Jews who accepted his gospel—Timothy (Phil 2:19-24) and Mark (Col 4:10; 2 Tim 4:11; Philem 24)—"a remnant (*leimma*), according to the election (*kat' eklogēn*) by grace (*kharitos*)." And if the election is due to God's sheer grace, then the remnant among the Jews were "chosen" not because they have done the works prescribed by the Law (Rom 11:6; see earlier 9:30-31; see also Phil 2:13; 3:5-9). Thus one cannot speak of a total failure on Israel's part in its seeking the righteousness desired by God (Rom 9:31; 10:3). For although Israel in its totality did not reach what it was seeking after, "the elect (*eklogē*) did reach while the rest

---

[1] The numeral ten and its multiples (100/1000/10,000) reflect the totality of all those referred to. The numeral seven indicates usually that the matter at hand is under the control of God alone and thus is known only to him. See on scriptural numerology *NTI₃* 22-5.

were hardened" (11:7). By switching from "remnant" (v.5) to
"election/elect" (v.7) to speak of that remnant, Paul is
underscoring that the size of the remnant's constituency is totally
God's domain and no one else is privy to it. And, as usual, to
explain this, Paul defers to scripture itself again in its entirety,
the Law and the Prophets (a combination of Deut 29:4 and Is
29:10 in Rom 11:8) and the Writings (Ps 69:22-23 in Rom
11:9-10).

Vv. 11-24 ¹¹ Λέγω οὖν, μὴ ἔπταισαν ἵνα πέσωσιν; μὴ
γένοιτο· ἀλλὰ τῷ αὐτῶν παραπτώματι ἡ σωτηρία τοῖς
ἔθνεσιν εἰς τὸ παραζηλῶσαι αὐτούς. ¹² εἰ δὲ τὸ παράπτωμα
αὐτῶν πλοῦτος κόσμου καὶ τὸ ἥττημα αὐτῶν πλοῦτος ἐθνῶν,
πόσῳ μᾶλλον τὸ πλήρωμα αὐτῶν. ¹³ ὑμῖν δὲ λέγω τοῖς
ἔθνεσιν· ἐφ᾽ ὅσον μὲν οὖν εἰμι ἐγὼ ἐθνῶν ἀπόστολος, τὴν
διακονίαν μου δοξάζω, ¹⁴ εἴ πως παραζηλώσω μου τὴν σάρκα
καὶ σώσω τινὰς ἐξ αὐτῶν. ¹⁵ εἰ γὰρ ἡ ἀποβολὴ αὐτῶν
καταλλαγὴ κόσμου, τίς ἡ πρόσλημψις εἰ μὴ ζωὴ ἐκ νεκρῶν;
¹⁶ εἰ δὲ ἡ ἀπαρχὴ ἁγία, καὶ τὸ φύραμα· καὶ εἰ ἡ ῥίζα ἁγία,
καὶ οἱ κλάδοι. ¹⁷ Εἰ δέ τινες τῶν κλάδων ἐξεκλάσθησαν, σὺ
δὲ ἀγριέλαιος ὢν ἐνεκεντρίσθης ἐν αὐτοῖς καὶ συγκοινωνὸς
τῆς ῥίζης τῆς πιότητος τῆς ἐλαίας ἐγένου, ¹⁸ μὴ κατακαυχῶ
τῶν κλάδων· εἰ δὲ κατακαυχᾶσαι οὐ σὺ τὴν ῥίζαν βαστάζεις
ἀλλὰ ἡ ῥίζα σέ. ¹⁹ ἐρεῖς οὖν· ἐξεκλάσθησαν κλάδοι ἵνα ἐγὼ
ἐγκεντρισθῶ. ²⁰ καλῶς· τῇ ἀπιστίᾳ ἐξεκλάσθησαν, σὺ δὲ τῇ
πίστει ἕστηκας. μὴ ὑψηλὰ φρόνει ἀλλὰ φοβοῦ· ²¹ εἰ γὰρ ὁ
θεὸς τῶν κατὰ φύσιν κλάδων οὐκ ἐφείσατο, [μή πως] οὐδὲ
σοῦ φείσεται. ²² ἴδε οὖν χρηστότητα καὶ ἀποτομίαν θεοῦ·
ἐπὶ μὲν τοὺς πεσόντας ἀποτομία, ἐπὶ δὲ σὲ χρηστότης θεοῦ,
ἐὰν ἐπιμένῃς τῇ χρηστότητι, ἐπεὶ καὶ σὺ ἐκκοπήσῃ.   ²³
κἀκεῖνοι δέ, ἐὰν μὴ ἐπιμένωσιν τῇ ἀπιστίᾳ,
ἐγκεντρισθήσονται· δυνατὸς γάρ ἐστιν ὁ θεὸς πάλιν
ἐγκεντρίσαι αὐτούς. ²⁴ εἰ γὰρ σὺ ἐκ τῆς κατὰ φύσιν ἐξεκόπης
ἀγριελαίου καὶ παρὰ φύσιν ἐνεκεντρίσθης εἰς καλλιέλαιον,
πόσῳ μᾶλλον οὗτοι οἱ κατὰ φύσιν ἐγκεντρισθήσονται τῇ ἰδίᾳ
ἐλαίᾳ.

¹¹So I ask, have they stumbled so as to fall? By no means! But through their trespass salvation has come to the Gentiles, so as to make Israel jealous. ¹²Now if their trespass means riches for the world, and if their failure means riches for the Gentiles, how much more will their full inclusion mean! ¹³Now I am speaking to you Gentiles. Inasmuch then as I am an apostle to the Gentiles, I magnify my ministry ¹⁴in order to make my fellow Jews jealous, and thus save some of them. ¹⁵For if their rejection means the reconciliation of the world, what will their acceptance mean but life from the dead? ¹⁶If the dough offered as first fruits is holy, so is the whole lump; and if the root is holy, so are the branches. ¹⁷But if some of the branches were broken off, and you, a wild olive shoot, were grafted in their place to share the richness of the olive tree, ¹⁸do not boast over the branches. If you do boast, remember it is not you that support the root, but the root that supports you. ¹⁹You will say, "Branches were broken off so that I might be grafted in." ²⁰That is true. They were broken off because of their unbelief, but you stand fast only through faith. So do not become proud, but stand in awe. ²¹For if God did not spare the natural branches, neither will he spare you. ²²Note then the kindness and the severity of God: severity toward those who have fallen, but God's kindness to you, provided you continue in his kindness; otherwise you too will be cut off. ²³And even the others, if they do not persist in their unbelief, will be grafted in, for God has the power to graft them in again. ²⁴For if you have been cut from what is by nature a wild olive tree, and grafted, contrary to nature, into a cultivated olive tree, how much more will these natural branches be grafted back into their own olive tree.

The rhetorical question, "Have they stumbled so as to fall (*pesōsin* from the verb *piptō*)?" (Rom 11:11) was already answered in 9:6: "But it is not as though the word of God had

failed (*ekpeptōken* from the verb *ekpiptō*)." Since God is in
charge, the failing of his people does not necessarily translate into
the failing of his word as consigned in scripture. Unexpectedly,
from a human standpoint, the sins of Israel had a double positive
result: salvation unto the Gentiles, whose effect in turn was to
render the Jews jealous (*parazēlōsai*), which was precisely God's
plan from the beginning (Deut 32:21 quoted earlier in Rom
10:19). If the sinfulness of the Jews translated into God's
pouring "the riches of his kindness and forbearance and
patience" (Rom 2:4) onto Gentiles and thus the entire Roman
world, imagine, says Paul, what the acceptance of the message by
the majority of the Jews (their fullness) would mean (11:12).
Then he proceeds to elaborate on this matter by addressing
specifically his Gentile hearers (13a).

Since God's entire plan hinges on his graceful call, then from
the perspective of the Gentiles of Rome the entire matter hinges
on Paul himself, the messenger who carried to them the divine
invitation: "So long (inasmuch as) I am an apostle to Gentiles, it
is I who glorify *my* ministry (*diakonian*)." (v.13b) This choice of
vocabulary is pertinent. *Diakonia* is literally service at table
fellowship. So here Paul is reminding his hearers that, were it not
for him, they would never have shared in the table fellowship of
Israel. Furthermore, it is he who fought that battle at Antioch
(Gal 2:11-14). Hence, the channel for God's stirring the Jews'
jealousy is not the Gentiles, but rather Paul himself who is trying
to "save some of them [the Jews]" (Rom 11:14). This verse
corroborates what I said earlier regarding numbers in scripture
where "many" is tantamount to "all" and vice versa. Hence the
frequent use of *hosoi* (as many as they be) both in Paul and in the

rest of the New Testament.[2] Numbers are thus metaphorical and refer always to the *pars pro toto*. The phrase "(I) save some" occurs once more in the classic text on Paul's apostleship in 1 Corinthians:

> For though I am free from all men, I have made myself a slave to all, that I might win the more. To the Jews I became as a Jew, in order to win Jews; to those under the law I became as one under the law—though not being myself under the law—that I might win those under the law. To those outside the law I became as one outside the law—not being without law toward God but under the law of Christ—that I might win those outside the law. To the weak I became weak, that I might win the weak. I have become all things to all men, that *I might by all means save some*. I do it all for the sake of the gospel, that I may share in its blessings. (9:19-23)

Romans 11:13-14 is Paul's way of reminding his hearers that it is not the number of those who hearken to God's call that matters, but rather the call itself, since even the response is ultimately God's doing: "Therefore, my beloved, as you have always obeyed, so now, not only as in my presence but much more in my absence, work out your own salvation with fear and trembling; *for God is at work in you, both to will and to work for his good pleasure*." (Phil 2:12-13)

Furthermore, throughout scripture God realizes his plans in adversity, in spite of what his presumed followers do. When God threw to the wayside the Judahites by destroying their city and scattering them among the nations, he ended by spreading his law among those same nations and thus inviting them to reconciliation with him (Is 40-55). So here also, God's initial

---

[2] See e.g. Mt 14:36; Mk 3:10; 6:56; Acts 3:24; 4:6, 34; Rom 6:3; 8:14; Gal 3:10, 27; 6:12, 16; Phil 3:15; 2:1.

apobolē (throwing away [to the sideway])[3] of the Jews, due to
their refusal of the gospel, ends in reconciling to himself Gentiles
who submitted to that same gospel (Rom 11:15). Now imagine,
proceeds Paul, what would happen when a larger number of Jews
repent and are received by God. That would be a sign that he
had fully realized his plan, and it is time for "life out of (the
domain of) the dead," that is to say, life eternal that comes after
the raising of the dead and their judgment. Paul detailed this in
1 Corinthians 15:12-55 where he ended his argumentation with
the combined scriptural quotation that speaks of the end of
death itself: "Death is swallowed up in victory (Is 25:8). O death,
where is thy victory? O death, where is thy sting? (Hos 13:14)."
(1 Cor 15:54c-55) This is not to be taken, as is often done, as
meaning that Paul is setting a tight timetable linked to
observable and measurable events. That would contradict what
he wrote in 1 Thessalonians 4:13-5:11. It rather means that the
end will not come until everyone, Jew and Gentile alike, has had
enough opportunity to heed the gospel (2 Thess 2:1-12). In
other words, it is a caveat to Paul's addressees that they are not to
imagine that they are the only ones that count in God's plan of
salvation. And as in 1 Corinthians, the entire success of the plan
is linked to the *aparkhē* (first fruits; 15:20, 23), which functions
as an indication that the success process has already begun and
even is well and alive, since the first fruits are indeed full and
mature fruits.

It is clear that the term "first fruits" was introduced due to the
mention of life from among the dead, thus corresponding to the
terminology of 1 Corinthians. It also facilitated the introduction

---

[3] The choice of *apobolē* from the verb *apoballō* (throw away) here over the verb
apotheomai (11:1-2) is in view of the imagery of breaking off branches (and thus
throwing them away) in vv.17-24.

of the agricultural terminology of root and branches, which will take central place in the following argument (Rom 11:17-25). However, whereas root and branches fit together, first fruits and lump do not. Furthermore, in 1 Corinthians 5:6-8 and Galatians 5:9, the only other New Testament instances of "lump" outside Romans, the corresponding term is "leaven" and not "first fruits." So "lump" here must correspond to its earlier and only use in this letter, which occurs within the same context (Romans 9-11):

> But who are you, o man, to answer back to God? Will what is molded say to its molder, "Why have you made me thus?" Has the potter no right over the clay, to make out of the same lump one vessel for beauty and another for menial use? What if God, desiring to show his wrath and to make known his power, has endured with much patience the vessels of wrath made for destruction, in order to make known the riches of his glory for the vessels of mercy, which he has prepared beforehand for glory, even us whom he has called, not from the Jews only but also from the Gentiles? (9:20-24)

The message of this passage, as I explained earlier, is that God has total and absolute freedom to decide our fate. He can either doom us to destruction or maintain us through his mercy, and yet his choice, or rather his decision, is to deal mercifully with us. But this is precisely, as we shall see, the message concerning the branches of the olive tree (11:17-24). Hence the function of 11:16 is to prepare for the following vv.17-24 by reminding the hearer of what was said earlier. Put otherwise, whereas the first part of Romans 11:16 (If the first fruits is holy, so is the whole lump) looks backward, the second part (if the root is holy, so are the branches) looks forward. Such is the literary construct of *inclusio* whereby the author brackets his presentation by revisiting at the end his initial argument, thus stressing the issue

to the hearer. One is always to remember that letters are meant
to be heard, not read or studied by each individual. The
repetition of the beginning at the end ensures that the hearer be
again subject to the message of the sender so that it not be
misunderstood.

So, the question that remains is, "To whom does the term
"root" refer?" Given the parallelism with first fruits, the first
choice would be Jesus Christ, especially when one takes into
consideration a similar metaphor of the vine and its branches in
the New Testament (Jn 15:1-5). One can also add that the (new)
"leaven" of the "lump" (of sincerity and truth) in 1 Corinthians
5:6-8 is Christ. And finally, the fact that the basis of holiness of
the believers is the holiness of Christ, which was secured through
his resurrection from the dead (Rom 1:4), adds more weight to
the argument since what is said concerning the holiness of the
first fruits and the root in 11:16 immediately follows the
mention of "life from the (domain of the) dead" (v.15). The
difficulty, however, with this option is that neither Jesus nor
Christ is mentioned once in this chapter, while the term "Lord"
appears twice but only in Old Testament quotations where the
intended is obviously God (11:3, 34). Consequently, to consider
that the "root" refers to Jesus Christ is improbable since it would
be asking an unusual literary leap on the part of the hearer. In
the Old Testament, the olive tree is a metaphor for Israel per se
without any reference to the Messiah (Is 17:4-6; 24:13; Jer
11:16; Hos 14:5-6), as is precisely the case in Romans 11:17-24.
And it is this passage (11:17-24) that will confirm that the root
spoken of is indeed Abraham.

The aim of the metaphor of the one tree and the two kinds of
branches (11:17-24) is to underscore the ultimate oneness of
state between Jews and Gentiles. This is evident from the

conclusion in v.32 (For God has consigned both to disobedience, that he may have mercy upon all). A similar detailed discussion of the oneness between Jews and Gentiles in chapter 4 was shown to be "rooted" in Abraham. This oneness, as I indicated earlier in my discussion of Romans 11:13-15, was secured through the apostolic activity of Paul, who earlier introduced himself as "an Israelite, of the progeny of Abraham," which is the topic of discussion in the second part of chapter 4 (vv.13, 16, 18). More importantly, in spite of his opponents' being "enemies (of God) according of the gospel, they are still beloved (by God) according to the election *for the sake of the fathers*" (11:28), and Paul has earlier presented them as "Israelites" (9:4) and "the fathers as being theirs" (v.5), that is to say, as being on the same footing as he, the apostle to the Gentiles (11:13), is (v.1).

Noticeable in vv.17-24 is Paul's use of the diatribe style second person singular, this time against the Gentile rather than the Jew. The roles are reversed: it is the Gentile who is potentially the arrogant (v.18) and self-righteous one, forgetting that all, in God's plan, happens out of his gracefulness. The statements in vv.17-18 are the basis for the further developments and conclusions in the rest of the passage. A close analysis of the original Greek of v.17 is of utmost importance. A literal translation sounds thus: "If some of the branches were broken off and you, still (being) wild olive shoots, were grafted in their stead and became partaker (*synkoinōnos*; member of the fellowship) of the root of the fatness[4] (oiliness) of the olive tree..." The phrase

---

[4] *tēs rhizēs tēs piotētos* is clearly the *lectio difficilior* and thus most definitely the original reading.

"of the root of the fatness" sounds strange[5] and thus is definitely intentional. The syntax is heavy due to the series of three genitives (noun complements): "of the root of the fatness of the olive tree." The simpler phrase after "partaker" would have been either "of the root of the olive tree" or "of the fatness of the olive tree." Given that "root" fits the context and is part of the concluding remark (v.18), it is the latter term, "fatness," unique to the New Testament, that has been forced into the equation. The question is why. The fatness of an olive tree is obviously visible through the oiliness of its olives. In other words, it is through its fruits that a tree is valued and also judged. This is a classic metaphor in the New Testament.[6] Consequently, a branch is broken off for a reason and a goal, and not whimsically. The reason is that it is not producing fruit (Jn 15:1-6), and the goal is to save the entire tree from being uprooted and burned down (Mt 3:10; 7:19; Lk 3:9; 13:7).[7] By the same token, Paul is preparing his hearers for the eventuality of their being broken off the same tree to which they were grafted if they cease to be productive (Rom 11:24). Not only that, but the original broken off branches will be re-grafted if and when they prove to be ready to submit to God's will that they be productive (v.23).

One might object, however, that the argument revolves around faith and unbelief, not around fruits and the lack thereof. The resolution for this lies, I am convinced, in appealing to Galatians,

---

[5] Witness the manuscript tradition that reflects an effort at elucidation: "of the root and the fatness" (which is the most frequent option); "of the fatness"; "of the fatness and the root."

[6] Mt 3:10; 7:17-19; 12:33; Lk 3:9; 6:43-44; 13:7.

[7] In scripture, God's goal is to maintain his community and not each and every individual. When necessary he does so by excising some individuals (Ex 12:15, 19; 30:33, 38; 31:14; Lev 7:20, 21, 25, 27; 17:4, 9, 14; 18:29; 19:8; 20, 17, 18; 23:29; etc...).

which functions as the blueprint for Romans. The "fruitfulness" of the believer is the express topic of Galatians 5:13-23 where Paul speaks of the love for the neighbor as the first expression of "the fruit of the Spirit" (v.22). In turn, the topic of love was introduced, just before the aside where Paul castigates the Galatians for their change of mind (vv.7-12), in the following terms: "*For through the Spirit, by faith,* we wait for the hope of righteousness. For in Christ Jesus neither circumcision nor uncircumcision is of any avail, *but faith working through love.*" (vv.5-6) Both the Spirit and love, as its fruit, are linked to faith. Thus, the Spirit's work in the believer is to produce, through obedience to that same Spirit (vv.16 and 18), the required trust (faith) in God's commandments in order to do them. These commandments are subsumed in the injunction of love for one's neighbor (vv.13-15).

What seals the connection between Romans and Galatians are two more features, one very striking and the other more subtle. The first is the use of the rare "lump" in both Galatians 5:9 and Romans 11:16. Since "a little leaven leavens the whole lump" is readily understandable in the context of Galatians, one can safely conclude by its unexpected use in Romans that the author of Romans 11:13-24 had in mind Galatians 5:5-26. On the other hand, in his discussion of the struggle between God's spirit and our flesh Paul writes: "I warn you, as I warned you before, that those who do such things [viz. the works of the flesh] shall not inherit the kingdom of God." (Gal 5:21) God's kingdom is functionally equivalent to his glory as is evident from 1 Thessalonians: "for you know how, like a father with his children, we exhorted each one of you and encouraged you and charged you to lead a life worthy of God, who calls you into his own kingdom and glory." (2:11-12) Earlier in Romans Paul wrote:

> For he [God] will render to every man according to his works: to
> those who by patience in well-doing seek for glory and honor and
> immortality, he will give eternal life; but for those who are factious
> and do not obey the truth, but obey wickedness, there will be
> wrath and fury. There will be tribulation and distress for every
> human being who does evil, the Jew first and also the Greek, but
> glory and honor and peace for every one who does good, the Jew
> first and also the Greek. (2:6-10)

Considering the equivalence between God's kingdom and glory,
this verdict sounds like an expanded version of Galatians 5:21.
However, the attaining of the glory for either Jew or Gentile is
made possible only through God's kindness (*makrothymia*; long-
suffering, patience), as we are told in Romans 2:4. And this is
precisely what Paul reiterates in 11:22-23: "Note then the
kindness and the severity of God: severity toward those who have
fallen, but God's *kindness* to you, *provided you persevere in his
kindness; otherwise you too will be cut off.* And even the others, if
they do not persist in their unbelief, will be grafted in, for God
has the power to graft them in again."

In light of all the preceding discussion let us revisit vv.17-18.
Gentiles are grafted in the place of (*en avtois*) Jewish branches
that are broken off so that they can produce the good fruits
expected from God's olive tree. This is possible because they
have become sharers, partakers, of the root, which is Abraham,
to whom the promise was made (Rom 4:13-25). The Gentiles
ought not to look down on the Jews who were cut off from that
promise because of their disobedience to the truth of the gospel
(2:8). There is no reason for the Gentiles to be arrogant, since it
is the root that sustains them, and not they the root. If they were
grafted in place of the original branches (Rom 11:19), then their
new status would depend on God's promise to Abraham, not on
their own merit or value. Their arrogance would be a mistake,

since it would show that they did not heed the reason behind the fall of the others (v.20). To be arrogant would be repeating the mistake of Israel who thought that the gift of the land had to do with their special value in God's eyes. In reality, the original inhabitants of the land were punished for their own sins. Furthermore, Israel's misunderstanding led them to suffer the same fate of destruction as divine punishment for their disobedience. Only "the fear of the Lord," which translates into bearing the fruits expected by him, would have spared Israel. That is why the Gentiles are to "fear" God (v.20), lest he not spare them (v.21). They are to remain faithful to his kindness (v.22) by obeying his commandments, since "neither circumcision counts for anything *nor uncircumcision*, but *keeping the commandments of God*" (1 Cor 7:19). Whenever the broken off branches are ready to cease their mistrust in the gospel, then they will be grafted in again. God is able (*dynatos*) to do this (Rom 11:23), just as he was able (*dynatos*) to keep his promise to Abraham (4:21). In fact, it will be comparatively easier for him to accomplish this task than it is for him to graft in the Gentiles! The reason is that grafting wild olive branches is *para physin* (contrary to nature, in a way different than the habitual manner, in an unorthodox manner; v.24). Usually one grafts a shoot from a good (cultivated) olive tree into a wild one in order to cultivate the latter. In doing otherwise, God has risked "infecting" his olive tree with the wild olive shoots. But all is well so long as the original branches and the grafted ones remember that they are "partakers of the root." It is insofar they all remember they are Abraham's children and act accordingly (4:11-12) that they will be safe.

Vv. 25-36 [25] *Οὐ γὰρ θέλω ὑμᾶς ἀγνοεῖν, ἀδελφοί, τὸ μυστήριον τοῦτο, ἵνα μὴ ἦτε [παρ᾽] ἑαυτοῖς φρόνιμοι, ὅτι πώρωσις ἀπὸ μέρους τῷ Ἰσραὴλ γέγονεν ἄχρι οὗ τὸ πλήρωμα*

τῶν ἐθνῶν εἰσέλθῃ ²⁶ καὶ οὕτως πᾶς Ἰσραὴλ σωθήσεται,
καθὼς γέγραπται· ἥξει ἐκ Σιὼν ὁ ῥυόμενος, ἀποστρέψει
ἀσεβείας ἀπὸ Ἰακώβ. ²⁷ καὶ αὕτη αὐτοῖς ἡ παρ᾽ ἐμοῦ
διαθήκη, ὅταν ἀφέλωμαι τὰς ἁμαρτίας αὐτῶν. ²⁸ κατὰ μὲν τὸ
εὐαγγέλιον ἐχθροὶ δι᾽ ὑμᾶς, κατὰ δὲ τὴν ἐκλογὴν ἀγαπητοὶ
διὰ τοὺς πατέρας· ²⁹ ἀμεταμέλητα γὰρ τὰ χαρίσματα καὶ ἡ
κλῆσις τοῦ θεοῦ. ³⁰ ὥσπερ γὰρ ὑμεῖς ποτε ἠπειθήσατε τῷ
θεῷ, νῦν δὲ ἠλεήθητε τῇ τούτων ἀπειθείᾳ, ³¹ οὕτως καὶ οὗτοι νῦν ἠπείθησαν τῷ ὑμετέρῳ ἐλέει, ἵνα καὶ αὐτοὶ [νῦν]
ἐλεηθῶσιν. ³² συνέκλεισεν γὰρ ὁ θεὸς τοὺς πάντας εἰς
ἀπείθειαν, ἵνα τοὺς πάντας ἐλεήσῃ. ³³ Ὦ βάθος πλούτου καὶ
σοφίας καὶ γνώσεως θεοῦ· ὡς ἀνεξεραύνητα τὰ κρίματα
αὐτοῦ καὶ ἀνεξιχνίαστοι αἱ ὁδοὶ αὐτοῦ. ³⁴ τίς γὰρ ἔγνω νοῦν
κυρίου; ἢ τίς σύμβουλος αὐτοῦ ἐγένετο; ³⁵ ἢ τίς προέδωκεν
αὐτῷ, καὶ ἀνταποδοθήσεται αὐτῷ; ³⁶ ὅτι ἐξ αὐτοῦ καὶ δι᾽
αὐτοῦ καὶ εἰς αὐτὸν τὰ πάντα· αὐτῷ ἡ δόξα εἰς τοὺς αἰῶνας,
ἀμήν.

²⁵*Lest you be wise in your own conceits, I want you to
understand this mystery, brethren: a hardening has come upon
part of Israel, until the full number of the Gentiles come in,
²⁶and so all Israel will be saved; as it is written, "The Deliverer
will come from Zion, he will banish ungodliness from Jacob";
²⁷"and this will be my covenant with them when I take away
their sins." ²⁸As regards the gospel they are enemies of God, for
your sake; but as regards election they are beloved for the sake of
their forefathers. ²⁹For the gifts and the call of God are
irrevocable. ³⁰Just as you were once disobedient to God but now
have received mercy because of their disobedience, ³¹so they have
now been disobedient in order that by the mercy shown to you
they also may receive mercy. ³²For God has consigned all men to
disobedience, that he may have mercy upon all. ³³O the depth of
the riches and wisdom and knowledge of God! How
unsearchable are his judgments and how inscrutable his ways!
³⁴"For who has known the mind of the Lord, or who has been
his counselor?" ³⁵"Or who has given a gift to him that he might*

be repaid?" [36]*For from him and through him and to him are all
things. To him be glory for ever. Amen.*

At the start of the letter, speaking of his plan to bring the
message of the gospel to the patricians of Rome, Paul wrote: "*I
do not want you to be ignorant, brethren,* that I have often
intended to come to you, but thus far have been prevented, in
order that I may reap some harvest among you as well as among
the rest of the Gentiles." (1:13) Fearing that he might not be
able to pay them that intended visit (15:22-25), Paul expanded
on this gospel in writing. In so doing, he revealed to them God's
"mystery" from beginning to end. Having arrived at the end of
his exposition, he writes: "For *I do not want you to be ignorant,
brethren,* of this mystery ... that a hardening has come upon part
of Israel, until the fullness of the Gentiles comes in, and so all
Israel will be saved." (11:25-26a) God alone is in control of his
plan, including its timing and outcome, and no one is privy to
the knowledge of that plan except his plenipotentiary emissary:
"Surely the Lord God does nothing, without revealing his
(secret) counsel (*sod*) to his servants the prophets. The lion has
roared; who will not fear? The Lord God has spoken; who can
but prophesy? Proclaim to the strongholds in Assyria, and to the
strongholds in the land of Egypt, and say..." (Am 3:7-9a) False
prophets, on the other hand, are not part of the council of God:

> Thus says the Lord of hosts: "Do not listen to the words of the
> prophets who prophesy to you, filling you with vain hopes; they
> speak visions of their own minds, not from the mouth of the Lord.
> They say continually to those who despise the word of the Lord,
> 'It shall be well with you'; and to every one who stubbornly
> follows his own heart, they say, 'No evil shall come upon you.' For
> who among them has stood in the council (*sod*) of the Lord to
> perceive and to hear his word, or who has given heed to his word
> and listened? Behold, the storm of the Lord! Wrath has gone

forth, a whirling tempest; it will burst upon the head of the wicked. The anger of the Lord will not turn back until he has executed and accomplished the intents of his mind. In the latter days you will understand it clearly. I did not send the prophets, yet they ran; I did not speak to them, yet they prophesied. But if they had stood in my council (*sod*), then they would have proclaimed my words to my people, and they would have turned them from their evil way, and from the evil of their doings." (Jer 23:16-22)

It is clear that the emissary's mission is to reveal to his addressees God's counsel to which only the *true* members of the divine council are privy. This explains why Isaiah had to become one of those members before he could propose himself as a divine emissary:

And I said: "Woe is me! For I am lost; for I am a man of unclean lips, and I dwell in the midst of a people of unclean lips; for my eyes have seen the King, the Lord of hosts!" Then flew one of the seraphim to me, having in his hand a burning coal which he had taken with tongs from the altar. And he touched my mouth, and said: "Behold, this has touched your lips; your guilt is taken away, and your sin forgiven." And I heard the voice of the Lord saying, "Whom shall I send, and *who will go for us*?" Then I said, "*Here am I! Send me*." And he said, "Go, and say to this people…" (Is 6:5-9a)

It stands to reason then that Paul, the sole true apostle to the nations, would be the one to "reveal" God's divine plan (counsel) to the Roman Gentiles. Thus "mystery" is not to be understood as something mystifying as though a mystery remains inexplicable even after it is revealed. Rather, it is similar to a secret that is hidden from those who do not know about it until it is shared with them. Consequently, one is not to take the term "mystery" in Romans 11:25 as referring exclusively to the following verses, as is done more often than not. The mystery actually applies to the *entire* gospel that Paul has been explicating for the last eleven chapters. Further, his comments in Ephesians parallel this:

> For this reason I, Paul, a prisoner for Christ Jesus on behalf of you Gentiles—assuming that you have heard of the stewardship of God's grace that was given to me for you, how the mystery was made known to me by revelation, as I have written briefly. When you read this you can perceive my insight into the mystery of Christ, which was not made known to the sons of men in other generations as it has now been revealed to his holy apostles and prophets by the Spirit; that is, how the Gentiles are fellow heirs, members of the same body, and partakers of the promise in Christ Jesus through the gospel. Of this gospel I was made a minister according to the gift of God's grace which was given me by the working of his power. To me, though I am the very least of all the saints, this grace was given, to preach to the Gentiles the unsearchable riches of Christ, and to make all men see what is the plan of the mystery hidden for ages in God who created all things; that through the church the manifold wisdom of God might now be made known to the principalities and powers in the heavenly places. (3:1-10)

Consider also the following:

1. The phrase "I do not want you to be ignorant, brethren" forms an *inclusio* bracketing the entire exposition of the letter (Rom 1:13; 11:25).

2. The ironic request that his hearers not falsely consider themselves as wise (11:25)[8] is a fitting conclusion to what he expanded on in vv.17-24.

---

[8] See my comments below on this matter.

3. The terminology of "hardening" and "fullness" (*plērōma*) in v.25 harks back to vv.7 and 12.

4. The salvation of Israel (v.26) recalls the introduction of the letter (1:16).

5. The conclusion in Romans 11:28-32 recalls elements that were part of that total exposition.

6. If vv.25-27 contained secret information Paul intended to share only with the Romans, then he would not have shared this with the Ephesians and other Gentiles.

Unfortunately, relegating the "mystery" to the "end times" as is usually done, especially since the founding of the state of Israel in 1948, has created havoc in that many people did and continue to do what the Lord as well as the Apostle expressly forbade *to all* (Mk 13:32-37; 1 Thess 5:1-2), that is, trying to figure out not only the timetable of the end times, but also attempting to force that timetable on God, thus giving God "a helping hand!"

Paul, who already cautioned his hearers not to be conceited or arrogant (Rom 11:17-24), repeats that request in an ironic manner: "Do not assume yourselves as wise when you are wise only to yourselves (in your own eyes)." (v.25) Israel's hardening of mind and heart is partial (*apo merous*; v.25) as he already indicated in v.7. More importantly, it is functional in God's plan: it is to give enough time for Gentiles to accept the gospel and repent in order to ensure that "their fullness (as large a number as can be)[9] enter (go in)" (v.25). The crux to be figured out here is the "place" that the Gentiles would enter. The most

---

[9] See my comments earlier on *plērōma* (fullness) in Rom 11:12.

plausible answer is to be sought out in the immediate context. The scriptural text appealed to in vv.26b-27 in support of Paul's statement in vv.25-26a is "The Deliverer will come from Zion, he will banish ungodliness from Jacob; and this will be my covenant with them when I take away their sins." This is mainly from Isaiah 59:20-21, with an addition from Isaiah 27:9. It is then Zion, God's heavenly city, which is the intended place the Gentiles will enter. This fits perfectly the thesis of the latter part of Isaiah, foreseen in Isaiah 2:2-5, where the light of God's teaching in his law will shine forth to the Gentiles as well as to the exiled of Israel, both of whom will be attracted, through that teaching, to "the mountain of the house of the Lord" (2:2):

> For thus says the Lord: "To the eunuchs who keep my sabbaths, who choose the things that please me and hold fast my covenant, I will give in my house and within my walls a monument and a name better than sons and daughters; I will give them an everlasting name which shall not be cut off. And the foreigners who join themselves to the Lord, to minister to him, to love the name of the Lord, and to be his servants, every one who keeps the sabbath, and does not profane it, and holds fast my covenant— these I will bring to my holy mountain, and make them joyful in my house of prayer; their burnt offerings and their sacrifices will be accepted on my altar; for my house shall be called a house of prayer for all peoples. Thus says the Lord God, who gathers the outcasts of Israel, I will gather yet others to him besides those already gathered." (56:4-8)

Thus, according to Isaiah, the "fullness" of the Gentiles, together with "all Israel," will be saved (Rom 11:25-26).

Let us examine more closely the terminology of v.26. First of all, the phrase "all Israel" need not mean *all* the Jews, as very often it is taken to denote. In scripture the fullness of the number of those who are finally saved is always assumed. The classic passage regarding this is found in Ezekiel 20. Although his plan of salvation entails judgment (vv.33-37) followed by a purge (I will purge out the rebels from among you, and those who transgress against me; *I will bring them out of the land where they sojourn, but they shall not enter the land of Israel.* Then you will know that I am the Lord; v.38), yet those who will reach God's holy mountain where they will abide in safety are *all the house of Israel, all of it* (*in its entirety*):

> For on my holy mountain, the mountain height of Israel, says the Lord God, there all the house of Israel, all of it, shall serve me in the land; there I will accept them, and there I will require your contributions and the choicest of your gifts, with all your sacred offerings. As a pleasing odor I will accept you, when I bring you out from the peoples, and gather you out of the countries where you have been scattered; and I will manifest my holiness among you in the sight of the nations. And you shall know that I am the Lord, when I bring you into the land of Israel, the country which I swore to give to your fathers. (vv.40-42)

Consequently, "all" in "all Israel" in Romans 11:26 corresponds in meaning to the "fullness" of the Gentiles as well as to Israel's own "fullness" (v.12). Thus it refers to all those who would ultimately be saved by following in the footsteps of the very small number that had accepted the call of the gospel at the time of its writing.

Secondly, we have "and thus (instead of "then") will all Israel be saved." While "then" (*eita, epeita*) means simply "afterwards," "thus" (*houtōs*) connotes a chronological sequence and also implies a result, as in "consequently." This reflects the point Paul developed earlier: the repentance of a larger number of Jews will be the result of a "jealousy" triggered by the repentance of a large number of Gentiles.

Thirdly, in quoting Isaiah in Romans 11:26a-27, Paul appeals to Psalm 14:7 (LXX 13:7), changing the preposition *heneken* (on account of, for the sake of) before Zion into *ex* (from, out of):[10] "Who will give deliverance for Israel *out of* Zion? When the Lord restores the fortunes of his people, Jacob shall rejoice, Israel shall be glad." Such a change does not affect the meaning of the original in Isaiah since Zion is the abode of God which he upholds and where he invites his followers. In the particular context of Romans 11:25-28, Paul is referring to that point in time when a large number of Gentiles will have accepted the gospel call and will "have entered God's city." In order for Paul to keep them in check, as he has been trying to do, he reminds them that, at that point in time when *their* part of the story ends, God's story has not necessarily reached its end, since his promise to Abraham still stands.

Can one say more concerning Paul's double intention to rouse the jealousy of his colleagues in Jerusalem while keeping in check the arrogance of his addressees? One of the major reasons for the consistent misunderstanding, if not, manipulation, of scripture lies in our proclivity to project the scriptural story or argument into our world. Case in point are the perennial debates concerning the "factuality" of the scriptural exodus, the conquest of Canaan including the decimation of its inhabitants, and the

---

[10] Ps 14:7 has "O that deliverance for Israel would come *out of* (*ek*) Zion! When the Lord restores the fortunes of his people, Jacob shall rejoice, Israel shall be glad" whereas in Is 59:20 we hear "And he will come *on account* of (*heneken*) Zion as Redeemer, to those in Jacob who turn from transgression, says the Lord."

return from exile to the pre-exilic Jerusalem.[11] Ezekiel has taught us that his "stories" of Samaria and Jerusalem (chs.16 and 23) and even Israel (ch.20) are actually "parables" intended to prompt the hearers to action, namely, to repentance away from the sins of their progenitors.[12] This is the same teaching that is evident in the story of Israel in Psalm 78:

> A Maskil (wisdom teaching) of Asaph. Give ear, O my people, to my teaching; incline your ears to the words of my mouth! I will open my mouth in a parable; I will utter dark sayings from of old, things that we have heard and known, that our fathers have told us. We will not hide them from their children, but tell to the coming generation the glorious deeds of the Lord, and his might, and the wonders which he has wrought. He established a testimony in Jacob, and appointed a law in Israel, which he commanded our fathers to teach to their children; that the next generation might know them, the children yet unborn, and arise and tell them to their children, so that they should set their hope in God, and not forget the works of God, but keep his commandments; and that they should not be like their fathers, a stubborn and rebellious generation, a generation whose heart was not steadfast, whose spirit was not faithful to God. (vv.1-8)[13]

When one remains within the initial hearers' parameters, which are posited in the text of the letter itself, then one develops a more realistic understanding of what Paul is actually saying. He is definitely not describing the "end times." He is

---

[11] A similar classic case in the New Testament is the debate surrounding the "factuality" of Jesus' and Peter's walking on the water.

[12] Ezek 2:3; 20:18, 24, 27, 30, 36.

[13] What is further interesting and pertinent to our discussion in the case of this psalm is its ending: "He rejected the tent of Joseph, he did not choose the tribe of Ephraim; but *he chose* the tribe of Judah, *Mount Zion*, which he loves. *He built his sanctuary like the high heavens*, like the earth, which he has founded for ever." (vv.67-69)

teaching his addressees, through his letter to them, the "end goal" of God's plan: "But thanks be to God, that you who were once slaves of sin have become obedient from the heart to *the teaching* which was handed to you and of which you have a type in this letter (*eis hon paredothēte typon didakhēs*)." (Rom 6:17)[14] Given what he will say at the end of the letter *regarding the future beyond the end of the letter* (15:22-33), one has a better grasp of what Paul means by "fullness" and "all (the entirety of)." In this letter he is sharing, in writing, the gospel with the patricians of Rome, in case he will not be able to see them face to face. He is telling them that the entire eastern part of the empire has been evangelized, and thus the number of Gentiles who submitted to the gospel has grown. The "fullness" of the Gentiles will be attained when many residents of the western part of the empire are also evangelized. Through this letter and for this purpose, he is starting with Rome and Italy. This way he will not have to linger too long in Rome and will be able to proceed, as quickly as possible, to Spain, the westernmost region of the empire. Should the Roman addressees accept his message, then the number of the obedient Gentiles would swell and that, in turn, will put pressure on the Jerusalemite leaders whom he is planning to visit after having penned the letter; however, the response of those Jerusalemite leaders to the offering from the Gentiles he is bringing them (15:25-27) is uncertain. If their response proves to be negative, the Romans are not to be puffed up and assume that their acceptance of the gospel brings the number of required Gentiles to its "fullness" since those in Spain have yet to hear the gospel. Further, the "fullness" of Israel is required, and this will not be settled with Paul's visit to Jerusalem, and consequently not at the time of his projected visit to Rome. The Romans will

---

[14] See my comments on this verse.

have to *wait* for there is still hope for Israel to repent in larger numbers. Indeed, although the Jews have been proven to be God's enemies by their refusal of the gospel message, they are so *for your [the Romans'] sake* (*di' hymas*) (11:28a). However, in accordance with God's election that takes place through the forefathers, especially Abraham, they are God's beloved because of those forefathers (*dia tous pateras*) (v.28b). For God's gifts (*kharismata*; expression of his grace) and his call to all are irrevocable (unregrettable) (v.29). Otherwise, hope, even that of the Romans, will be in vain.

As I indicated in discussing 9:13-15, God allowed matters to go the way of humans in order that all, Gentiles as well as Jews, comprehend that, ultimately, God controls our world and our destiny through *his mercy toward all.* Further, no one is entitled to that mercy since "all men, both Jews and Greeks, are under the power of sin" (3:9) and thus are condemnable:

> Just as you were once disobedient (*ēpeithēsate*) to God but now have received mercy because of their disobedience (*apeitheia*), so they have now been disobedient (*ēpeithēsan*) in order that by the mercy shown to you they also may receive mercy. For God has consigned all (both Jews and Gentiles)[15] to disobedience (*apeitheian*), that he may have mercy upon all. (11:30-32)

Both Gentiles and Jews are guilty of disobedience (*apeitheia*; mistrust): the former to the truth of God (2:8), and the latter to (the truth of) the gospel, thus becoming enemies of God (11:28) just as the Gentiles were.

At this point, Paul has no further recourse except to laud God for his judgments beyond reproach—for he is by definition the

---

[15] See my comments in *Gal* 156-9.

judge (3:5-6)—and, more importantly, for the inscrutable ways in which he goes about exercising his prerogative for our own good (11:33-36).

Chapter 12

Vv. 1-8 ¹ Παρακαλῶ οὖν ὑμᾶς, ἀδελφοί, διὰ τῶν οἰκτιρμῶν τοῦ θεοῦ παραστῆσαι τὰ σώματα ὑμῶν θυσίαν ζῶσαν ἁγίαν εὐάρεστον τῷ θεῷ, τὴν λογικὴν λατρείαν ὑμῶν· ² καὶ μὴ συσχηματίζεσθε τῷ αἰῶνι τούτῳ, ἀλλὰ μεταμορφοῦσθε τῇ ἀνακαινώσει τοῦ νοὸς εἰς τὸ δοκιμάζειν ὑμᾶς τί τὸ θέλημα τοῦ θεοῦ, τὸ ἀγαθὸν καὶ εὐάρεστον καὶ τέλειον. ³ Λέγω γὰρ διὰ τῆς χάριτος τῆς δοθείσης μοι παντὶ τῷ ὄντι ἐν ὑμῖν μὴ ὑπερφρονεῖν παρ᾽ ὃ δεῖ φρονεῖν ἀλλὰ φρονεῖν εἰς τὸ σωφρονεῖν, ἑκάστῳ ὡς ὁ θεὸς ἐμέρισεν μέτρον πίστεως. ⁴ καθάπερ γὰρ ἐν ἑνὶ σώματι πολλὰ μέλη ἔχομεν, τὰ δὲ μέλη πάντα οὐ τὴν αὐτὴν ἔχει πρᾶξιν, ⁵ οὕτως οἱ πολλοὶ ἓν σῶμά ἐσμεν ἐν Χριστῷ, τὸ δὲ καθ᾽ εἷς ἀλλήλων μέλη. ⁶ ἔχοντες δὲ χαρίσματα κατὰ τὴν χάριν τὴν δοθεῖσαν ἡμῖν διάφορα, εἴτε προφητείαν κατὰ τὴν ἀναλογίαν τῆς πίστεως, ⁷ εἴτε διακονίαν ἐν τῇ διακονίᾳ, εἴτε ὁ διδάσκων ἐν τῇ διδασκαλίᾳ, ⁸ εἴτε ὁ παρακαλῶν ἐν τῇ παρακλήσει· ὁ μεταδιδοὺς ἐν ἁπλότητι, ὁ προϊστάμενος ἐν σπουδῇ, ὁ ἐλεῶν ἐν ἱλαρότητι.

¹I appeal to you therefore, brethren, by the mercies of God, to present your bodies as a living sacrifice, holy and acceptable to God, which is your spiritual worship. ²Do not be conformed to this world but be transformed by the renewal of your mind, that you may prove what is the will of God, what is good and acceptable and perfect. ³For by the grace given to me I bid every one among you not to think of himself more highly than he ought to think, but to think with sober judgment, each according to the measure of faith which God has assigned him. ⁴For as in one body we have many members, and all the members do not have the same function, ⁵so we, though many, are one body in Christ, and individually members one of another. ⁶Having gifts that differ according to the grace given to us, let us use them: if prophecy, in proportion to our faith; ⁷if

*service, in our serving; he who teaches, in his teaching; ⁸he who
exhorts, in his exhortation; he who contributes, in liberality; he
who gives aid, with zeal; he who does acts of mercy, with
cheerfulness.*

Having steered the Romans away from unwarranted
arrogance that would ultimately bring them under God's
condemnation as it did the scriptural Israel, Paul embarks on a
lengthy series of requests concerning the new life they are
supposed to lead, come what may, in order for them to "enter"
the new Zion. Romans 12:1-15:6 is a detailed coverage of the
rules of their new household (Rom 6) issued by Paul, the
household chief steward (*oikonomos*). He begins with God's
mercy, a long argument he discussed in chapters 9-11. The two
terms *eleos* (11:31) and *oiktirmoi* (12:1) are related and connote
the feeling of mercy and compassion.[1] The merciful God is,
nevertheless, the judge, and the Romans understand this reality
all too well: their emperor is their judge and *that is why* they look
for his mercy. One day they will have to stand before God as
their judge; indeed "we shall all stand (*parastēsai*; appear) before
the judgment seat of God" (14:10). Here in 12:1 is the only
other occurrence of the verb *parastēsai* in Romans,[2] and the
context is one of standing before the divine judgment since the
Romans are asked to "prove what is the will of God, what is
good and acceptable and perfect (in his eyes)" (12:2b). What
they are to offer is themselves "as a living sacrifice, holy and

[1] Often in the Old Testament *oiktirmōn* (merciful; Hebrew *raḥum*) and *eleēmōn*
(gracious; Hebrew *ḥannun*) are coupled: Ex 34:6; Neh 9:17; Ps 86:15 (85:15 LXX);
102:8 (103:8 LXX); 110:4 (111:4 LXX); 112:4 (111:4 LXX); 145:8 (144:8 LXX); Joel
2:13; Jonah 4:2.
[2] In this case, it is transitive since it is followed by the object complement "your
bodies." The result is, nevertheless, the same since the "body" in scripture represents
the actual living being.

acceptable to God" (v.1).[3] "Living sacrifice" is a contradiction in terms, especially if it is heard in the original Hebrew where the meaning would be "living slaughtered animal." This would make sense only in the setting of temple terminology where the animal about to be slaughtered is referred to as a "sacrifice." This rejoins the scriptural quotation Paul referred to earlier in conjunction with a court setting, just as we have here: "For thy sake we are being killed all the day long; we are regarded as sheep to be slaughtered." (8:36) Here again, to be killed *all day long* is a factual impossibility unless one takes it in a metaphorical sense, just as one must take Luke's "If any man would come after me, let him deny himself and take up his cross *daily* and follow me" (Lk 9:23). Yet, Paul provides the solution to this apparent impasse in the appositional phrase to "living sacrifice": "(which is) your *logic-al* (verbal) worship (*tēn logikēn latreian*)." I purposely kept the original in the transliteration to avoid *eisegeting* (reading into the text) as witnessed in the different translations: "reasonable worship" (KJV); "spiritual worship" (RSV); "intelligent worship" (Phillips); "worship offered by mind and heart" (NEB); "spiritual act of worship" (NIV).

The Greek adjective *logikēn* is from the noun *logos* (word [of teaching]) which is another term for the gospel in Paul's letters. In discussing Romans 1:8-9, I mentioned that, *as apostle to the Gentiles*, Paul viewed himself as their high priest. He clearly states this in 15:15-16: "But on some points I have written to you very boldly by way of reminder, because of the grace given me by God to be a minister (*leitourgos*; liturg; someone performing a liturgical [priestly] act) of Christ Jesus to the Gentiles in the priestly service of the gospel (*hierourgounta ton*

---

[3] The parallelism between the two requirements is evident in that both use the adjective "acceptable" (*evareston*; pleasing, according to God's pleasure).

evangelion; hierourgizing the gospel; handling the gospel as a priest would) of God, so that the offering (*prosphora*; temple offering) of the Gentiles may be acceptable (*evprosdektos*), sanctified (*hēgiasmenē*) by the Holy Spirit."[4] One can imagine the practical impossibility of translating v.16 since the Greek terminology is technical. Suffice it to say that the thread that holds together the entire picture is the temple worship background. However, Paul was not a priest serving in the Jerusalem temple, let alone in pagan temples. His combining gospel terminology with temple worship phraseology reflects the fact that he perceived his apostolic "verbal" (*logikēn*) ministry as a high priestly one. Consequently, here in 12:1, he is requesting that the Romans join him in that same kind of service, however, he as the apostle, as will be confirmed in v.3 (For by the grace given to me I say to every one among you), and they as the disciples implementing his teaching. In other words, Paul is asking the Romans to live the life he is about to detail to them in the following chapters. His letter to them, after all, is the gospel he is teaching them.

This new kind of life is unlike the one they have been living. *As Romans*, they are bound to the will of the emperor to do what is pleasing to him. However, *as Paul's disciples*, they are to "prove what is the will of God, what is good and acceptable and perfect" in God's eyes (v.2). Becoming disciples requires that they cease to conform (*syskhēmatizesthe*) to this world, the world ruled by the emperor, and that their view of matters be *transformed* (transshaped; *metamorphousthe*) through the renewing of their mind (v.2).[5] This renewal is to take place "day in day out" (2 Cor

---

[4] Notice the terminological closeness between the two texts: "acceptable" (12:1; 15:16); "the grace given me" (12:3; 15:15).

[5] *skhēma* and *morphē* bear the same connotation as I discussed in my commentary on Philippians; see *C-Phil* 116-7. The parallelism in meaning between *skhēma* and *morphē*

4:16). Such transformation takes place by following the commandments of God inscribed in his law. For how would one know what the will of God is all about unless one is "instructed (catechized) in the law" (Rom 2:18) which is "the embodiment (*morphōsin*; shaping) of the knowledge and the truth (of God)" (v.20). Indeed, "neither circumcision counts for anything nor uncircumcision, but keeping the commandments of God" (1 Cor 7:19). To be conformed to the will of a non-iconic God cannot be done except through obedience to his teaching, since he cannot be seen and thus communicated with. Philippians expands on this topic by requesting that the Philippians, mainly Roman soldiers, become "citizens" of God's kingdom. In order for them to do so requires that they behave in a way worthy of such citizenry while "awaiting from heaven a Savior, the Lord Jesus Christ, who will transform (*metaskhēmatisei*) our lowly body to have a similar form as (*symmorphon*) his glorious body, by the power which enables him even to subject all things to himself" (Phil 3:20-21). However, earlier in the letter, the Philippians were told that the same Christ Jesus "though he was in the form (*morphē*) of God, did not count equality with God a thing to be grasped, but emptied himself, taking the form (*morphēn*) of a servant, being born in the likeness of men. And being found in human form (*skhēmati*) he humbled himself and became *obedient* unto death, even death on a cross" (2:6-8). And Paul has just asked to "have this mind among yourselves, which is yours in Christ Jesus" (v.5). All the aforementioned boils down to behaving as obedient slaves of God, and not of the emperor,

---

is further evidenced in the switch of the prepositions *sys*— and *meta*— before them in the two letters: "Do not be conformed (*syskhēmatizesthe*) to this world but be transformed (*metamorphousthe*) by the renewal of your mind" (Rom 12:2); "[the Lord Jesus Christ] who will change (*metaskhēmatisei*) our lowly body to be like (*symmorphon*) his glorious body, by the power which enables him even to subject all things to himself." (Phil 3:21)

which is precisely what Paul asked for earlier in Romans 6 after having spoken of Jesus as having done this in chapter 5.

A look at the only other place where the adjective *logic-al* (verbal) occurs in the New Testament will confirm our findings:

> So put away all malice and all guile and insincerity and envy and all slander. Like newborn babes, long for the pure *logic-al* (*logikon*) milk, that by it you may grow up to salvation; for you have tasted the kindness of the Lord. Come to him, to that living stone, rejected by men but in God's sight chosen and precious; and like living stones be yourselves built into a spiritual house, to be a holy *priesthood*, to offer spiritual *sacrifices acceptable* to God through Jesus Christ. For it stands in scripture: "Behold, I am laying in Zion a stone, a cornerstone chosen and precious, and he who believes in him will not be put to shame."[6] To you therefore who believe, he is precious, but for those who do not believe, "The very stone which the builders rejected has become the head of the corner," and "A stone that will make men stumble, a rock that will make them fall"; for they stumble because *they disobey (mistrust) the word* (*tō logō apeithountes*), as they were destined to do. (1 Pet 2:1-8)

The correspondence between 1 Peter and Romans is evident. Not only is the terminology of 1 Peter 2:1-8 close to the one extant in Romans, but we have the same quotation from Isaiah 28:16 found elsewhere in the New Testament only in Romans 9:33. As important is that the meaning of *logikon* (*logic-al*) in 1 Peter 2:2 is corroborated as being "conform to the (gospel) word (*logos*)" (v.8). Of note also is the use in v.8 of the root *apeith*— (disobedience, mistrust) with the gospel as was the case in Romans 11:28-31: "As regards the *gospel* they are enemies of God, for your sake … but now [you] have received mercy

---

[6] Is 28:16.

because of their disobedience (*apeitheia*), so they have now been disobedient (*ēpeithēsan*)…"

Having succinctly reminded his addressees that they are standing before God and not Caesar (Rom 12:1-2), Paul speaks as God's *oikonomos* (1 Cor 4:1-2; 9:17) and begins delivering to them the "word" (Rom 12:3-15:7) through which he invites them to lead a life worthy of that word. The "I say" (*legō*; from the same root as *logos*) with which he starts (v.3) that lengthy admonition is clearly apostolic since it is followed by "the grace given to me." This apostolic "I say" holds together the following three chapters. The next instance of "I say" is not until 15:8. What is still more impressive is that the Greek *legō* is from the same root as the noun *logos* (word); thus Paul's *logic-al* (verbal; word-y) instructions call for a *logic-al* response on the part of his hearers.

Continuing his message of Romans 9-11, Paul starts here by attacking the potentially deadly arrogance: "For by the grace given to me I say to every one among you not to think of himself more highly (*hyperphronein*) than he ought to think (*phronein*), but to think (*phronein*) in a way that produces sobriety (*eis to sōphronein*), each according to the measure of faith which God has assigned him." (12:3)[7] Then he appeals to the metaphor of the one body and its many members, which he uses extensively in 1 Corinthians 12 and on which he builds his teaching concerning the differing gifts in consort for the one cause. All these gifts (*kharismata*) are expressions or reflections of the same grace (*kharis*) that was granted to the Romans (Rom 12:6) as well as to Paul (v.3). Since Paul singled himself in v.3, he omits the mention of apostleship among the gifts and begins with

---

[7] The wordplay in the original is impressive.

prophecy: "Having gifts that differ according to the grace given to us, let us use them: if prophecy, in analogy with the faith (*kata tēn analogian tēs pisteōs*)." (v.6) Here again, we have a similar case to v.1 whereby this last phrase is translated differently: "whether prophecy, *let us prophesy* according to the proportion of faith" (KJV); "if prophecy, in proportion to our faith" (RSV); "If our gift is preaching, let us preach to the limit of our vision" (Phillips); "the gift of inspired utterance, for example, in proportion to a man's faith" (NEB); "If a man's gift is prophesying, let him use it in proportion to his faith" (NIV). Hence I kept my translation as close as possible to the original. To add the possessive adjective "his" is misleading since it makes of the prophet an individual preacher not bound by anything except "his vision or view." In my comments on Galatians 1:23 and 3:2, I argued extensively to show that "the faith" refers to the gospel, given that its message requires a trusting response.[8] So, as is the case in 1 Corinthians 12 and 14, the church prophet is to keep the apostolic word alive and well. Consequently, "analogy" can only mean "in accordance with, corresponding to" and not "in proportion." By assuming that "the faith" refers to the prophet's personal (level of) faith and not the gospel, all adduced translations understandably opt for "proportion" or "limit" to render "analogy." Actually, I am convinced that Paul's choice of the rare term "analogy" has to do with its being from the same root as *logos*. Thus, in our case, *analogia* is tantamount to "using the terminology (vocabulary) of." In Greek the preposition *ana* (upward) functions similarly to *kata* (downward) when it is part of a noun or verb; they both express the fullness of an action, as in analysis and catalysis, for instance. Thus, *analogia* (ana-logy) would be a verbal process using the *katalogos*

---

[8] *Gal* 54-55 and 100-1.

(cata-logue),[9] that to say, the thesaurus, of the gospel. My reading is corroborated by Paul's use of the preposition *kata* (according to) only before "the analogy of the faith," whereas he uses the preposition *en* (in) in all other instances of the differing gifts. Thus, he intended to single out the importance of the gift of prophecy, just as he does in 1 Corinthians 14. One can find further corroboration in how the only other instance of the root *analog*— in the New Testament functions: "Consider (*analogisasthe*) him who endured from sinners such hostility (*antilogian*; adverse stance) against himself, so that you may not grow weary or fainthearted." (Heb 12:3) Here the opposing attitude is referred to as *anti-logy*, a stance using an incompatible vocabulary and thus a conflicting manner of thinking. Consequently, the addressees are invited to behave *analogically*, not *anti-logically*, to Christ.

In 1 Corinthians the gift that has the place of honor after prophecy is teaching. However, here in Romans, mention is made of service or ministry (*diakonia*) immediately after prophecy and before teaching. The reason is that *diakonia* controls the remainder of the letter. Paul already viewed his apostolic mission as a *diakonia* (11:13), confirming that Paul's primary concern is the behavior of his addressees. He is not interested in teaching them "theology."[10] In chapter 13, even the emperor, who is granted full authority (*exousia*) from God himself (vv.1-3), is nevertheless to function as a minister (*diakonos*; servant) of that same God (v.4). Although in chapter 14 nouns and verbs from the root *diakon*— are not to be found, the entire chapter deals with table fellowship which is the

---

[9] Both terms are from the same root *log*— as *logos*.

[10] One of the major calamities that crept into the church tradition, under the influence of the erudite among those who endorsed the Christian faith, was using the Pauline letters as though they were a source of information about God.

diakonia par excellence, since the *diakonos* is, by definition, the house slave assigned to the service of tables. In 15:8, even Christ is presented as a *diakonos*. The mission of Paul to Jerusalem, on which the smoothness of his apostolic endeavor to the western parts of the empire hinges, is cast in terms of *diakonia* (vv.25, 31). Finally, at the top of the list of those whose greetings Paul is transmitting to the Romans, is Phoebe, "a *diakonos*[11] of the church at Cenchreae" (16:1).

The phraseology with which *diakonia* is presented intends to make out of it a bridge between prophecy that precedes it and the series of other gifts that follow it. On the one hand, only *diakonia* and prophecy are mentioned as nouns referring to the function itself (prophecy; service/ministry [*diakonia*]). The rest of the gifts are introduced in the form of the present participle of the verb, thus referring to the person dispensing that gift (the one who teaches; the one who exhorts; etc.). On the other hand, whereas the mention of prophecy is followed by the preposition "according," *diakonia* stands together with the other gifts in that they are followed by the preposition "in." Thus, *diakonia* connects prophecy with the rest of the gifts. As in 1 Corinthians, with the exception of apostleship, prophecy holds the highest honor. However, since Paul the Apostle is himself—let alone any church prophet—a *diakonos* (Rom 11:13; 15:25, 31) then the functions of the other five church leaders (or kinds of leadership), by the same token, are subsumed under the aegis of *diakonia*, that is to say, they are to dispense their duties as though they were the lesser. In case his addressees are uneasy

---

[11] In Greek the noun *diakonos* is a generic term for table servants in the same manner as the noun "servant" in English. When preceded by the masculine definite article *ho* it denotes a male servant; when it is introduced with the feminine definite article *hē*, then it refers to a female servant. The article functions in a similar manner as the "he" and "she" in our "he-servant" and "she-servant."

about this, Paul is reserving a surprise for them when, a few verses later, he will be referring to the emperor himself as *diakonos* and no less than twice in the same verse (13:4)!

The first two activities are teaching and exhortation. They go hand in hand with the ministry of the "word," as is evident from 1 Corinthians. The teachers are third in line after the apostles and the prophets (12:8), and all three dispense their duties using intelligible words. Exhortation (*paraklēsis*) pertains to the domain of prophecy: "On the other hand, he who prophesies speaks to men for their upbuilding and exhortation (*paraklēsin*; encouragement) and consolation." (14:3) Furthermore, functionally, it is linked to learning, and thus teaching: "For you can all prophesy one by one, so that all may *learn* and all be exhorted (*parakalōntai*; encouraged)." (v.31)

The last three activities are not necessarily expressed through words of exhortation or teaching. Consequently, instead of mentioning the area of activity with the preposition *en* (in) followed by the definite article, as in the case of *diakonia*, teaching, and exhortation (if *diakonia*, in (*en*) the *diakonia*; he who teaches, in (*en*) *the* teaching; he who exhorts, in (*en*) *the* exhortation; Rom 12:7-8a), we have the same preposition *en* (in) introducing an attitude and thus without the definite article. In this case, the preposition *en* is instrumental, which explains its possible translation into "with": "he who shares, with (in) simplicity; he who leads, with (in) assiduity; he who does acts of mercy, with (in) cheerfulness." (my translation; v.8b) The first and the third attitudes (simplicity and cheerfulness) reflect a total absence of arrogance on the part of the one who helps someone else in need. The second quality (*spoudē*; assiduity) is usually associated with the position of an inferior serving a superior; in this particular case, it is required from someone in a position of leadership. Thus the general picture in vv.6-8 is one of pressure on the seniors to behave in a spirit of humility in spite of their higher position.

Vv. 9-21 ⁹ Ἡ ἀγάπη ἀνυπόκριτος. ἀποστυγοῦντες τὸ πονηρόν, κολλώμενοι τῷ ἀγαθῷ, ¹⁰ τῇ φιλαδελφίᾳ εἰς ἀλλήλους φιλόστοργοι, τῇ τιμῇ ἀλλήλους προηγούμενοι, ¹¹ τῇ σπουδῇ μὴ ὀκνηροί, τῷ πνεύματι ζέοντες, τῷ κυρίῳ δουλεύοντες, ¹² τῇ ἐλπίδι χαίροντες, τῇ θλίψει ὑπομένοντες, τῇ προσευχῇ προσκαρτεροῦντες, ¹³ ταῖς χρείαις τῶν ἁγίων κοινωνοῦντες, τὴν φιλοξενίαν διώκοντες. ¹⁴ εὐλογεῖτε τοὺς διώκοντας [ὑμᾶς], εὐλογεῖτε καὶ μὴ καταρᾶσθε. ¹⁵ χαίρειν μετὰ χαιρόντων, κλαίειν μετὰ κλαιόντων. ¹⁶ τὸ αὐτὸ εἰς ἀλλήλους φρονοῦντες, μὴ τὰ ὑψηλὰ φρονοῦντες ἀλλὰ τοῖς ταπεινοῖς συναπαγόμενοι. μὴ γίνεσθε φρόνιμοι παρ᾽ ἑαυτοῖς. ¹⁷ μηδενὶ κακὸν ἀντὶ κακοῦ ἀποδιδόντες, προνοούμενοι καλὰ ἐνώπιον πάντων ἀνθρώπων· ¹⁸ εἰ δυνατὸν τὸ ἐξ ὑμῶν, μετὰ πάντων ἀνθρώπων εἰρηνεύοντες· ¹⁹ μὴ ἑαυτοὺς ἐκδικοῦντες, ἀγαπητοί, ἀλλὰ δότε τόπον τῇ ὀργῇ, γέγραπται γάρ· ἐμοὶ ἐκδίκησις, ἐγὼ ἀνταποδώσω, λέγει κύριος. ²⁰ ἀλλὰ ἐὰν πεινᾷ ὁ ἐχθρός σου, ψώμιζε αὐτόν· ἐὰν διψᾷ, πότιζε αὐτόν· τοῦτο γὰρ ποιῶν ἄνθρακας πυρὸς σωρεύσεις ἐπὶ τὴν κεφαλὴν αὐτοῦ. ²¹ μὴ νικῶ ὑπὸ τοῦ κακοῦ ἀλλὰ νίκα ἐν τῷ ἀγαθῷ τὸ κακόν.

⁹*Let love be genuine; hate what is evil, hold fast to what is good;* ¹⁰*love one another with brotherly affection; outdo one another in showing honor.* ¹¹*Never flag in zeal, be aglow with the Spirit, serve the Lord.* ¹²*Rejoice in your hope, be patient in tribulation, be constant in prayer.* ¹³*Contribute to the needs of the saints, practice hospitality.* ¹⁴*Bless those who persecute you; bless and do not curse them.* ¹⁵*Rejoice with those who rejoice, weep with those who weep.* ¹⁶*Live in harmony with one another; do not be haughty, but associate with the lowly; never be conceited.* ¹⁷*Repay no one evil for evil, but take thought for what is noble in the sight of all.* ¹⁸*If possible, so far as it depends upon you, live*

peaceably with all. ¹⁹Beloved, never avenge yourselves, but leave it to the wrath of God; for it is written, "Vengeance is mine, I will repay, says the Lord." ²⁰No, "if your enemy is hungry, feed him; if he is thirsty, give him drink; for by so doing you will heap burning coals upon his head." ²¹Do not be overcome by evil, but overcome evil with good.

In 1 Corinthians, after mentioning the gifts related to positions of leadership (ch.12), Paul points out the path of love which is common to and required from all (ch.13). He does so again in Romans. Love is to be unfeigned (*anypokritos*; non-hypocritical; genuine): it is to be expressed through doing good and avoiding evil (Rom 12:9), since love is not an inner feeling, but rather an attitude toward the others, *philadelphia*, love *toward* our fellow human (v.10a). And such attitude is rooted in our honoring and respecting (*timē*) the other (v.10b). The following three items ("Never flag in zeal [*spoude*; assiduity], be aglow with the Spirit, serve the Lord" v.11) are interconnected in that the assiduity is that of a slave in the service of his lord. Given that the believers have become members of God's household, their behavior is kindled by his spirit through whom they have been included in that household (8:15-17) since "all who are led by the Spirit of God are sons of God" (v.14). Still, this new life is on hope (8:24) which requires patience (v.25), in spite of tribulation (12:12ab). Actually, tribulation is an integral part of the life on hope (5:2-4), and what sustains the believers on that path is holding fast to the common prayer gathering (12:12c).[12] Yet this brotherly love

---

[12] The "prayer" (*prosevkhē*) here denotes the common gathering rather than the individual prayer as is evident from the other occurrences of the parallel phrase (*tē prosevkhē proskarterountes*) in the Book of Acts: Acts 1:14 (All these with one accord *devoted* themselves to *prayer*, together with the women and Mary the mother of Jesus, and with his brothers); 2:42 (And they *devoted* themselves to the apostles' teaching and fellowship, to the breaking of bread and *the prayers*); 2:46 (And day by day, *persevering*

and concern is not to be restricted to the members of their immediate community, but it should include the Jews of Judea (12:13a)[13] and even the strangers (v.13b).[14] "Pursuing (*diōkontes*) the care for strangers" forms the bridge with the following verse where Paul requires the maximum: to bless those who pursue (*tous diōkontas*) and thus persecute us, since our call is to bless and not to curse (v.14). The reason, as Paul explains in v. 19, is that only the judge of all has the right to avenge. We are to share with others their pain as well as their joy (v.15). To be able to do so, Paul reminds his hearers, as he did in 11:25, requires that they not be conceited (12:16). Instead of gazing and yearning upwards, they are to associate with the lowly.

In all the preceding Paul's aim is to curb the arrogance of the patricians of Rome, the incontrovertible masters of the Roman empire. However, the proverbial "death blow" against them is in 12:17-21 where he turns the tables against the pride of Rome, the *pax Romana*, the internal peace within the boundaries of the Roman empire, which was realized through forceful subjugation of opponents within and enemies without by the "Roman sword" referred to obliquely in 8:35. If love is to be truly genuine and unfeigned, then one is to be good at all cost and not repay evil with evil, but "having always in mind good things

---

in the temple together and breaking bread in their homes, they partook of food with glad and generous hearts); 6:2-4 (And the twelve summoned the body of the disciples and said, "It is not right that we should give up preaching the word of God to serve tables. Therefore, brethren, pick out from among you seven men of good repute, full of the Spirit and of wisdom, whom we may appoint to this duty. But we will *devote ourselves to prayer* and to the ministry of the word.")

[13] This seems to be the meaning of "saints" here in view of the parallel phraseology between Rom 12:13a (Contribute [*koinōnountes*] to the needs of the saints) and 15:26 (For Macedonia and Achaia have been pleased to make some contribution [*koinōnian*] for the poor among the saints at Jerusalem). See also 2 Cor 8:1-4.

[14] The Greek *philoxenia* means "love, care for strangers."

openly, in the sight of all men" (12:17). If at all possible, *yet definitely on our part*, we are to live peaceably with all men (v.18), without ever allowing the possibility for ire or revenge (v.19a). And since such behavior is quite against the grain in a society built on law, on the one hand, and on might, on the other hand, Paul appeals to God's law in scripture: "'Vengeance is mine, I will repay (*antapodōsō*),'[15] says the Lord." (Rom 12:19b). As to the behavior required, the quotation is taken from Proverbs 25:21-22a: "If your enemy is hungry, feed him; if he is thirsty, give him drink; for by so doing you will heap burning coals upon his head." (Rom 12:20). The connection between these two quotations hinges on the verb "repay" (*antapodidōmi*) which occurs at the end of the quotation from Proverbs "and the Lord will repay (*antapodōsei*) you with good things (*agatha*)" (25:22b). The "good things" allow Paul to end on the same note with which he started the passage: "Let love be genuine; hate what is evil, hold fast to what is good (*tō agathō*)" (12:9); "Do not be overcome (*nikō*) by evil, but overcome (*nika*) evil with good (*tō agathō*)." (v.21)

Reading Romans 12:17-21 as being anti-imperial is borne out by the use of the verb *nikaō* (prevail; overcome; be victorious) which occurs in Romans here, in 8:37, and in the quotation from Psalms in Romans 3:4 (That thou mayest be justified in thy words, and prevail [*nikēseis*; be victorious] when thou judgest). "We shall be more than conquerors (*hypernikōmen*; super-victorious) through him who loved us" (8:37) clearly has an anti-Roman empire connotation, and given that their super-victory lay in God as universal judge (vv.31-33), the hearers could not fail to make the connection with 3:4 where God is "victorious" as universal judge (vv.5-6). If this is so, then the

---

[15] Deut 32:35.

believers are to behave after the manner of his love for us while
we were still sinners and his enemies (5:1-11). Thus while
awaiting *his* judgment (12:19), we are to treat our enemies and
persecutors with the same kind of love (v.14).

Chapter 13

Vv. 1-7 ¹ *Πᾶσα ψυχὴ ἐξουσίαις ὑπερεχούσαις ὑποτασσέσθω. οὐ γὰρ ἔστιν ἐξουσία εἰ μὴ ὑπὸ θεοῦ, αἱ δὲ οὖσαι ὑπὸ θεοῦ τεταγμέναι εἰσίν.* ² *ὥστε ὁ ἀντιτασσόμενος τῇ ἐξουσίᾳ τῇ τοῦ θεοῦ διαταγῇ ἀνθέστηκεν, οἱ δὲ ἀνθεστηκότες ἑαυτοῖς κρίμα λήμψονται.* ³ *οἱ γὰρ ἄρχοντες οὐκ εἰσὶν φόβος τῷ ἀγαθῷ ἔργῳ ἀλλὰ τῷ κακῷ. θέλεις δὲ μὴ φοβεῖσθαι τὴν ἐξουσίαν· τὸ ἀγαθὸν ποίει, καὶ ἕξεις ἔπαινον ἐξ αὐτῆς·* ⁴ *θεοῦ γὰρ διάκονός ἐστιν σοὶ εἰς τὸ ἀγαθόν. ἐὰν δὲ τὸ κακὸν ποιῇς, φοβοῦ· οὐ γὰρ εἰκῇ τὴν μάχαιραν φορεῖ· θεοῦ γὰρ διάκονός ἐστιν ἔκδικος εἰς ὀργὴν τῷ τὸ κακὸν πράσσοντι.* ⁵ *διὸ ἀνάγκη ὑποτάσσεσθαι, οὐ μόνον διὰ τὴν ὀργὴν ἀλλὰ καὶ διὰ τὴν συνείδησιν.* ⁶ *διὰ τοῦτο γὰρ καὶ φόρους τελεῖτε· λειτουργοὶ γὰρ θεοῦ εἰσιν εἰς αὐτὸ τοῦτο προσκαρτεροῦντες.* ⁷ *ἀπόδοτε πᾶσιν τὰς ὀφειλάς, τῷ τὸν φόρον τὸν φόρον, τῷ τὸ τέλος τὸ τέλος, τῷ τὸν φόβον τὸν φόβον, τῷ τὴν τιμὴν τὴν τιμήν.*

¹*Let every person be subject to the governing authorities. For there is no authority except from God, and those that exist have been instituted by God.* ²*Therefore he who resists the authorities resists what God has appointed, and those who resist will incur judgment.* ³*For rulers are not a terror to good conduct, but to bad. Would you have no fear of him who is in authority? Then do what is good, and you will receive his approval,* ⁴*for he is God's servant for your good. But if you do wrong, be afraid, for he does not bear the sword in vain; he is the servant of God to execute his wrath on the wrongdoer.* ⁵*Therefore one must be subject, not only to avoid God's wrath but also for the sake of conscience.* ⁶*For the same reason you also pay taxes, for the authorities are ministers of God, attending to this very thing.* ⁷*Pay all of them their dues, taxes to whom taxes are due, revenue to whom revenue is due, respect to whom respect is due, honor to whom honor is due.*

Having expanded on love as the rule of life for *all* believers and what such life entails, Paul will make the point that the reason behind this is that by following that rule the believers would be actually fulfilling God's entire law (13:8-10). Thus, it would behoove them to be obedient to that Law since God's judgment day is not only coming but is actually nearing (vv.11-14). On the other hand, the freedom granted us by God is not to be equated with unruliness (Gal 5:13-26; Rom 8:12-13). That is why Paul reminds the Philippians, who are Roman citizens, that basic decent behavior is required: "Finally, brethren, whatever is true, whatever is honorable, whatever is just, whatever is pure, whatever is lovely, whatever is gracious, if there is any excellence, if there is anything worthy of praise, think about these things. What you have learned and received and heard and seen in me, do; and the God of peace will be with you." (Phil 4:8-9) If the believers cannot conform to basic social rules of decency, then they have no hope of following the intransigence of the gospel, and no chance of passing the test on the Lord's Day. Hence, Roman authority can be viewed as good training for the real and much harsher judgment that will be administered by God (Rom 13:1-7).

Paul applies to the Roman empire the hierarchical terminology of a household, which revolves around the verb *tassō* (ordain; institute order) with its cognates *hypotassō* (sub-ordain), *antitassō* (take a stand against the order) and the noun *diatagē* (ordinance) which occur no less than five times in vv.1-5.[1] Since all fatherly authority (*patria*) has its source in God (Eph 3:15), so does the authority of the emperor and his helpers. If the Roman believer is to submit (*hypotassesthō*; be sub-ordained) to those

---

[1] See Eph 5:21, 24 and Col 3:18 for the use of the verb *hypotassō* in a household context.

authorities it is *because* they are ordained (*tetagmenoi*) as such by God himself (Rom 13:1). Consequently, anyone who contravenes (*antitassomenos*) that authority is actually opposing the ordinance (*diatagē*) of God himself; and those who do so are liable to judgment (v.2). For the rulers do not instill fear except toward the evil, not the good, deed (v.3a). So, to forego the fear of the authorities, one is to do the good (v.3b), which the believers are supposed to do anyway (12:9, 21). More importantly, from that perspective, the authority actually functions as a *diakonos* of God unto the good (13:4), which is exactly what Paul himself is all about.[2] He used his authority to excise an evildoer from the community in order to "save" him (1 Cor 5:1-5). Put otherwise, he executed preemptively God's wrath as a means of correction; the alternative was that the evildoer would come under God's non-appealable condemnation.[3] So, says Paul, the authority of the Roman rulers is to be viewed by his addressees as doing the same thing: "But if you do wrong, be afraid, for he does not bear the sword in vain; he is the servant of God to execute his wrath on the wrongdoer." (Rom 13:4) Consequently, it is a dutiful necessity (*anankē*) to submit to those authorities, not only out of fear of reprisal, but for the sake of our conscience (v.5) since it is the conscience that prepares for the ultimate test: "They show that what the law requires is written on their hearts, while their conscience also

---

[2] The intended parallelism between the two is corroborated in that two verses later (13:6) the Roman authorities are even called "liturgs (*leitourgoi*; temple servants) of God" just as Paul will refer to himself in 15:16.

[3] Later, in the same letter, Paul contends that God himself acts preemptively for our instruction with the hope that, should we heed, we would not be condemned: "For any one who eats and drinks without discerning the body eats and drinks judgment upon himself. That is why many of you are weak and ill, and some have died. But if we judged ourselves truly, we should not be judged. But when we are judged by the Lord, we are chastened so that we may not be condemned along with the world." (11:29-32)

bears witness and their conflicting thoughts accuse or perhaps excuse them on that day when, according to my gospel, God judges the secrets of men by Christ Jesus." (2:15-16)[4]

Furthermore, the Roman citizens should not complain since they reap great benefits from the Roman governance: legal system, business, commerce, roads, protection from thieves, etc. However, in exchange for such benefits, they are to fulfill their monetary dues, especially tax and toll payments (*phorous teleite*; 13:6).[5] It is striking, at this point, that Paul uses the liturgical and thus communitarian terminology he links to church gatherings: "for the authorities are *liturgs* (*leitourgoi*; liturgical ministers) of God, attending (*proskarterountes*)[6] to this very thing." (v.6b) Here again, we see how Paul is presenting the Roman empire to his hearers as an extended household. Consequently, what one is paying (*apodote*) to the authorities is simply what is due to them (*tas opheilas*): payment (*phoron*) and tax (*telos*) as expressions of the awe (*phobon*; fear) and respect (*timēn*; honor) that one owes them (v.7).

Vv. 8-10 8 Μηδενὶ μηδὲν ὀφείλετε εἰ μὴ τὸ ἀλλήλους ἀγαπᾶν· ὁ γὰρ ἀγαπῶν τὸν ἕτερον νόμον πεπλήρωκεν. 9 τὸ γὰρ οὐ μοιχεύσεις, οὐ φονεύσεις, οὐ κλέψεις, οὐκ ἐπιθυμήσεις, καὶ εἴ τις ἑτέρα ἐντολή, ἐν τῷ λόγῳ τούτῳ ἀνακεφαλαιοῦται [ἐν τῷ]· ἀγαπήσεις τὸν πλησίον σου ὡς σεαυτόν. 10 ἡ ἀγάπη τῷ πλησίον κακὸν οὐκ ἐργάζεται· πλήρωμα οὖν νόμου ἡ ἀγάπη.

---

[4] These are the only instances of "conscience" in Romans besides 9:1 which I discussed earlier and showed that it harked back to 2:15-16.

[5] *phoros*, from the verb *pherō* (carry) refers to the payments, such a rents, that one "carries" and thus has to fulfill (*teleō*). Conversely, from the verb *teleō* we have the noun *telos* that has the same connotation as *phoros* but seems to refer more specifically to the assigned taxes (see e.g. Mt 17:24-25), whence *telōnēs* (tax collector).

[6] See my comments on 12:12 above.

> *⁸Owe no one anything, except to love one another; for he who loves his neighbor has fulfilled the law. ⁹The commandments, "You shall not commit adultery, You shall not kill, You shall not steal, You shall not covet," and any other commandment, are summed up in this sentence, "You shall love your neighbor as yourself." ¹⁰Love does no wrong to a neighbor; therefore love is the fulfilling of the law.*

Speaking of "dues," Paul hurries to say that the believers' only actual due is love, meaning that they are to respect the authorities not out of fear of them, but out of the fear of the Lord. Indeed, loving the other is the fulfillment of God's law. In other words, the believers are to offer the Roman authorities what is due them, as though they are offering God what is due him. We have yet another indication that Paul is looking at the empire as being a mega-Roman household, when we consider what he wrote in Colossians and Ephesians concerning the behavior within a believer's household:

> And whatever you do, in word or deed, *do everything in the name of the Lord Jesus,* giving thanks to God the Father through him. Wives, be subject to your husbands, as is fitting *in the Lord.* Husbands, love your wives, and do not be harsh with them. Children, obey your parents in everything, for *this pleases the Lord.* Fathers, do not provoke your children, lest they become discouraged. Slaves, obey in everything those who are your earthly masters, not with eyeservice, as men-pleasers, but in singleness of heart, *fearing the Lord.* Whatever your task, work heartily, as *serving the Lord* and not men, knowing that *from the Lord* you will receive the inheritance as your reward; *you are serving the Lord Christ.* (Col 3:17-24; see also Eph 5:22-6:9)

It is clear that his instruction revolves around the premise that the Lord Jesus Christ, not the paterfamilias, is the master of the house. And so it is on the level of the Roman empire: the master is not the emperor, but God. Whatever the believers do, they do not out of submission to the emperor's will, but to that of God expressed in his law, and "love is the (fullness) fulfilling of the Law" (Rom 13:10b).

Vv. 11-14 ¹¹ Καὶ τοῦτο εἰδότες τὸν καιρόν, ὅτι ὥρα ἤδη ὑμᾶς ἐξ ὕπνου ἐγερθῆναι, νῦν γὰρ ἐγγύτερον ἡμῶν ἡ σωτηρία η᾽ ὅτε ἐπιστεύσαμεν. ¹² ἡ νὺξ προέκοψεν, ἡ δὲ ἡμέρα ἤγγικεν. ἀποθώμεθα οὖν τὰ ἔργα τοῦ σκότους, ἐνδυσώμεθα [δὲ] τὰ ὅπλα τοῦ φωτός. ¹³ ὡς ἐν ἡμέρᾳ εὐσχημόνως περιπατήσωμεν, μὴ κώμοις καὶ μέθαις, μὴ κοίταις καὶ ἀσελγείαις, μὴ ἔριδι καὶ ζήλῳ, ¹⁴ ἀλλὰ ἐνδύσασθε τὸν κύριον Ἰησοῦν Χριστὸν καὶ τῆς σαρκὸς πρόνοιαν μὴ ποιεῖσθε εἰς ἐπιθυμίας.

> ¹¹*Besides this you know what hour it is, how it is full time now for you to wake from sleep. For salvation is nearer to us now than when we first believed;* ¹²*the night is far gone, the day is at hand. Let us then cast off the works of darkness and put on the armor of light;* ¹³*let us conduct ourselves becomingly as in the day, not in reveling and drunkenness, not in debauchery and licentiousness, not in quarreling and jealousy.* ¹⁴*But put on the Lord Jesus Christ, and make no provision for the flesh, to gratify its desires.*

In the same Law, one follows God's commandments by "walking" on "the (right) way" until the Lord "comes" to judge us on his "day." The combination of these three metaphors allows Paul to write that "salvation is nearer to us now than when we first believed, that the night is far gone, the day is at hand" (vv.11c-12a) Consequently, "it is full time now for you to be raised (waken up) from sleep" (v.11b). By using the verb "raised" (*egerthēnai*) Paul is clearly drawing attention to the fact that he is referring to the "last (final) judgment." However, since he is addressing hearers who are living, Paul speaks of being raised from sleep and thus "awake" in the sense of being diligent.

In 1 Thessalonians he also uses the opposition of night and day
in conjunction with the coming Lord's "day":

> But as to the times and the seasons, brethren, you have no need to
> have anything written to you. For you yourselves know well that
> the day of the Lord will come like a thief in the night. When
> people say, "There is peace and security," then sudden destruction
> will come upon them as travail comes upon a woman with child,
> and there will be no escape. But you are not in *darkness*, brethren,
> for that day to surprise you like a thief. For you are all sons of *light*
> and sons of the day; we are not of the night or of *darkness*. So then
> *let us not sleep*, as others do, but let us keep *awake* and be sober.
> For those who *sleep sleep* at night, and those who *get drunk are
> drunk* at night. But, since we belong to the day, let us be sober,
> and *put on* the breastplate of faith and love, and for a helmet the
> hope of *salvation*. For God has not destined us for wrath, but to
> obtain *salvation* through our Lord Jesus Christ, who died for us so
> that whether we *wake* or *sleep* we might live with him. (5:1-10)

The same vocabulary is found in Romans, where, besides "day,"
"night," "sleeping," and "awake," we hear of "salvation" (13:11),
"darkness" and "light" (v.12), "putting on an armor" (v.12), and
"drunkenness" (v.13). On the other hand, we also have the
vocabulary of "works" (v.12), "walk" (v.13), "reveling
(carousing)" (*methai*; v.13), "licentiousness" (v.13), "quarelling
(strife)" (*eris*; v.13), "jealousy" (v.13), "flesh" (v.14), "desires"
(*epithymias*; v.14) which, together with "drunkenness" (v.13), are
found in Galatians 5:16-24. One should add that the metaphor
of "putting on Christ" occurs only in these two letters in the
New Testament (Rom 13:14 and Gal 3:27). The closeness
between the two passages is also evident in their intent. They
both invite us to move away from works that would result in our
condemnation on judgment day to a "way" that leads into the
kingdom of God, just as in 1 Thessalonians. In other words, they

both stress behavior, not creedal or theological formulae, as the muster for the judgment. More importantly, they both come after their respective passages where Paul makes his point that love for the other is the fulfillment of the Law.

So the closeness between the two letters is not only "theological," as has been said throughout the centuries, but more importantly lies in that they both stress behavioral expectations. What is more striking still is that the test in this matter is table fellowship between Jew and Gentile, which will be discussed lengthily in the following chapter (Rom 14). For Paul to single out this matter and even discuss it at such great length with a community he has yet to meet is unexpected, to say the least. Or is it? Throughout Romans 12 and 13, Paul was dealing with his addressees' behavior in the Roman empire as if it were a large household. The most important aspect of a Roman household, or of any household for that matter, is the *symposion*, the table fellowship when all guests, as well as family members, are "one." This was precisely the "practical" setting at Antioch (Gal 2:11-14) when the "theoretical" agreement of Jerusalem (vv.7-10) was tested and unfortunately fell through. Consequently, to make sure that the community of believers in the great city of the West not fall prey to what happened in the great city of the East, Paul dedicates a very lengthy passage to this matter (14:1-15:13), before engaging his travel plans (15:14-32) and the final greetings (ch.16).

Chapter 14

Vv. 1-12 ¹ Τὸν δὲ ἀσθενοῦντα τῇ πίστει προσλαμβάνεσθε, μὴ εἰς διακρίσεις διαλογισμῶν. ² ὃς μὲν πιστεύει φαγεῖν πάντα, ὁ δὲ ἀσθενῶν λάχανα ἐσθίει.ὃς μὲν πιστεύει φαγεῖν πάντα, ὁ δὲ ἀσθενῶν λάχανα ἐσθίει. ³ ὁ ἐσθίων τὸν μὴ ἐσθίοντα μὴ ἐξουθενείτω, ὁ δὲ μὴ ἐσθίων τὸν ἐσθίοντα μὴ κρινέτω, ὁ θεὸς γὰρ αὐτὸν προσελάβετο. ⁴ σὺ τίς εἶ ὁ κρίνων ἀλλότριον οἰκέτην; τῷ ἰδίῳ κυρίῳ στήκει η᾽ πίπτει· σταθήσεται δέ, δυνατεῖ γὰρ ὁ κύριος στῆσαι αὐτόν. ⁵ Ὃς μὲν [γὰρ] κρίνει ἡμέραν παρ᾽ ἡμέραν, ὃς δὲ κρίνει πᾶσαν ἡμέραν· ἕκαστος ἐν τῷ ἰδίῳ νοῒ πληροφορείσθω. ⁶ ὁ φρονῶν τὴν ἡμέραν κυρίῳ φρονεῖ· καὶ ὁ ἐσθίων κυρίῳ ἐσθίει, εὐχαριστεῖ γὰρ τῷ θεῷ· καὶ ὁ μὴ ἐσθίων κυρίῳ οὐκ ἐσθίει καὶ εὐχαριστεῖ τῷ θεῷ. ⁷ οὐδεὶς γὰρ ἡμῶν ἑαυτῷ ζῇ καὶ οὐδεὶς ἑαυτῷ ἀποθνῄσκει· ⁸ ἐάν τε γὰρ ζῶμεν, τῷ κυρίῳ ζῶμεν, ἐάν τε ἀποθνῄσκωμεν, τῷ κυρίῳ ἀποθνῄσκομεν. ἐάν τε οὖν ζῶμεν ἐάν τε ἀποθνῄσκωμεν, τοῦ κυρίου ἐσμέν. ⁹ εἰς τοῦτο γὰρ Χριστὸς ἀπέθανεν καὶ ἔζησεν, ἵνα καὶ νεκρῶν καὶ ζώντων κυριεύσῃ. ¹⁰ Σὺ δὲ τί κρίνεις τὸν ἀδελφόν σου; η᾽ καὶ σὺ τί ἐξουθενεῖς τὸν ἀδελφόν σου; πάντες γὰρ παραστησόμεθα τῷ βήματι τοῦ θεοῦ, ¹¹ γέγραπται γάρ· ζῶ ἐγώ, λέγει κύριος, ὅτι ἐμοὶ κάμψει πᾶν γόνυ καὶ πᾶσα γλῶσσα ἐξομολογήσεται τῷ θεῷ. ¹² ἄρα [οὖν] ἕκαστος ἡμῶν περὶ ἑαυτοῦ λόγον δώσει [τῷ θεῷ].

¹*As for the man who is weak in faith, welcome him, but not for disputes over opinions.* ²*One believes he may eat anything, while the weak man eats only vegetables.* ³*Let not him who eats despise him who abstains, and let not him who abstains pass judgment on him who eats; for God has welcomed him.* ⁴*Who are you to pass judgment on the servant of another? It is before his own master that he stands or falls. And he will be upheld, for the Master is able to make him stand.* ⁵*One man esteems one day as better than another, while another man esteems all days alike. Let every one be fully convinced in his own mind.* ⁶*He who*

observes the day, observes it in honor of the Lord. He also who eats, eats in honor of the Lord, since he gives thanks to God; while he who abstains, abstains in honor of the Lord and gives thanks to God. ⁷None of us lives to himself, and none of us dies to himself. ⁸If we live, we live to the Lord, and if we die, we die to the Lord; so then, whether we live or whether we die, we are the Lord's. ⁹For to this end Christ died and lived again, that he might be Lord both of the dead and of the living. ¹⁰Why do you pass judgment on your brother? Or you, why do you despise your brother? For we shall all stand before the judgment seat of God; ¹¹for it is written, "As I live, says the Lord, every knee shall bow to me, and every tongue shall give praise to God." ¹²So each of us shall give account of himself to God.

To make sure that the Roman patricians heed his instructions concerning oneness at table fellowship, Paul cajoles them by addressing them as "the strong ones" and their Jewish counterparts, "the weak ones." This approach is known as *captatio benevolentiae*, captivating (ensuring) the benevolence (goodwill) of the addressees, putting them in the right mood or mental state, before communicating to them a message that puts the onus on them rather on their counterparts.

We are to receive and welcome (into our home; *proslambanesthe*) the one who is weak in faith without the ulterior motive of debating opinions (*dialogismōn*; thoughts) (14:1) since thoughts will be revealed and judged on that day when God will judge all according to the gospel of Paul (2:15-16), that is to say, according to the rule of love, and not whether we are technically or theoretically right or wrong. Let the one who eats everything not despise the one who eats only vegetables

in order not to risk eating meat offered to idols (1 Cor 8:7-13).[1]
Conversely, let not the latter pass judgment on the former.
Either action is unacceptable and will be criticized in the
following verses.

The use of the verb "judge" (*krinetō*) to describe the action of
the Jew corresponds to the terminology used earlier by Paul
(Rom 2:1, 3); the reason is that the Jew knows God's law (3:1-2,
17-20). However, since God alone is the ultimate judge,
subsequent terminology referring to either the action of the Jew
or of the Gentile is subsumed under the verb "judge." Because
God himself is the host and he has received and welcomed
(*proselabeto*) each (14:3), the Gentile is not to despise others, nor
is the Jew to judge others. Each is the "foreign (belonging to
another person) house servant" (*allotrion oiketēn*) to those around
him and as such those who are gathered at table do not belong to
one another, but to the Lord. It is he who will decide who shall
have withstood or failed the last test. Even more, we most
probably shall stand because the Lord is able to make it happen
(14:4) through his mercy (11:30-31). The connection between
Romans 14 and 11 can be seen in the similar terminology:

> It is before his own master that he stands fast (*stēkei*) or falls
> (*piptei*). And he will end up standing (*stathēsetai*),[2] for the Master
> (Lord) is able (*dynatei*) to make him stand (*stēsai*).[3] (14:4)

> They were broken off because of their unbelief, but you stand fast
> (*hestēkas*)[4] only through faith. So do not become proud, but fear.

---

[1] The connection between Romans and 1 Corinthians is evident in the close
parallelism between the following two statements: "If *your brother* is being injured by
what you eat, you are no longer walking in love. Do not let what you eat cause the
ruin of one *for whom Christ died*" (Rom 14:15); "And so by your knowledge this weak
man is destroyed, *the brother for whom Christ died*." (1 Cor 8:11)

[2] From the verb *histēmi*.

[3] From the verb *histēmi*.

For if God did not spare the natural branches, neither will he spare you. Note then the kindness and the severity of God: severity toward those who have fallen (*pesontas*),[5] but God's kindness to you, provided you continue in his kindness; otherwise you too will be cut off. And even the others, if they do not persist in their unbelief, will be grafted in, for God is able (*dynatos estin*) to graft them in again. (11:20-23)

With the parenthetical mention of "days" to be taken into consideration (14:5-6a), Paul makes it clear, throughout this passage, that he is referring to potential tensions between Jews and Gentiles (compare with Gal 4:10). Still, the main topic remains "food" as is clear from the remainder of Romans 14:6. Moreover, the "days" at the beginning of v.6 is phrased in a way that it goes hand in hand with the phraseology concerning "eating" in the remainder of the verse: "He who observes (takes into consideration) the day, observes it (takes it into consideration) *for (in honor of) the Lord*. He also who eats, eats *for (in honor of) the Lord*, since he gives thanks to God; while he who abstains, abstains *for (in honor of) the Lord* and gives thanks to God." Thus, the topic "days" is secondary to that of "eating." When one considers the expansion of Galatians 4:10 (You observe days, and months, and seasons, and years!) in Colossians 2:16 (Therefore let no one pass judgment [*krinetō*] on you in questions of food and drink or with regard to a festival or a new moon or a sabbath), it becomes clear that "days" include and refer primarily to sabbaths. What is noticeable in the Colossians text is the use of the verb "judge" and the linkage between the matter of "food and drink," on the one hand, and with that of "days," on the other hand. In all probability, here in Romans, Paul was asking the Roman Gentiles not to impose any food on

---

[4] From the verb *histēmi* and yet sounds like *stēkei*.
[5] From the verb *piptō*.

their fellow Jews, and, by the same token, he was asking them
not to interfere with the Jews' keeping the sabbath rule of not
traveling more than the prescribed distance. By extension, Paul
was also asking the Romans to excuse the Jews if on sabbaths
they did not accept an invitation to a common meal, so long as
both the Gentile and the Jew render thanksgiving to God. After
all, the table fellowship of the believers is a thanksgiving
(eucharist; *evkharistia*) meal for the Lord's sacrificing himself for
us (1 Cor 11:24). Actually, in the immediate following verses
(Rom 14:7-10) Paul will be referring to Christ's sacrificial death.

Since food is the sustenance of life, the mention of eating
versus abstinence allows Paul to move to life and death. Here
again, as slaves in the household of God (6:22) whatever we do,
including life and death, we do unto (in honor of) the Lord since
we are his (Rom 14:7-8). However, Christ not only died, but
came alive again (*ezēsen*) so that he could lord over both the dead
and the living (*zōntōn*) (v.9). That, in turn, will entail bringing
everyone to stand before the judgment seat of God; and if so,
then, coming back to where he started, Paul asks why would one
despise the other and the other judge the one (v.10; compare
with v.3). Instead of spending energy to no avail, let everyone
prepare to render account to God (v.12).

Vv. 13-23 ¹³ Μηκέτι οὖν ἀλλήλους κρίνωμεν· ἀλλὰ τοῦτο
κρίνατε μᾶλλόν τὸ μὴ τιθέναι πρόσκομμα τῷ ἀδελφῷ ἢ
σκάνδαλον ¹⁴ οἶδα καὶ πέπεισμαι ἐν κυρίῳ Ἰησοῦ ὅτι οὐδὲν
κοινὸν δι' ἑαυτοῦ, εἰ μὴ τῷ λογιζομένῳ τι κοινὸν εἶναι,
ἐκείνῳ κοινόν. ¹⁵ εἰ γὰρ διὰ βρῶμα ὁ ἀδελφός σου λυπεῖται,
οὐκέτι κατὰ ἀγάπην περιπατεῖς· μὴ τῷ βρώματί σου ἐκεῖνον
ἀπόλλυε ὑπὲρ οὗ Χριστὸς ἀπέθανεν. ¹⁶ μὴ βλασφημείσθω οὖν
ὑμῶν τὸ ἀγαθόν. ¹⁷ οὐ γάρ ἐστιν ἡ βασιλεία τοῦ θεοῦ
βρῶσις καὶ πόσις ἀλλὰ δικαιοσύνη καὶ εἰρήνη καὶ χαρὰ ἐν
πνεύματι ἁγίῳ· ¹⁸ ὁ γὰρ ἐν τούτῳ δουλεύων τῷ Χριστῷ

εὐάρεστος τῷ θεῷ καὶ δόκιμος τοῖς ἀνθρώποις. ¹⁹ Ἄρα οὖν
τὰ τῆς εἰρήνης διώκωμεν καὶ τὰ τῆς οἰκοδομῆς τῆς εἰς
ἀλλήλους. ²⁰ μὴ ἕνεκεν βρώματος κατάλυε τὸ ἔργον τοῦ θεοῦ.
πάντα μὲν καθαρά, ἀλλὰ κακὸν τῷ ἀνθρώπῳ τῷ διὰ
προσκόμματος ἐσθίοντι. ²¹ καλὸν τὸ μὴ φαγεῖν κρέα μηδὲ
πιεῖν οἶνον μηδὲ ἐν ᾧ ὁ ἀδελφός σου προσκόπτει. ²² σὺ
πίστιν [ἣν] ἔχεις κατὰ σεαυτὸν ἔχε ἐνώπιον τοῦ θεοῦ.
μακάριος ὁ μὴ κρίνων ἑαυτὸν ἐν ᾧ δοκιμάζει· ²³ ὁ δὲ
διακρινόμενος ἐὰν φάγῃ κατακέκριται, ὅτι οὐκ ἐκ πίστεως·
πᾶν δὲ ὃ οὐκ ἐκ πίστεως ἁμαρτία ἐστίν.

¹³Then let us no more pass judgment on one another, but rather
decide never to put a stumbling block or hindrance in the way of
a brother. ¹⁴I know and am persuaded in the Lord Jesus that
nothing is unclean in itself; but it is unclean for any one who
thinks it unclean. ¹⁵If your brother is being injured by what you
eat, you are no longer walking in love. Do not let what you eat
cause the ruin of one for whom Christ died. ¹⁶So do not let your
good be spoken of as evil. ¹⁷For the kingdom of God is not food
and drink but righteousness and peace and joy in the Holy
Spirit; ¹⁸he who thus serves Christ is acceptable to God and
approved by men. ¹⁹Let us then pursue what makes for peace
and for mutual upbuilding. ²⁰Do not, for the sake of food,
destroy the work of God. Everything is indeed clean, but it is
wrong for any one to make others fall by what he eats; ²¹it is
right not to eat meat or drink wine or do anything that makes
your brother stumble. ²²The faith that you have, keep between
yourself and God; happy is he who has no reason to judge
himself for what he approves. ²³But he who has doubts is
condemned, if he eats, because he does not act from faith; for
whatever does not proceed from faith is sin.

Instead of judging one another, then, we are to judge the
situation so as not to put a stumbling block (*proskomma*) or a
hindrance (*skandalon*) in the way of the brother (v.13), since

these are God's prerogative (9:32-33), given that he alone is the tester and judge. In itself nothing is unclean, yet it might be so for someone who considers it as such (14:14). Consequently, the matter is not an issue of food. Actually, the matter at stake is a triple jeopardy. First, the one who makes the other feel sorrow (*lypeitai*) "is not walking according to the rule of love" (v.15a) and thus is at risk of losing the Kingdom. Secondly, the one who is scandalized may act incorrectly and thus will perish (*apollye*), which is the opposite of salvation,[6] in spite of the fact that Christ died to ensure him the latter. Thirdly and most importantly, the result would be that the name of God will be blasphemed among the nations (2:14) in that the intended good he brought about has failed since neither the Gentile offender nor the scandalized Jew will be saved (14:16). The kingdom of God is not a matter of food and drink, but rather a matter of eschatological peace and the ensuing joy that is attained only through righteous behavior. This is ensured if we follow the lead of Holy Spirit (v.17) as Paul instructed in detail in Galatians 5:13-26. Indeed, anyone who follows that path is a true servant of Christ and will prove to be acceptable (pleasing) in God's eyes and, as a bonus, will be viewed as wise by men (Rom 14:18). We are thus to pursue the matter of the eschatological peace of the Kingdom as seriously and as eagerly as the Roman citizens pursue the *pax Romana*. The way toward that peace (v.17) is our mutual building up (v.19) of one another, which ultimately is the work of God's spirit (1 Cor 14:12).

One should not undo God's work because of misunderstanding about food. Everything is clean. However, this reality ought not to become an opportunity to do evil by making someone else stumble through our reckless behavior of eating

---

[6] See 1 Cor 1:18; 2 Cor 2:15; 2 Thess 2:10; 1 Pet 1:7-9. See also Mt 8:25.

anything at will (Rom 14:20). Actually, the better thing to do is "to overcome evil with good" and "not eat meat or drink wine or do anything that makes the brother stumble" (v.21; see also 1 Cor 8:13).[7] This is clearly an extreme measure meant to make the hearers realize the gravity of not caring for the brother. Ultimately the judge of our trust in God is God himself, not ourselves, let alone our feelings (Rom 14:22a). God will judge if our trust is real, that is to say "working through love" for the other (Gal 5:6). And since judgment is reserved to God alone, blessed is the one who, until then, tests (*dokimazei*) himself to see where he stands, yet does not emit judgment (*krinōn*) on himself (Rom 14:22b). Furthermore, if one truly trusts in the gospel teaching that "the kingdom of God is not food and drink but righteousness and peace and joy in the Holy Spirit" (v.17), "then he is not to keep debating in his mind (*diakrinomenos*) what to eat or not eat; otherwise he is already liable of condemnation (*katakekritai*), since the lack of trust (faith) is tantamount to sin" (v.23), the sin of disobedience (5:19).

It is worth noting that the vocabulary of the concluding remarks of Romans 14:22-23—*krinōn*; *dokimazei*; *diakrinomenos*; *katakekritai*—parallel those of 1 Corinthians 11:27-34, which also contains Paul's concluding remarks on the mishandling of table fellowship. This confirms that Romans 14 is not discussing dietary issues in general, but rather doing so in conjunction with the oneness of the fellowship table. The seriousness of this matter has already been laid down in Galatians 2:11-14.

---

[7] The parallelism between Rom 14 and 1 Cor 8 is actually corroborated in the addition "for whom Christ died" to speak of the scandalized brother in both instances (Rom 14:15; 1 Cor 8:11).

Chapter 15

Vv. 1-6 ¹ Ὀφείλομεν δὲ ἡμεῖς οἱ δυνατοὶ τὰ ἀσθενήματα τῶν ἀδυνάτων βαστάζειν καὶ μὴ ἑαυτοῖς ἀρέσκειν. ² ἕκαστος ἡμῶν τῷ πλησίον ἀρεσκέτω εἰς τὸ ἀγαθὸν πρὸς οἰκοδομήν· ³ καὶ γὰρ ὁ Χριστὸς οὐχ ἑαυτῷ ἤρεσεν, ἀλλὰ καθὼς γέγραπται· οἱ ὀνειδισμοὶ τῶν ὀνειδιζόντων σε ἐπέπεσαν ἐπ᾽ ἐμέ. ⁴ ὅσα γὰρ προεγράφη, εἰς τὴν ἡμετέραν διδασκαλίαν ἐγράφη, ἵνα διὰ τῆς ὑπομονῆς καὶ διὰ τῆς παρακλήσεως τῶν γραφῶν τὴν ἐλπίδα ἔχωμεν. ⁵ ὁ δὲ θεὸς τῆς ὑπομονῆς καὶ τῆς παρακλήσεως δῴη ὑμῖν τὸ αὐτὸ φρονεῖν ἐν ἀλλήλοις κατὰ Χριστὸν Ἰησοῦν, ⁶ ἵνα ὁμοθυμαδὸν ἐν ἑνὶ στόματι δοξάζητε τὸν θεὸν καὶ πατέρα τοῦ κυρίου ἡμῶν Ἰησοῦ Χριστοῦ.

¹We who are strong ought to bear with the failings of the weak, and not to please ourselves; ²let each of us please his neighbor for his good, to edify him. ³For Christ did not please himself; but, as it is written, "The reproaches of those who reproached thee fell on me." ⁴For whatever was written in former days was written for our instruction, that by steadfastness and by the encouragement of the scriptures we might have hope. ⁵May the God of steadfastness and encouragement grant you to live in such harmony with one another, in accord with Christ Jesus, ⁶that together you may with one voice glorify the God and Father of our Lord Jesus Christ.

This passage concludes the section on the love for one another that was discussed in Romans 14. To begin, Paul reiterates the point he made earlier concerning love as fulfillment of the Law, namely, that love is a due: "Owe (*opheilete*) no one anything, except to love one another; for he who loves his neighbor has fulfilled the law." (13:8) Here he writes: "We who

257

are strong ought (*opheilomen*;[1] owe it) to bear with the failings of
the weak, and not to please ourselves." (15:1) This confirms that
the love Paul is speaking about is essentially that toward the
lesser, the junior, the needy. The same thought is further
corroborated in the use of "bear with" (*bastazein*); earlier we
heard that it is the root that supports (*bastazeis*) the branch and
not vice versa (11:18b). The expression of love consists
essentially in "pleasing" the lesser, as is evident in the fact that
"pleasing" is mentioned no less than three times in three verses
(15:1-3). When one considers that "pleasing" occurs earlier only
in conjunction with God (8:8; 12:1, 2; 14:18), then one realizes
the seriousness of the matter. God's judgment will rest on how
one behaves toward the needy neighbor, which "God's prophets
in the holy scriptures" (1:2) upheld time and again. Even Christ
had to go through that ordeal as intimated in scripture itself
(15:3; see also 5:6-11). That is why scripture is ultimately our
only hope: it teaches us that God consoles us through the
promise of the Kingdom and grants us the necessary patience to
proceed on that path (15:4; see also 5:1-5). We are to follow the
example of the Christ Jesus in our behavior toward one another,
as Paul stated in Romans 5:6-11 (15:5). And should we do so,
then "the God and Father of our Lord Jesus Christ," who is also
our God and Father (Gal 1:4) shall be glorified (Rom 15:6; see
also Phil 2:5-11). The "together (*homothymadon*) with one voice
(*en heni stomati*; in one mouth)" is inclusive of both Jews and
Gentiles and prepares for Romans 15:8-9 as we shall see.

Vv. 7-13 [7] Διὸ προσλαμβάνεσθε ἀλλήλους, καθὼς καὶ ὁ
Χριστὸς προσελάβετο ὑμᾶς εἰς δόξαν τοῦ θεοῦ. [8] λέγω γὰρ
Χριστὸν διάκονον γεγενῆσθαι περιτομῆς ὑπὲρ ἀληθείας θεοῦ,
εἰς τὸ βεβαιῶσαι τὰς ἐπαγγελίας τῶν πατέρων, [9] τὰ δὲ ἔθνη

---

[1] These are the only instances of the verb *opheilō* in Romans before its occurrence in
15:27. Besides looking back to 13:8, Rom 15:1 also prepares for 15:27.

ὑπὲρ ἐλέους δοξάσαι τὸν θεόν, καθὼς γέγραπται· διὰ τοῦτο
ἐξομολογήσομαί σοι ἐν ἔθνεσιν καὶ τῷ ὀνόματί σου ψαλῶ. ¹⁰
καὶ πάλιν λέγει· εὐφράνθητε, ἔθνη, μετὰ τοῦ λαοῦ αὐτοῦ. ¹¹
καὶ πάλιν· αἰνεῖτε, πάντα τὰ ἔθνη, τὸν κύριον καὶ
ἐπαινεσάτωσαν αὐτὸν πάντες οἱ λαοί. ¹² καὶ πάλιν Ἡσαΐας
λέγει· ἔσται ἡ ῥίζα τοῦ Ἰεσσαὶ καὶ ὁ ἀνιστάμενος ἄρχειν
ἐθνῶν, ἐπ’ αὐτῷ ἔθνη ἐλπιοῦσιν. ¹³ Ὁ δὲ θεὸς τῆς ἐλπίδος
πληρώσαι ὑμᾶς πάσης χαρᾶς καὶ εἰρήνης ἐν τῷ πιστεύειν, εἰς
τὸ περισσεύειν ὑμᾶς ἐν τῇ ἐλπίδι ἐν δυνάμει πνεύματος
ἁγίου.

*⁷Welcome one another, therefore, as Christ has welcomed you,
for the glory of God. ⁸For I tell you that Christ became a servant
to the circumcised to show God's truth, in order to confirm the
promises given to the patriarchs, ⁹ and in order that the Gentiles
might glorify God for his mercy. As it is written, "Therefore I
will praise thee among the Gentiles, and sing to thy name";
¹⁰and again it is said, "Rejoice, O Gentiles, with his people";
¹¹and again, "Praise the Lord, all Gentiles, and let all the
peoples praise him"; ¹²and further Isaiah says, "The root of Jesse
shall come, he who rises to rule the Gentiles; in him shall the
Gentiles hope." ¹³May the God of hope fill you with all joy and
peace in believing, so that by the power of the Holy Spirit you
may abound in hope.*

If the previous passage is the conclusion to the section on love
for the neighbor, this passage wraps up Paul's magisterial
scriptural "instruction" (*didaskalia*; Rom 15:4) laid down in the
entire letter,[2] before he moves on to speak of his upcoming plans
(15:14-33). Building up on the terminology of Romans 12-14,
the passage incorporates the thesis of Romans 1-11, especially 9-
11. Indeed, Romans 15:7 recapitulates Romans 14:1-15:6 by
combining Romans 14:1-3 and 15:6:

---

² See also "teaching" (*didakhē*) in Rom 6:17 and my comments there.

Welcome (*proslambanesthe*) one another, therefore, as Christ *has welcomed* (*proselabeto*) you, for the *glory of God*. (15:7)

As for the man who is weak in faith, *welcome* (*proslambanesthe*) him, but not for disputes over opinions. One believes he may eat anything, while the weak man eats only vegetables. Let not him who eats despise him who abstains, and let not him who abstains pass judgment on him who eats; for God *has welcomed* (*proselabeto*) him. (14:1-3)

... that together you may with one voice *glorify* the *God* and Father of our Lord Jesus Christ. (15:6)

Then Romans 15:8-9a ends with the glory due to God, using the terminology as well as the thesis of Romans 9-11: the truth of the gospel is addressed first to the circumcision in order to validate the promises to the fathers and then to the nations so that, though mercy, they also might glorify God (Romans 9-11). Then a series of quotations taken from the entire scripture—the Law, the Prior Prophets, the Latter Prophets, and Psalms—(Rom 15:9a-12) seals the announcement at the beginning of the letter that, indeed, Paul is the "servant of Jesus Christ, called to be an apostle, set apart for the gospel of God which he promised beforehand through his prophets in the holy scriptures, the gospel concerning his Son ... Jesus Christ our Lord, through whom we have received grace and apostleship to bring about the obedience of faith for the sake of his name among all the nations, including yourselves who are called to belong to Jesus Christ" (1:1-6); and, furthermore, that he has just fulfilled his mission *by writing this letter*. In so doing, Paul seals Romans as scripture in the same way he did with Galatians (6:11).

The choice of the quotations is ingenious. On the one hand, they are taken from the four sections of scripture: Romans 15:9b is from 2 Samuel 22:50 as well as Ps 18:49 (LXX 19:50); Romans 15:10 from Deuteronomy 32:43; Romans 15:11 from Ps 117:1 (LXX 116:1); and Romans 15:12 from Isaiah 11:10. On the other hand, they all pertain to the nations and are all introduced with the one "as it is written" of Romans 15:9b. Their inclusion under one umbrella is corroborated by the repeated "again" (*palin*) before each of the last three quotations.[3] Still, since each scriptural section abounds with adequate quotations, the choice was expressly made in a way that their terminology conform to the earlier phraseology of Romans, especially that of chapters 9-14 which have just been recapitulated in 15:7-9a. The correspondence in phraseology is more specifically found in the first and last quotations (vv.9b and 12) that bracket the entire set of quotations. V.9b (Therefore *I will confess* [*exomologēsomai*] *thee* among the Gentiles, and sing to thy name) is the answer of God's call in 14:11 (As I live, says the Lord, every knee shall bow to me, and every tongue shall *confess* [*exomologēsetai*] *God*) and 15:12 (The *root* of Jesse shall come, he who rises to rule the Gentiles; in him shall the Gentiles hope) harks back to the passage about the "root" in 11:16-18. Given all of the above, the lasting impression is that the "holy scriptures" are fulfilled in the "scripture" of this letter to the Romans. Just as Paul launched with Galatians (6:11) the tradition in his mainly Gentile churches that his letter be read in the gatherings following the reading of the Old Testament passages, and thus *as scripture*, so also here in Romans he is confirming that usage in the western parts of the empire. Having accomplished *his* mission as apostle, Paul asks the God of the hope just referred to at the end of Romans 15:12, to lead his hearers, *in hope*, on the road toward the eschatological peace of the Kingdom (v.13).

---

[3] RSV has "further" instead of "again" in Romans 15:12 but the original is *palin*.

Moreover, his hearers' itinerary, just as his and Christ's (1:4), is to be done "by the power of the Holy Spirit." Here again one detects how Paul masterfully recapitulated the entire letter in these few verses (15:7-13).

Still, there is another twist to this mastery. Besides looking backward as a conclusion should, this same passage prepares for the ending of the letter (vv.14-32) through the phrase "Christ became a minister to the circumcised (*diakonon tēs peritomēs*) to show God's truth" (v.8), which is inscribed in the Law (2:20) and thus propounded through Paul's gospel (1:1-2). This unique instance in the New Testament where Christ is referred to in a positive manner as *diakonos* appears suddenly in a context filled with phraseology consistent with that of Romans. The other occurrence, with a negative connotation, is found in Gal 2:17 where Paul is accused by his peers of making of Christ a "*diakonos* of sin." As I explained in my commentary on Galatians,[4] Paul was defending himself by explaining that if Christ is a *diakonos* to the sinful Gentiles (2:17), it does not ensue that he is a *diakonos* of sin. In Galatians it is clear that this ministry (*diakonia*) of Christ is effected through that of Paul: "But when he who had set me apart before I was born, and had called me through his grace, was pleased to reveal his Son *in me* (*en emoi*; through my agency), in order that I might preach him among the Gentiles" (1:15-16); "they only heard it said, 'He who once persecuted us is now preaching the faith he once tried to destroy.' And they glorified God *in me* (*en emoi*; for what he did through my agency)." (vv.23-24)[5] Since the gospel is one, then the apostolic ministry is also one (2:7-8). By the same token, if Christ, through the apostle, is *diakonos* to the Gentiles,

---

[4] *Gal* 86.
[5] See my comments on "in me" (*en emoi*) in *Gal* 46-8 and 56.

then according to Romans 9-11, he has been first *diakonos* to the circumcised for the sake of the Gentiles (15:8-9a). And it is this *diakonia* of offering the Christ of the gospel first to the Jew, but also to the Gentile, that Paul is introducing here in view of the subsequent passage where he speaks of his going up to Jerusalem to share with them the fruits of such gospel: "At present, however, I am going to Jerusalem *diakonōn* (ministering; with a ministry) to the saints" (v.25); "that I may be delivered from the unbelievers in Judea, and that my *diakonia* (ministry) for Jerusalem may be acceptable to the saints." (v.31)

Vv. 14-33 ¹⁴ Πέπεισμαι δέ, ἀδελφοί μου, καὶ αὐτὸς ἐγὼ περὶ ὑμῶν ὅτι καὶ αὐτοὶ μεστοί ἐστε ἀγαθωσύνης, πεπληρωμένοι πάσης [τῆς] γνώσεως, δυνάμενοι καὶ ἀλλήλους νουθετεῖν. ¹⁵ τολμηρότερον δὲ ἔγραψα ὑμῖν ἀπὸ μέρους ὡς ἐπαναμιμνῄσκων ὑμᾶς διὰ τὴν χάριν τὴν δοθεῖσάν μοι ὑπὸ τοῦ θεοῦ ¹⁶ εἰς τὸ εἶναί με λειτουργὸν Χριστοῦ Ἰησοῦ εἰς τὰ ἔθνη, ἱερουργοῦντα τὸ εὐαγγέλιον τοῦ θεοῦ, ἵνα γένηται ἡ προσφορὰ τῶν ἐθνῶν εὐπρόσδεκτος, ἡγιασμένη ἐν πνεύματι ἁγίῳ. ¹⁷ ἔχω οὖν [τὴν] καύχησιν ἐν Χριστῷ Ἰησοῦ τὰ πρὸς τὸν θεόν· ¹⁸ οὐ γὰρ τολμήσω τι λαλεῖν ὧν οὐ κατειργάσατο Χριστὸς δι᾽ ἐμοῦ εἰς ὑπακοὴν ἐθνῶν, λόγῳ καὶ ἔργῳ, ¹⁹ ἐν δυνάμει σημείων καὶ τεράτων, ἐν δυνάμει πνεύματος [θεοῦ]. ὥστε με ἀπὸ Ἰερουσαλὴμ καὶ κύκλῳ μέχρι τοῦ Ἰλλυρικοῦ πεπληρωκέναι τὸ εὐαγγέλιον τοῦ Χριστοῦ, ²⁰ οὕτως δὲ φιλοτιμούμενον εὐαγγελίζεσθαι οὐχ ὅπου ὠνομάσθη Χριστός, ἵνα μὴ ἐπ᾽ ἀλλότριον θεμέλιον οἰκοδομῶ, ²¹ ἀλλὰ καθὼς γέγραπται· οἷς οὐκ ἀνηγγέλη περὶ αὐτοῦ ὄψονται, καὶ οἳ οὐκ ἀκηκόασιν συνήσουσιν. ²² Διὸ καὶ ἐνεκοπτόμην τὰ πολλὰ τοῦ ἐλθεῖν πρὸς ὑμᾶς· ²³ νυνὶ δὲ μηκέτι τόπον ἔχων ἐν τοῖς κλίμασι τούτοις, ἐπιποθίαν δὲ ἔχων τοῦ ἐλθεῖν πρὸς ὑμᾶς ἀπὸ πολλῶν ἐτῶν, ²⁴ ὡς ἂν πορεύωμαι εἰς τὴν Σπανίαν· ἐλπίζω γὰρ διαπορευόμενος θεάσασθαι ὑμᾶς καὶ ὑφ᾽ ὑμῶν προπεμφθῆναι ἐκεῖ ἐὰν ὑμῶν πρῶτον ἀπὸ μέρους ἐμπλησθῶ. ²⁵ Νυνὶ δὲ πορεύομαι εἰς Ἰερουσαλὴμ διακονῶν τοῖς ἁγίοις. ²⁶ εὐδόκησαν γὰρ Μακεδονία καὶ Ἀχαΐα κοινωνίαν τινὰ ποιήσασθαι εἰς τοὺς πτωχοὺς τῶν ἁγίων τῶν ἐν Ἰερουσαλήμ. ²⁷ εὐδόκησαν γὰρ καὶ ὀφειλέται εἰσὶν αὐτῶν· εἰ γὰρ τοῖς πνευματικοῖς αὐτῶν ἐκοινώνησαν τὰ ἔθνη, ὀφείλουσιν καὶ ἐν τοῖς σαρκικοῖς λειτουργῆσαι αὐτοῖς. ²⁸ τοῦτο οὖν ἐπιτελέσας καὶ σφραγισάμενος αὐτοῖς τὸν καρπὸν τοῦτον, ἀπελεύσομαι δι᾽ ὑμῶν εἰς Σπανίαν· ²⁹ οἶδα δὲ ὅτι ἐρχόμενος πρὸς ὑμᾶς ἐν πληρώματι εὐλογίας Χριστοῦ ἐλεύσομαι. ³⁰ Παρακαλῶ δὲ ὑμᾶς[, ἀδελφοί,] διὰ τοῦ κυρίου ἡμῶν Ἰησοῦ Χριστοῦ καὶ διὰ τῆς ἀγάπης τοῦ πνεύματος συναγωνίσασθαί μοι ἐν ταῖς προσευχαῖς ὑπὲρ ἐμοῦ πρὸς τὸν θεόν, ³¹ ἵνα ῥυσθῶ ἀπὸ τῶν ἀπειθούντων ἐν τῇ Ἰουδαίᾳ καὶ ἡ διακονία μου ἡ εἰς Ἰερουσαλὴμ εὐπρόσδεκτος τοῖς ἁγίοις γένηται, ³² ἵνα ἐν χαρᾷ ἐλθὼν πρὸς ὑμᾶς διὰ θελήματος θεοῦ συναναπαύσωμαι ὑμῖν. ³³ Ὁ δὲ θεὸς τῆς εἰρήνης μετὰ πάντων ὑμῶν, ἀμήν.

¹⁴*I myself am satisfied about you, my brethren, that you yourselves are full of goodness, filled with all knowledge, and able to instruct one another. ¹⁵But on some points I have written to you very boldly by way of reminder, because of the grace given me by God ¹⁶to be a minister of Christ Jesus to the Gentiles in the priestly service of the gospel of God, so that the offering of the Gentiles may be acceptable, sanctified by the Holy Spirit. ¹⁷In Christ Jesus, then, I have reason to be proud of my work for God. ¹⁸For I will not venture to speak of anything except what Christ has wrought through me to win obedience from the Gentiles, by word and deed, ¹⁹by the power of signs and wonders, by the power of the Holy Spirit, so that from Jerusalem and as far round as Illyricum I have fully preached the gospel of Christ, ²⁰thus making it my ambition to preach the gospel, not where Christ has already been named, lest I build on another man's foundation, ²¹but as it is written, "They shall see who have never been told of him, and they shall understand who have never heard of him." ²²This is the reason why I have so often been hindered from coming to you. ²³But now, since I no longer have any room for work in these regions, and since I have*

longed for many years to come to you, ²⁴I hope to see you in passing as I go to Spain, and to be sped on my journey there by you, once I have enjoyed your company for a little. ²⁵At present, however, I am going to Jerusalem with aid for the saints. ²⁶For Macedonia and Achaia have been pleased to make some contribution for the poor among the saints at Jerusalem; ²⁷they were pleased to do it, and indeed they are in debt to them, for if the Gentiles have come to share in their spiritual blessings, they ought also to be of service to them in material blessings. ²⁸When therefore I have completed this, and have delivered to them what has been raised, I shall go on by way of you to Spain; ²⁹and I know that when I come to you I shall come in the fulness of the blessing of Christ. ³⁰I appeal to you, brethren, by our Lord Jesus Christ and by the love of the Spirit, to strive together with me in your prayers to God on my behalf, ³¹that I may be delivered from the unbelievers in Judea, and that my service for Jerusalem may be acceptable to the saints, ³²so that by God's will I may come to you with joy and be refreshed in your company. ³³The God of peace be with you all. Amen.

Now that the addressees are filled with both the goodness that they are to use for the sake of the weaker brother and the knowledge to do so, knowledge which Paul has just imparted to them through his letter, they are empowered (*dynamenoi*) to instruct one another (v.14). Having said all he wanted to say to the Romans, and in detail, Paul uses the same literary device as he did in 1:10-15 to excuse himself for having done so, that is, a combination of delays in his plans to visit them and his duty to share with them "some aspects of" the gospel, in a way we would say nowadays, "to share a couple of items with you." At the beginning of the letter he wrote "that I may impart to you *some* spiritual gift" (1:11); here he writes "on *some* points (*apo merous*)" (15:15). In either case, he did what he did, actually wrote what he wrote, *as assigned apostle to the Gentiles*. It is precisely his apostleship that accounts for his boldness to indulge in writing so lengthily: "On some points I have written to you more boldly (*tolmēroteron*) ... For I will not be so bold (*tolmēsō*) as to speak of anything except what Christ has wrought through me..." (vv.15, 18) Paul has already covered the eastern parts of the empire (v.19), and his hope and plan is to visit and preach in its western parts, all the way to Spain (vv.22-24). However, he is also planning to give his preaching a better chance in the west— bringing along the fullness of the blessing of God in Christ (vv.28-29)—by having his peers in Jerusalem officially endorse what he accomplished in the east by accepting the gift of fellowship (*koinōnian*) of the two major eastern provinces of Macedonia and Achaia (vv.25-26). Conversely, when he goes up to Jerusalem, if he can show that his gospel has borne "some" fruit in the west as it did the east (v.27), then that would give his position more clout in the eyes of his peers. So writing to the Romans ahead of his visit to Jerusalem makes sense. If matters go wrong and he finds his end in Jerusalem, then the gospel seed will have already been planted in Rome and, through the Romans, hopefully in Spain. If, on the other hand, his letter would have already borne some fruit before his ascent to Jerusalem, then it would bolster his case. And if his peers are convinced, he might not have to travel to Rome and Spain; his letter would continue to be read in the table fellowship gatherings and that ultimately is all that matters in his eyes. That he had in mind some eventual fruit in Rome through his letter can be gathered from the indirect pressure he put on his addressees. After having said that Macedonia and Achaia had been "well pleased" (*evdokēsan*) to share in the *koinōnia* for Jerusalem (v.26), he adds: "they were pleased to do it, and *indeed they are in debt* (opheilousin) *to them*, for if the Gentiles have come to share in their spiritual blessings, they ought also to be of service to them in material blessings." (v.27) At any rate, reiterating what he already said at the start of the chapter (v.1) was meant to break any residue arrogance on the part of the Roman addressees: though the entire habitation is indebted to the patricians of Rome, now the patricians themselves are in debt because of Christ (v.3).

Summing up what he said in vv.14-29, Paul asks that the Romans join him in his "race" to propagate the gospel (*synagōnisasthai moi*) by praying for him during his upcoming mission to Jerusalem (v.30).[6] The mention of Judea next to Jerusalem is interesting. When referring to his going up to Jerusalem from Macedonia, Paul mentions either Jerusalem (1 Cor 16:3-5) or Judea (2 Cor 1:16), but never both, except here in Romans 15:31.[7] So it seems that Paul intentionally added Judea besides Jerusalem, the site referred to throughout chapter 15 (vv.19, 25, 26). The clue to understanding this lies in the phrase "the unbelievers (*apeithountōn*) in Judea." On the one hand, it contrasts with "the saints (in Jerusalem)" and thus must refer to the Jews in the Roman province Judea, and those "at large" throughout the empire, who oppose Paul's gospel. On the other hand, however, this unbelief is an attitude that could qualify the Gentiles as well as the Jews (11:30-32). Nonetheless, I believe Paul's intention is to leave the door open, in the minds of the Romans, for God's re-grafting the unbelieving Jews into his olive tree whenever they would repent (11:23-24). It is, after all, the will of the God of peace that should prevail (15:33). For

---

[6] The root *agōn* (race: sport competition; effort spent in such competition) is used in this sense in Paul (1 Cor 9:25; Phil 1:30; Col 1:29; 2:1; 4:12; 1 Thess 2:2; 1 Tim 4:10; 2 Tim 4:7).

[7] The other two instances of Judea in the Pauline corpus are Gal 1:22 and 1 Thess 2:14 where we have "the churches of Judea."

the time being, Paul is still hoping that his mission in Jerusalem will prove successful, and he will be granted to share rest, in God's peace, with the Romans (v.32).

Chapter 16

Vv. *1-16* ¹ *Συνίστημι δὲ ὑμῖν Φοίβην τὴν ἀδελφὴν ἡμῶν, οὖσαν [καὶ] διάκονον τῆς ἐκκλησίας τῆς ἐν Κεγχρεαῖς,* ² *ἵνα αὐτὴν προσδέξησθε ἐν κυρίῳ ἀξίως τῶν ἁγίων καὶ παραστῆτε αὐτῇ ἐν ᾧ ἂν ὑμῶν χρῄζῃ πράγματι· καὶ γὰρ αὐτὴ προστάτις πολλῶν ἐγενήθη καὶ ἐμοῦ αὐτοῦ.* ³ *Ἀσπάσασθε Πρίσκαν καὶ Ἀκύλαν τοὺς συνεργούς μου ἐν Χριστῷ Ἰησοῦ,* ⁴ *οἵτινες ὑπὲρ τῆς ψυχῆς μου τὸν ἑαυτῶν τράχηλον ὑπέθηκαν, οἷς οὐκ ἐγὼ μόνος εὐχαριστῶ ἀλλὰ καὶ πᾶσαι αἱ ἐκκλησίαι τῶν ἐθνῶν,* ⁵ *καὶ τὴν κατ᾽ οἶκον αὐτῶν ἐκκλησίαν. ἀσπάσασθε Ἐπαίνετον τὸν ἀγαπητόν μου, ὅς ἐστιν ἀπαρχὴ τῆς Ἀσίας εἰς Χριστόν.* ⁶ *ἀσπάσασθε Μαρίαν, ἥτις πολλὰ ἐκοπίασεν εἰς ὑμᾶς.* ⁷ *ἀσπάσασθε Ἀνδρόνικον καὶ Ἰουνιᾶν τοὺς συγγενεῖς μου καὶ συναιχμαλώτους μου, οἵτινές εἰσιν ἐπίσημοι ἐν τοῖς ἀποστόλοις, οἳ καὶ πρὸ ἐμοῦ γέγοναν ἐν Χριστῷ.* ⁸ *ἀσπάσασθε Ἀμπλιᾶτον τὸν ἀγαπητόν μου ἐν κυρίῳ.* ⁹ *ἀσπάσασθε Οὐρβανὸν τὸν συνεργὸν ἡμῶν ἐν Χριστῷ καὶ Στάχυν τὸν ἀγαπητόν μου.* ¹⁰ *ἀσπάσασθε Ἀπελλῆν τὸν δόκιμον ἐν Χριστῷ. ἀσπάσασθε τοὺς ἐκ τῶν Ἀριστοβούλου.* ¹¹ *ἀσπάσασθε Ἡρῳδίωνα τὸν συγγενῆ μου. ἀσπάσασθε τοὺς ἐκ τῶν Ναρκίσσου τοὺς ὄντας ἐν κυρίῳ.* ¹² *ἀσπάσασθε Τρύφαιναν καὶ Τρυφῶσαν τὰς κοπιώσας ἐν κυρίῳ. ἀσπάσασθε Περσίδα τὴν ἀγαπητήν, ἥτις πολλὰ ἐκοπίασεν ἐν κυρίῳ.* ¹³ *ἀσπάσασθε Ῥοῦφον τὸν ἐκλεκτὸν ἐν κυρίῳ καὶ τὴν μητέρα αὐτοῦ καὶ ἐμοῦ.* ¹⁴ *ἀσπάσασθε Ἀσύγκριτον, Φλέγοντα, Ἑρμῆν, Πατροβᾶν, Ἑρμᾶν καὶ τοὺς σὺν αὐτοῖς ἀδελφούς.* ¹⁵ *ἀσπάσασθε Φιλόλογον καὶ Ἰουλίαν, Νηρέα καὶ τὴν ἀδελφὴν αὐτοῦ, καὶ Ὀλυμπᾶν καὶ τοὺς σὺν αὐτοῖς πάντας ἁγίους.* ¹⁶ *ἀσπάσασθε ἀλλήλους ἐν φιλήματι ἁγίῳ. ἀσπάζονται ὑμᾶς αἱ ἐκκλησίαι πᾶσαι τοῦ Χριστοῦ.*

¹I commend to you our sister Phoebe, a deaconess of the church at Cenchreae, ²that you may receive her in the Lord as befits the saints, and help her in whatever she may require from you, for she has been a helper of many and of myself as well. ³Greet Prisca and Aquila, my fellow workers in Christ Jesus, ⁴who risked their necks for my life, to whom not only I but also all the churches of the Gentiles give thanks; *⁵greet also the church in their house. Greet my beloved Epaenetus, who was the first convert in Asia for Christ.* *⁶Greet Mary, who has worked hard among you.* *⁷Greet Andronicus and Junias, my kinsmen and my fellow prisoners; they are men of note among the apostles, and they were in Christ before me.* *⁸Greet Ampliatus, my beloved in the Lord.* *⁹Greet Urbanus, our fellow worker in Christ, and my beloved Stachys.* *¹⁰Greet Apelles, who is approved in Christ. Greet those who belong to the family of Aristobulus.* *¹¹Greet my kinsman Herodion. Greet those in the Lord who belong to the family of Narcissus.* *¹²Greet those workers in the Lord, Tryphaena and Tryphosa. Greet the beloved Persis, who has worked hard in the Lord.* *¹³Greet Rufus, eminent in the Lord, also his mother and mine.* *¹⁴Greet Asyncritus, Phlegon, Hermes, Patrobas, Hermas, and the brethren who are with them.* *¹⁵Greet Philologus, Julia, Nereus and his sister, and Olympas, and all the saints who are with them.* *¹⁶Greet one another with a holy kiss. All the churches of Christ greet you.*

My reading of the long list of greetings is in line with my view of personal and geographical names in scripture: they all are metaphorical and thus functional within the context in which they appear. I have used this methodology extensively in my four-volume Introduction to the New Testament.[1]

First and foremost is Phoebe (*Phoibē*), who stands apart from all the others in that she is neither the object nor the subject of a greeting; rather, Paul commends her to the Romans. *Phoibē* is the feminine of *Phoibos* ([the] luminous) which is the surname of the god Apollo. Apollo's twin sister is Artemis, the patroness of

---

[1] *NTI₁, NTI₂, NTI₃, NTI₄.*

the city of Ephesus where a temple in her honor was erected and was counted among the seven wonders of the ancient world. Paul's gospel produced a stir among Artemis' followers because it succeeded to attract many citizens and threatened the lucrative trade that sustained the temple (Acts 19:23-41). A few verses earlier, in reporting Paul's success, Luke writes: "So the word of the Lord grew and prevailed mightily. Now after these events Paul resolved in the Spirit to pass through Macedonia and Achaia and go to Jerusalem, saying, 'After I have been there, I must also see Rome.'" (vv.20-21) This is precisely the plan Paul spoke of in Romans 15:22-29. So it seems reasonable to assume that, in Romans 16:1-2, Paul was commending Phoebe, a servant of the gospel in the eastern parts of the empire, to his Roman hearers as the example to follow. The new "luminous" is the light of the gospel instead of the light of the Greco-Roman deities. My understanding of Phoebe is corroborated in that she is said to be of "the church that is in Cenchreae" (16:2). It is, at face value, rather odd that such a primary importance be given to this port town of Corinth, which is mentioned in passing only once more in the New Testament: "After this Paul stayed many days longer, and then took leave of the brethren and sailed for Syria, and with him Priscilla and Aquila. At Cenchreae he cut his hair, for he had a vow. And they came to Ephesus, and he left them there; but he himself went into the synagogue and argued with the Jews." (Acts 18:18-19) The vow taken at Cenchreae would be fulfilled in Jerusalem (21:23-24) which Paul would visit after his farewell to the church of Ephesus (20:17-38). If we give Cenchreae a symbolic value as we do Phoebe, then matters would begin to make sense. Cenchreae is the port whence Paul sailed *to Ephesus* with Priscilla and Aquila, who are mentioned with equal importance (two full verses [Rom 16:3-4]) as that given to Phoebe (vv.1-2).[2] More important, however, is the immediate connotation of the Greek *Kenkhreai* to the hearers' ears, just as was the case with Phoebe. Sound-wise *Kenkhreai* is very close to the adjective *kenkhriaiai* meaning "as little as a grain of millet (*kenkhros*)." This connotation fits both Acts and Romans. In Acts, Cenchreae is the insignificant point of departure of Paul's first visit to Ephesus, the city that would become his headquarters, and from which he would eye Rome itself (Acts 19:21). Here also in Romans, the patricians of Rome are reminded that the conquest of the city of Artemis was done through the little seed of the gospel and, in turn, they are asked to welcome this small seed with all due honors (Rom 16:2).[3] This would explain Paul's choice of Cenchreae over Ephesus in Romans.

Further, in order to keep the Roman patricians in check, the honor due to Phoebe lies in that her worth is that of the "saints" (v.2a). In the immediate context, the saints refer to the leaders of the Jerusalem church (15:25, 26, 31). Here then Paul is equating in value the church of Ephesus with that of Jerusalem, thus giving Ephesus the highest possible honor in the eyes of the Romans. The reason is that Ephesus, for all intent and purposes, has become the earthly seat of the Jerusalem above, the mother of all, Gentiles as well as Jews (Gal 4:26). Indeed, Phoebe is said

[2] See further below on Aquila and Priscilla.

[3] Another less probable, yet attractive, proposition is to hear *Kenkhreai* as a combination of *ken*—, the first syllable of *kentron* (center) and *khreai* that sounds very much like *khreiai*, which is the plural of *khreia* whose meaning is "need" and also the "duty" serving that need as in Acts 6:3. Earlier in Rom 12:13, Paul used this term in conjunction with the *koinōnia* (table fellowship)—and thus *diakonia* (the service at table fellowship)—toward the "saints of Judea," which was an integral part of Paul's gospel (see above my comments on 12:7a). Consequently *Kenkhreai* can be a reference to the center (headquarters) of Paul's apostolic mission, Ephesus.

to be the *prostatis*[4] (chief, patron, one who stands at the head of) "of many, including myself" (Rom 16:2c). Thus Paul is inviting the Romans to consider the church of Ephesus his "locum tenens," even his "heir," in case they do not get to see him.

That is why the Romans are to extend a helping hand (*parastēte*)[5] to Phoebe in any matter (*pragmati*) she might be needing (*khrēzē*) (v.2b). Which "matter" can Paul possibly be talking about except that of the gospel? This is the only instance of *pragma* in Romans, and it occurs in a context that is close to what we find in Acts 18 and 19.[6] In the diptych Luke-Acts, the root *pragma* occurs three times. In Luke 1:1 it is clearly related to the gospel "word": "Inasmuch as many have undertaken to compile a narrative of the matters (*pragamtōn*) which have been accomplished among us, just as they were delivered to us by those who from the beginning were eyewitnesses and ministers of *the word*, it seemed good to me also, having followed all things closely for some time past, to write an orderly account for you, most excellent Theophilus, that you may know the truth concerning *the words* which you have been catechized." (1:1-4)[7] The second instance is the verb *pragmatevsasthe* where again the meaning is clear from the context: "A nobleman went into a far country to receive a kingdom and then return. Calling ten of his servants, he gave them ten pounds, and said to them, '*Handle the matter* (*pragmatevsasthe*) till I come.'" (Lk 19:12-13) The matter is the business of the nobleman who is to receive the *kingdom* and his servants are to handle his matter *until he comes*. The third instance is found in Acts 5:4 where Peter chides Ananias for

---

[4] Unique instance of that noun in the New Testament.
[5] Actually this verb is from the same root *histēmi* as the noun *prostatis*. So the Romans are to stand beside (*paristēmi*) the one who stands in front (*proistēmi*).
[6] See further below on Romans 16:3-4.
[7] See my detailed comments on this prologue to the Gospel of Luke in *NTI₂* 25-6.

having cheated in his donation to the common treasury: "How is it that you have contrived this *deed* (*pragma*) in your heart? You have not lied to men but to God." This story parallels the parable in Luke 19 where one of the servants did not attend to the "matter" of his "lord," the nobleman (vv.20-21).[8]

Thus, Phoebe as "minister" (*diakonos*; servant of the table fellowship) stands as the heir of both Paul, the "minister of the gospel" to the Gentiles (Rom 11:13; 15:25, 31) and Christ the "minister" of the same gospel toward the circumcision (15:8). In other words, it is at Ephesus that the full table fellowship between Jews and Gentiles is realized, after it was botched at Antioch (Gal 2:11-14). In turn, it is neither Antioch nor Jerusalem, but Ephesus which is the blueprint for Rome to follow.

The immediate mention of Prisca and Aquila after that of Phoebe confirms my reading of Romans 16:1-2. According to Acts, although Paul meets them in Corinth (18:2),[9] their actual co-working with him starts upon sailing from Cenchreae (vv.18-19) and is at its fullest in Ephesus where they introduce Apollos, Paul's helper in Corinth, into the fullness of the gospel (vv.24-

---

[8] In Acts, we have a further indication that the "matter" where Ananias failed was directly related to the gospel. A few verses earlier, we are told that "they had *all things in common* (*hapanta koina*)" (Acts 4:32). The only other occurrence of the phrase "all things in common" in the entire New Testament is found earlier in Acts in a context similar to that in Acts 4:32-37: "And they devoted themselves to the apostles' teaching and fellowship (*koinōnia*), to the breaking of bread and the prayers. And fear came upon every soul; and many wonders and signs were done through the apostles. And all who believed were together and had *all things in common* (hapanta koina); *and they sold their possessions and goods and distributed them to all, as any had need.*" (2:42-45) Yet here the same action is directly linked to the apostolic teaching and table fellowship, which are at the heart of Paul's gospel. Notice that "(table) fellowship" (*koinōnia*) and "in common" (*koina*) are from the same root *koin—*.

[9] Priscilla is the diminutive of Prisca.

28) *after* Paul's departure from Ephesus (vv.21-23). The fact that they functioned in his absence indicates that they were indeed fully his co-workers. Romans 16:4 seems to reflect that they shared with Paul the life-threatening riots against him in Ephesus (Acts 19:23-40). In 1 Corinthians 16:19 they are presented as part of the churches of the Roman province Asia whose capital was Ephesus. Being originally from Rome (Acts 18:2) it stands to reason that they decided to return there or were sent back by the Pauline entourage to either plant the seed of the gospel or help promote it in Rome. At any rate, what is important is that the gospel they were serving in Rome, they learned from Paul in Corinth or, more probably, in Ephesus. In this sense, they were the "face" of Phoebe in Rome and even her well established presence, since they headed a house church there (Rom 16:5a). Their mention at the head of the list of those to be greeted is significant. Not only were they Jews (Acts 18:2), but they bore Latin names, just as Paul did. Furthermore, their names are symbolic, again just as is Paul's. Prisca is an adjective meaning "pristine, age old, original" and Aquila is "eagle." Thus, between them, they represented the Roman empire as well as old Rome from its beginning to the rise of the empire. In other words, Paul meant them as a check to the potential arrogance of the patricians of Rome. Prisca and Aquila functioned as a constant reminder of what Paul taught earlier in Romans 11: the patricians of Rome shall always remain wild olive shoots grafted into the cultivated olive tree whose root is Abraham.

As reinforcement to the point made through Prisca and Aquila, the next in line in the list is Epaenetus, "the first fruits of Asia for Christ" (16:5b). Not only is Epaenetus "first fruits," corresponding to what Paul said in 11:16 of the root of the cultivated olive tree, but he is from Asia. Furthermore, his Greek name *Epainetos* means "(to be) commended, praised" indicating that his behavior is so perfect that ultimately he is bound to be commended and praised not only by the Roman authorities (13:13) but even by God himself (2:29; see also 1 Cor 4:5). Once more, the patricians of Rome, rulers of the world, are put in second position.

Following this we have the only instance of Mary outside the Gospels and Acts in the New Testament. Her mention here fits perfectly what I said repeatedly in my New Testament Introduction tetralogy concerning Mary being a symbol of the church, more specifically the Pauline church gathered around Timothy and John Mark, both Jews, headquartered at Ephesus. Thus Paul is reminding his hearers that that church has toiled to bring the gospel (*ekopiasen*)[10] unto them.

Now that he has established in his addressees' minds that, from the perspective of the gospel, Rome is second to Ephesus, he proceeds by listing symbolically all possible kinds of individuals and nations that live "in Rome," that is to say, under Roman rule and within the boundaries of its empire, who trusted in and obediently submitted to the gospel he is preaching (see Rom 1:5-6). Functionally, this list is comparable to that of Acts 2:9-11.

To start, we have two Jews (Paul's kinsmen) bearing a Greek (Andronicus) and a Latin (Junias or Junia) name, just as Peter and Timothy (Greek names), on the one hand, and Paul and Mark (Latin names), on the other hand. This combination of Jewish, Greek, and Latin elements accounts for the entirety of the empire, as in the case of the three languages (Hebrew, Greek, and Latin) Pilate ordered to be used on the inscription on Jesus'

---

[10] The verb *kopiō* (toil) in the New Testament, and especially in Paul, has the connotation of toiling in the gospel's service (see e.g. 1 Cor 4:12; 15:10; 16:16; Gal 4:11; Phil 2:16; Col 1:29; 1 Tim 4:10).

cross (Jn 19:20). Andronicus and Junias or Junia toiled so hard
for the gospel's sake that they ended as co-prisoners with Paul,
and for this they became prominent in the apostles' eyes or
among the apostles.[11] Paul held Epaphroditus in this same kind
of high esteem for the exceptional effort he expanded for the sake
of the gospel: "I have thought it necessary to send to you
Epaphroditus my brother and fellow worker and fellow soldier,
and your messenger (*apostolon*; apostle) and minister to my
need." (Phil 2:25) However the honor here is pushed to the
extreme in that "they were (had become) ahead of me in Christ."
Such a statement mirrors what Paul writes in 1 Corinthians 15:

> … and that he appeared to Cephas, then to the twelve. Then he
> appeared to more than five hundred brethren at one time, most of
> whom are still alive, though some have fallen asleep. Then he
> appeared to James, *then to all the apostles. Last of all,* as to one
> untimely born, *he appeared also to me.* For I am the least of the
> apostles, unfit to be called an apostle, because I persecuted the
> church of God. (vv.5-9)[12]

Given all the above, the literary value of Andronicus and Junias
or Junia functionally parallels that of the Jewish couple Prisca
and Aquila. The use, however, of a Greek and a Latin name, as
opposed to two Latin names, intends to cover the cultural
Greco-Roman legacy instead of the political Roman empire.
Symbolically the two names reflect the "power of God in the
gospel" (Rom 1:16). The Greek *Andronikos* means "vanquisher
of men" and the Latin Junias or Junia is an adjective linked to
the goddess Juno (Greek Hera), the main consort of the mighty
Jupiter (Greek Zeus), "the father of gods and men alike."

---

[11] The Greek *en tois apostolois* can have either meaning.
[12] Notice that the apostles here are a different category then the "twelve."

Then follows a long list of Greek as well as Latin names that reflect the over-indulgence in the power and wealth of the Roman empire, which was overcome and tamed *on hope* (Rom 5:2-5; 8:19-25; 12:12; 15:4, 13, 24) in submission to the gospel. Ampliatus is from the Latin *amplius* meaning vast, large. The Latin Urbanus means "pertaining to the city." The Greek *Stakhys* means thick, fat, and thus replete, overfed. The Greek *Apellēs* would be non-dark, non-somber and thus "luminous" and "happy (not in mourning)." The Greek Aristoboulos means the one who wants or desires to be the best. Paul's kinsman Herodion recalls Herod the King who calculatingly became a client of Rome in order to secure the kingship of Judea. Narcissus is the classic egotist who is enamored with himself. Tryphaena and Tryphosa are both from the Greek root *tryph*— that connotes indulgence, reveling, luxury, and splendor.

Persis is obviously a reference to the Persians who lived outside the eastern borders of the Roman empire and who were conquered by Alexander of Macedon whose empire preceded that of Rome. The Greeks and after them the Romans considered themselves the civilized "habitation" (*oikoumenē*) and referred to the peoples outside their bounderies as "barbarians." In discussing 1:14 (I am under obligation both to Greeks [Hellenes] and to barbarians, both to the wise and to the foolish) I explained that the phraseology was intended to put the patricians of Rome on par with the barbarians from the perspective of scripture, since they were both part of the "nations," and to keep in check any potential arrogance on the part of the elite among Roman citizenry. Here, at the end of the letter and functioning as an *inclusio* with 1:14, Paul deftly includes a Persian among those who submitted to the gospel and whose names reflect Roman power and wealth. As if to make his point more pertinent, Paul gives Persis the highest of honors in the entire list by qualifying her as "the beloved, who has toiled (*ekopiasen*) in the Lord" (16:12), which puts her on par with none less than Mary (v.7).

My understanding of the name Persis and its function is actually corroborated in the following statement "Greet Rufus, the elect in the Lord, also his mother and mine" (v.13). While Persis refers to the most powerful "barbarian" empire conquered by Alexander, Rufus is one of the most classical Latin names. However, here, the civilized Rufus is mentioned *after* Persis as if to say that the "foolish barbarian" accepted the gospel *before* the "wise Hellene (Greco-Roman)," although the sequence in 1:14 was the inverse.[13] Moreover, while Persis became "beloved (of God)" by toiling for the gospel's sake, Rufus is simply said to be "elect," someone who is idly enjoying the gift. In the list of names, the adjective "elect (chosen)"[14] qualifying Rufus may well be an intended wordplay since it has the connotation of "eminent." The patrician and thus "free" citizen Rufus is enjoying his status as though it is owed to him, whereas the conquered and thus "slave" Persis is expressing her gratitude for the undeserved status of being "beloved" by toiling for the "lord." It is as though she understood fully Paul's injunction in Galatians: "For you were called to freedom, brethren; only do not use your freedom as an opportunity for the flesh, but through love be servants (slaves) of one another" (5:13). And, in order to soften the blow against his addressees, Paul uses his being a Roman citizen to include himself along with them in the same "family" by writing that Rufus' mother is also his.

---

[13] See also a similar phenomenon in the sequence Gentile before Jew in 9-11 when compared to that in Rom 1:16; 2:9-10 where the Jew is put before the Gentile.
[14] "Beloved" is the most used epithet.

Once he reached Rufus, the quintessential representative of Rome and its empire, Paul underscores the "universal" value of Rufus' submission to the gospel, through two sets of five names each, the first set ending with "brethren" and the second set with "saints (holy ones)," the two major appellatives of the believers. In so doing, Paul is bringing the entire Roman empire unto "trusting obedience (*hypakoēn pisteōs*)" (1:6) to the message of "the gospel that was promised in the holy scriptures" (vv.1-2), the main expression of those scriptures being the Law in its five books. The corollary is that Paul is *on hope* yoking the entire Roman empire under God's will expressed in the Law (2:17-20) which is "holy" (7:12) and grafting them into the "holy" root of the fathers (11:16). The first set of five is conceived along the same lines of wealth and power as the previous names starting with Andronicus and Junia. The Greek Asyncritus means "incomparable." The Greek Phlegon means "ardent" and "brilliant." The Greek Hermes, whose other form is Hermas, is the messenger of the gods and thus denotes "eloquence." The Greek Patrobas means "descendant of the father" and thus "noble."

The second set of names is the most enigmatic cluster of names; thus any proposed solution is tentative. Since, however, all the other names are functional, by following a method of trial and error, we should find the most plausible solution. The only expression of Roman power that we have not yet detected in the list of those to be greeted in Rome is the imperial institution. Keeping that possibility in mind, one soon discovers the key that holds together both the second set of five names and the fact that they are divided into three units (Philologus and Julia, Nereus and his sister, and Olympas) whereas in the previous set the names are listed in sequence (Asyncritus, Phlegon, Hermes, Patrobas, Hermas). A feature of imperial authority, which started with Julius Caesar, is the apotheosis (divinization) of the emperors upon their death. This phenomenon seems to be hinted at in the last and single name to submit to the gospel, Olympas, which is from the same root as Olympus, the Mount of the Greek pantheon around Zeus. Once this premise is assumed then Julia and Nereus in the second set begin to make sense. Julia reflects the Julian "family" of Julius Caesar and the first emperors. By association, the Greek *Philologos* (lover of the [spoken] word, man of letters) would be an oblique reference to Julius Caesar himself, writer whose rhetoric and erudite style drew the praise of Cicero himself. Nereus is the ancient sea god and would have been used to reflect the famed Roman maritime power, especially under the early emperors. That unexpected choice of the name of an ancient deity seems to have been dictated by its assonance with Nero, the last of the emperors of the Julian dynasty. This, in turn, would easily explain the enigmatic "and his sister." It was well known that Nero married his step-sister Claudia Octavia.

My reading fits the context of the Roman imperial power of the times as well as that of the letter to the Romans itself in its dealing with that power. Earlier in Romans 13:1-7 Paul made the assertion that "there is no authority except from God, and those [authorities] that exist have been ordained by God" (v.1b). Here in Romans 16:15 he pushes the matter a substantial step further by saying that the "house of Caesar," at least in part, has submitted to the gospel.[15] The emperors, even those apotheosed, are indeed bound to be "subordained" to God. Still, in choosing to refer specifically to the Julian-Claudian *dynasty*, the first

---

[15] See also a similar statement in Phil 1:12-13 (I want you to know, brethren, that what has happened to me has really served to advance the gospel, so that it has become known throughout the whole praetorian guard and to all the rest that my imprisonment is for Christ).

imperial dynasty, Paul was drawing his hearers' attention to the fact that Roman imperial power as such is ultimately human, and not divine.[16]

Paul ends his first list of salutations by asking his addressees to give one another the "holy" kiss of brotherliness (v.16a) since they all are now "holy" (v.15). And since the church of Rome is part of the consortium of churches in the empire, Paul concludes by including all the churches of the eastern parts of the empire that join him in greeting the patricians of Rome.

Vv. 17-20 *¹⁷ Παρακαλῶ δὲ ὑμᾶς, ἀδελφοί, σκοπεῖν τοὺς τὰς διχοστασίας καὶ τὰ σκάνδαλα παρὰ τὴν διδαχὴν ἣν ὑμεῖς ἐμάθετε ποιοῦντας, καὶ ἐκκλίνετε ἀπ' αὐτῶν· ¹⁸ οἱ γὰρ τοιοῦτοι τῷ κυρίῳ ἡμῶν Χριστῷ οὐ δουλεύουσιν ἀλλὰ τῇ ἑαυτῶν κοιλίᾳ, καὶ διὰ τῆς χρηστολογίας καὶ εὐλογίας ἐξαπατῶσιν τὰς καρδίας τῶν ἀκάκων. ¹⁹ ἡ γὰρ ὑμῶν ὑπακοὴ εἰς πάντας ἀφίκετο· ἐφ' ὑμῖν οὖν χαίρω, θέλω δὲ ὑμᾶς σοφοὺς εἶναι εἰς τὸ ἀγαθόν, ἀκεραίους δὲ εἰς τὸ κακόν. ²⁰ ὁ δὲ θεὸς τῆς εἰρήνης συντρίψει τὸν σατανᾶν ὑπὸ τοὺς πόδας ὑμῶν ἐν τάχει. Ἡ χάρις τοῦ κυρίου ἡμῶν Ἰησοῦ μεθ' ὑμῶν.*

¹⁷I appeal to you, brethren, to take note of those who create dissensions and difficulties, in opposition to the doctrine which you have been taught; avoid them. ¹⁸For such persons do not serve our Lord Christ, but their own appetites, and by fair and flattering words they deceive the hearts of the simple-minded. ¹⁹For while your obedience is known to all, so that I rejoice over you, I would have you wise as to what is good and guileless as to what is evil; ²⁰then the God of peace will soon crush Satan under your feet. The grace of our Lord Jesus Christ be with you.

---

[16] See Rev 13:18: "This calls for wisdom: let him who has understanding reckon the number of the beast, for it is *a human number (a number of a man [human being])*, its number is six hundred and sixty-six."

However, before singling out a few prominent names, he digresses to draw the attention to the fact that the believers are still "on the way" (5:1-4) and their "hope" is continually under the "test" (*dokimē*) (v.4). Hence he is requesting them "to watch out for (*skopein*) those who create dissensions (*dikhostasias*) and scandals (scandalous teachings), beyond (the limits of) the teaching (*didakhēn*) which you learned, and avoid such" (16:17). Worth noting is the use of *skopein* and "teaching." The first is from the same root as *skopos* (aim, end, scope) and thus means that one is to keep watch with an eye on the end of the "way, road." The only other occurrence of "teaching" in Romans is found in 6:17 where it is a reference to the actual teaching Paul is expounding in the letter itself. So, as he did in Galatians, where we have the only other instance of "dissensions" (*dikhostasiai*) in the New Testament (5:20), Paul is warning his addressees to abide by the teaching he just committed in writing in his letter (compare with Gal 6:11, 16).

The mention of serving the *koilia* (stomach) instead of Christ betrays that the intended false teachers are Paul's opponents who had a different view regarding table fellowship (Rom 14; see also Gal 4:11-14). The two terms "fair talk" (*khrēstologias*) and "blessing" (*evlogias*), to speak of the method used by the opponents to lure the innocent (unsuspecting), are also revealing. The preceding and only other occurrence of "blessing" in Romans was just used in 15:29 which is to be understood as the blessing secured by the promise to Abraham, a matter that Paul discussed in detail in Galatians: Paul's opponents taught that, in order for someone to share in this blessing, one is to be circumcised. Circumcision was, besides table fellowship, the other matter of import discussed in detail in Galatians. So the mention of "blessing" in conjunction with "stomach" here is understandable. But what about "fair talk," which is unique in the New Testament? *Khrēstologia* is actually a combination of *khrēstos* (meek, loving, pleasant) and *logos* (word). Since *logos* is often specifically the gospel teaching in Paul, the use of *khrēstos*, which practically sounds like *Khristos* (Christ), must have been triggered by the preceding mention of "teaching" (Rom 16:17) in conjunction with "Christ" (v.18). Consequently *khrēstologia* is the false, yet alluring, teaching regarding the function of Christ.

Finally, as usual, Paul redirects his hearers' attention to the "way" they are treading: they are to proceed in doing the good and steering away from practicing the evil (v.19). At the end of the road leading to peace (2:10; 3:17; 5:1; 8:6; 14:17-19; 15:13), the God of peace (15:33) will soon subdue Satan, the opponent par excellence, under their feet (16:20) since "our salvation is nearer to us now than when we first believed" (13:11b).

Vv. 21-24 ²¹ Ἀσπάζεται ὑμᾶς Τιμόθεος ὁ συνεργός μου καὶ Λούκιος καὶ Ἰάσων καὶ Σωσίπατρος οἱ συγγενεῖς μου. ²² ἀσπάζομαι ὑμᾶς ἐγὼ Τέρτιος ὁ γράψας τὴν ἐπιστολὴν ἐν κυρίῳ. ²³ ἀσπάζεται ὑμᾶς Γάϊος ὁ ξένος μου καὶ ὅλης τῆς ἐκκλησίας. ἀσπάζεται ὑμᾶς Ἔραστος ὁ οἰκονόμος τῆς πόλεως καὶ Κούαρτος ὁ ἀδελφός.

> ²¹*Timothy, my fellow worker, greets you; so do Lucius and Jason and Sosipater, my kinsmen.* ²²*I Tertius, the writer of this letter, greet you in the Lord.* ²³*Gaius, who is host to me and to the whole church, greets you. Erastus, the city treasurer, and our brother Quartus, greet you.*[17]

At this point, in order to seal the interconnection between the eastern and western parts of the empire, which he has been trying to secure all along, Paul conveys the greetings of his fellow

---

[17] V. 24 (The grace of our Lord Jesus Christ be with you all. Amen) is missing from the more important manuscripts.

workers who are with him in the east. However, the choice of names and their structuring in two groups of four each are intended to convey the message that the gospel preaching has already been successful by reaching "the four ends (directions) of the (Roman) world," which will warrant the final doxology in praise of the scriptural God (16:25-27).

First and foremost is Timothy, then Lucius and Jason and Sosipater, Paul's kinsmen (v.21). The outstanding position of Timothy is evident in that the verb "greets" is in the singular and thus Timothy alone is its subject; the other three are appended: "Timothy, my fellow worker, greets you; also Lucius and Jason and Sosipater, my kinsmen." (v.21). Timothy is Paul's heir. Thus, as is masterfully expressed in Philippians, should even Paul die (1:20-24)—and eventually he will—Timothy will carry on the torch (2:19-24).[18] Timothy is "another" Paul, a Jew bearing a Gentile name: *Timotheos* is Greek and *Paulus* Latin. Between the two of them they cover the entire Greco-Roman habitation. Furthermore, what started as a small (*Paulus*) seed has now grown into a reality through which God is honored (*Timotheos*). The full success of the endeavor is expressed through the four names—the numeral four reflects universality. The names of the other three Jews who complement Timothy are also Latin and Greek. The Latin Lucius, from *lux* (light), symbolizes the light of the gospel. The Greek Jason is both the name of the seeker of the Golden Fleece and that of *Iasō*, the goddess of healing; he sought and found the healing gospel. The Greek *Sosipatros* means the saving father and thus refers to the divine salvation brought about by the gospel (1:16a) and in all four cases "to the Jew first, yet also to the Gentile" (v.16b).

---

[18] Notice that Philippians has Timothy as its co-author.

The second cluster of four names corroborates my reading that
the final intention, on hope, is the gospel's total and final success
through the submission in faith to it in the western parts of the
empire. The first is Tertius (third in Latin), the secretary who
wrote the letter (16:22). Given that, in the previous set, Timothy
alone is the greeter while the other three are just appended to
him, then Tertius is the third in line after Paul and Timothy. He
represents, as it were, the third phase of the gospel's growth. Paul
is the initiator; Timothy is the heir who, as Bishop of Ephesus (1
Tim 1:3) where Paul has his headquarters, will carry on the
"oral" teaching. Tertius is the one who consigns to writing for
the ages Paul's gospel to Rome and to the empire. This third
phase is the last since it scripturalizes the Pauline gospel,
canonizing it, and thus dismissing any addition as deceptive
teaching (Rom 16:18). Consequently, it is the letter itself that is
planting the seed among its addressees, the Romans. The
culmination of that phase, on hope, is Quartus (fourth in Latin)
the brother (v.23c). Since the numeral four indicates
universality, then, at the end, the brotherhood based on the
gospel will encompass the Roman empire. Still, what would
facilitate the process initiated by Tertius and culminating with
Quartus is the submission of the imperial house to the cause of
the gospel. This is precisely expressed through Gaius being the
"host" of Paul and the entire church (v.23a). Gaius was the name
of the emperor Claudius as well as of Julius Caesar and Octavian
Augustus Caesar. Yet, the actual implementation of the gospel is
through what lies at the heart of its message, the brotherly love
toward the others. Hence beside Gaius we hear of Erastus
(v.23b), the Greek *erastos* (from the root *eros* [love]) meaning
"amiable, one who loves." When Erastus the "caretaker
(*oikonomos*) of the city," presumably Rome, implements the

teaching of Paul, the "caretaker (*oikonomos*)"[19] of the Jerusalem above, God's city, then all shall be well.

With this hope in mind and in that of his hearers, Paul bursts into his third and final doxological ode (after 8:31-39 and 11:33-36) in which he recapitulates the teaching of his letter. Terminology wise, besides incorporating elements from the entire letter, the ode forms an *inclusio* with the overture of the letter (1:1-7) and is thus a befitting end to it:

Vv. 25-27 ²⁵ Τῷ δὲ δυναμένῳ ὑμᾶς στηρίξαι κατὰ τὸ εὐαγγέλιόν μου καὶ τὸ κήρυγμα Ἰησοῦ Χριστοῦ, κατὰ ἀποκάλυψιν μυστηρίου χρόνοις αἰωνίοις σεσιγημένου, ²⁶ φανερωθέντος δὲ νῦν διά τε γραφῶν προφητικῶν κατ' ἐπιταγὴν τοῦ αἰωνίου θεοῦ εἰς ὑπακοὴν πίστεως εἰς πάντα τὰ ἔθνη γνωρισθέντος, ²⁷ μόνῳ σοφῷ θεῷ, διὰ Ἰησοῦ Χριστοῦ, ᾧ ἡ δόξα εἰς τοὺς αἰῶνας, ἀμήν.

²⁵*Now to him who is able to strengthen you according to my gospel and the preaching of Jesus Christ, according to the revelation of the mystery which was kept secret for long ages* ²⁶*but is now disclosed and through the prophetic writings is made known to all nations, according to the command of the eternal God, to bring about the obedience of faith—*²⁷*to the only wise God be glory for evermore through Jesus Christ! Amen.*

---

[19] 1 Cor 4:1-2; 9:17; Eph 3:2, 9: Col 1:25.

Further Reading

Commentaries and Studies

John Chrysostom, Homilies on Romans in P. Schaff, ed., *The Nicene and Post-Nicene Fathers.* Grand Rapids, 1st Series, xi 1979: 335-564.

Arbanas, M. *The Chosen People of God in Paul's Epistle to the Romans.* M.Div thesis. St. Vladimir's Orthodox Theological Seminary, 1998.

Bryan, C. *A Preface to Romans: Notes on the Epistle in Its Literary and Cultural Setting.* Oxford-New York: Oxford University Press, 2000.

Byrne B. *Romans.* Sacra Pagina 6. Collegeville, MN: Liturgical Press, 2007. Persuasion designed to transform readers through a celebratory presentation of the gospel.

Cobb J. B. and Lull D. J. *Romans.* Chalice Commentaries for Today. St Louis, MO: Chalice, 2005. Salvation is as much social as theological.

Cosgrove, C. H. *Elusive Israel: The Puzzle of Election in Romans.* Louisville, KY: Westminster John Knox Press, 1997. Excellent discussion of Romans 9-11.

Cranfield, C. E. B. *Romans: A Shorter Commentary.* Grand Rapids, MI: Eerdmans, 1985.

Das, A. A. *Paul, the Law, and the Covenant.* Peabody, MA: Hendrickson 2001.

Elliott N. *The Arrogance of the Nations: Reading Romans in the Shadow of the Empire.* Paul in Critical Contexts. Minneapolis: Fortress Press, 2008. Explores Paul's interaction with imperial topoi throughout the rhetoric of Romans and God's injustice against Roman injustice.

Esler, P. F. *Conflict and Identity in Romans: The Social Setting of Paul's Letter.* Minneapolis, MN: Fortress Press, 2003. The letter is militating for a new common identity of the Christ-movement.

Fitzmyer J. A., S.J. *Romans: A New Translation with Introduction and Commentary.* The Anchor Bible. New York: Doubleday, 1993.

Horsley R. A., ed. *Paul and the Roman Imperial Order.* Harrisburg, PA: Trinity Press International, 2004.

Jewett, R. *Romans: A Commentary.* Hermeneia. Philadelphia: Fortress Press, 2006. Stressing equality and not superiority, Paul elicits support for a mission to the "barbarians" in Spain.

Keck, L. E. *Romans.* Abingdon New Testament Commentaries. Nashville, TN: Abingdon, 2005. The audacity of Paul is the reflection of the audacity of God.

McGinn, S. E., ed. *Celebrating Romans: Template for Pauline Theology. Essays in Honor of Robert Jewett.* Grand Rapids, MI-Cambridge, UK: Eerdmans, 2004.

Meeks, W. A. *The First Urban Christians: The Social World of the Apostle Paul.* 2nd ed. New Haven-London: Yale University Press, 2003.

Osborne, G. R. *Romans.* IVP New Testament Commentary Series, 6. Downers Grove, IL—Leicester, UK: InterVarsity Press, 2004.

Reasoner M. *Romans in Full Circle: A History of Interpretation.* Louisville: Westminster ohn Knox, 2005. Discussion of key texts.

Ross, A. and Stevenson M. *Romans.* Interpretation Bible Studies. Louisville, KY: Geneva, 1999.

Sabou, S. *Between Horror and Hope: Paul's Metaphorical Language of Death in Romans 6:1-11.* Paternoster Bible Monographs. Milton Keynes, UK: Paternoster 2005. The imagery is that of burial in the family tomb in order to rise to the newness of life.

Sampley, J. P., ed. *Paul in the Graeco-Roman World: A Handbook*. Harrisburg, PA: Trinity Press International, 2003.

Song, C. *Reading Romans as a Diatribe*. Studies in Biblical Literature, 59. NY-Bern: Lang, 2004. The letter's teaching was not for Romans but intrinsically universalized.

Talbert, C.H. *Romans*. Smyth & Helwys Bible Commentary. Macon, GA: Smyth & Helwys, 2002.

Witherington B. III with Hyatt D. *Paul's Letter to the Romans: A Socio-Rhetorical Commentary*. Grand Rapids, MI-Cambridge, UK: Eerdmans, 2004.

Wright, N. T. *Paul for Everyone. Romans*. 2 volumes [1-8 and 9-16]. Louisville, KY: Wetsminster John Knox, 2004.

Articles

Begasse de Daehm, A. "Israel et les nations: la miséricorde dans l'histoire. L'exégèse ambrosienne de Rom 9-11." *Nouvelle Revue Théologique* 129 (2007) 235-253

Boers, H. "The Sructure and Meaning of Rom 6:1-14." *Catholic Biblical Quarterly* 63 (2001) 664-682

Braten, L. J. 'The Groaning Creation: the Biblical Background for Tomans 8:22." *Biblical Research* 50 (2005) 19-39

Dillon, R. J. "The 'priesthood of St. Paul' in Romans 15:15-16." *Worship* 74 [2000] 156-168

Engberg-Pedersen, T. "Paul's Stoicizing Politics in Romans 12-13: the Role of 13.1-10 in the Argument." *Jounal for the Study of the New Testament* 29 (2006) 163-172

Esler, P. F. "Ancient Oleiculture and Ethnic Differentiation: The Meaning of the Olive-Tree Image in Romans 11." *Journal for the Study of the New Testament* 26 (2003) 103-124.

Inversion of the method of grafting in order to check the arrogance of the Gentiles.

Esler, P. F. "The Sodom Tradition in Romans 1:18-32." *Biblical Theology Bulletin* 34 (2004) 4-16

Gathercole S. J. "A Law unto Themselves: the Gentiles in Romans 2.14-15 Revisited." *Jounal for the Study of the New Testament* 85 (2002) 27-49. Paul intended the Christian Gentiles and not Gentiles in general.

Lowe, C. "'There is no Condemnation' (Romans 8:1): But Why Not?" *Journal of the Evangelical Theological Society* 42 (1999) 231-250. There is need for sanctification.

Ortopeza, B. J. "Paul and Theodicy: Intertextual Thoughts of God's Justice and Faithfulness to Israel in Romans 9-11." *New Testament Studies* 53 (2007) 57-80. It is God's mercy that prevails.

Quarles, C. L. "From Faith to Faith: a Fresh Examination of the Prepositional Series in Romans 1:17." *Novum Testamentum* 5 (2003) 1-21. Defends Chrysostom's understanding: from faith of Old Testament believer to the faith of New Testament believer.

Tanner, J. P. "The New Covenant and Paul's Quotations from Hosea in Romans 9:25-26." *Biblia Sacra* 162 (2005) 95-110. The saved community is not ethnic Israel but the believing remnant which includes Jews and Gentiles.

Thorsteinsson, R.M. "Paul and Roman Stoicism: Romans 12 and Contemporary Stoic Ethics." *Jounal for the Study of the New Testament* 29 (2006) 139-161

Wasserman, E. "Paul among the Philosophers: The Case of Sin in Romans 6-8." *Jounal for the Study of the New Testament* 30 (2008) 387-415. Use of certain Platonic traditions. Sin stands in for irrational passions and appetites that operate as an evil counter-ruler within the soul.

Weima, J. A. D. "The Reason for Romans: the Evidence of Its Epistolary Framework." *Review and Expositor* 100 (2003) 17-33. Acceptance of Paul's gospel as "laid down" in the letter.

Whitsett, C. G. "Son of God, Seed of David: Paul's Messianic Exegesis in Romans 1:3-4." *Journal of Biblical Literature* 119 (2000) 661-681

CPSIA information can be obtained
at www.ICGtesting.com
Printed in the USA
BVHW050215290622
640909BV00004B/22